Early praise for *Domain Modeling Made Functional*

Scott Wlaschin is one of the most important communicators in practical, applied programming today. In this book, he brings clarity and simplicity to the process of bridging the gap between requirements, customers, and concrete designs and code. Enjoy!

➤ **Don Syme**
   Researcher, Microsoft U.K.

Many books explain functional programming, but few describe domain modeling from a functional perspective. Scott Wlaschin's book is a brilliant extension of the concepts of domain-driven design to a contemporary context.

➤ **Michael Feathers**
   Director, R7K Research and Conveyance

A few years ago, Scott's blog was my first encounter with domain modeling in a functional language—and it's still my favorite. He has a knack for expressing abstract topics in a clear and approachable way.

➤ **Mathias Verraes**
   Domain-Driven Design Europe

This is a fantastic book that takes you through the process of making software from start to finish, both on a technical and a functional level. I loved reading it!

➤ **Gien Verschatse**
   Owner, Eight Point Squared

Domain Modeling Made Functional

Tackle Software Complexity with
Domain-Driven Design and F#

Scott Wlaschin

The Pragmatic Bookshelf

Raleigh, North Carolina

Many of the designations used by manufacturers and sellers to distinguish their products are claimed as trademarks. Where those designations appear in this book, and The Pragmatic Programmers, LLC was aware of a trademark claim, the designations have been printed in initial capital letters or in all capitals. The Pragmatic Starter Kit, The Pragmatic Programmer, Pragmatic Programming, Pragmatic Bookshelf, PragProg and the linking *g* device are trademarks of The Pragmatic Programmers, LLC.

Every precaution was taken in the preparation of this book. However, the publisher assumes no responsibility for errors or omissions, or for damages that may result from the use of information (including program listings) contained herein.

Our Pragmatic books, screencasts, and audio books can help you and your team create better software and have more fun. Visit us at *https://pragprog.com*.

The team that produced this book includes:

Publisher: Andy Hunt
VP of Operations: Janet Furlow
Managing Editor: Brian MacDonald
Supervising Editor: Jacquelyn Carter
Indexing: Potomac Indexing, LLC
Copy Editor: Molly McBeath
Layout: Gilson Graphics

For sales, volume licensing, and support, please contact *support@pragprog.com*.

For international rights, please contact *rights@pragprog.com*.

ISBN-13: 978-1-68050-254-1

Book version: P1.0—January 2018

Contents

Preface   ix

Part I — Understanding the Domain

1. **Introducing Domain-Driven Design**   3
   The Importance of a Shared Model   4
   Understanding the Domain Through Business Events   7
   Partitioning the Domain into Subdomains   14
   Creating a Solution Using Bounded Contexts   16
   Creating a Ubiquitous Language   21
   Summarizing the Concepts of Domain-Driven Design   22
   Wrapping Up   23

2. **Understanding the Domain**   25
   Interview with a Domain Expert   25
   Fighting the Impulse to Do Database-Driven Design   29
   Fighting the Impulse to Do Class-Driven Design   30
   Documenting the Domain   31
   Diving Deeper into the Order-Taking Workflow   33
   Representing Complexity in Our Domain Model   36
   Wrapping Up   42

3. **A Functional Architecture**   43
   Bounded Contexts as Autonomous Software Components   44
   Communicating Between Bounded Contexts   45
   Contracts Between Bounded Contexts   48
   Workflows Within a Bounded Context   50
   Code Structure Within a Bounded Context   52
   Wrapping Up   55
   What's Next   55

Part II — Modeling the Domain

4. **Understanding Types** 59
   Understanding Functions 59
   Types and Functions 61
   Composition of Types 64
   Working with F# Types 66
   Building a Domain Model by Composing Types 67
   Modeling Optional Values, Errors, and Collections 69
   Organizing Types in Files and Projects 73
   Wrapping Up 75

5. **Domain Modeling with Types** 77
   Reviewing the Domain Model 77
   Seeing Patterns in a Domain Model 78
   Modeling Simple Values 79
   Modeling Complex Data 82
   Modeling Workflows with Functions 85
   A Question of Identity: Value Objects 88
   A Question of Identity: Entities 89
   Aggregates 94
   Putting It All Together 98
   Wrapping Up 101

6. **Integrity and Consistency in the Domain** 103
   The Integrity of Simple Values 104
   Units of Measure 106
   Enforcing Invariants with the Type System 107
   Capturing Business Rules in the Type System 108
   Consistency 112
   Wrapping Up 117

7. **Modeling Workflows as Pipelines** 119
   The Workflow Input 120
   Modeling an Order as a Set of States 122
   State Machines 124
   Modeling Each Step in the Workflow with Types 128
   Documenting Effects 134
   Composing the Workflow from the Steps 136
   Are Dependencies Part of the Design? 137

The Complete Pipeline   138
Long-Running Workflows   140
Wrapping Up   142
What's Next   142

Part III — Implementing the Model

8. **Understanding Functions** **147**
Functions, Functions, Everywhere   147
Functions Are Things   149
Total Functions   154
Composition   156
Wrapping Up   160

9. **Implementation: Composing a Pipeline** **161**
Working with Simple Types   162
Using Function Types to Guide the Implementation   163
Implementing the Validation Step   165
Implementing the Rest of the Steps   172
Composing the Pipeline Steps Together   178
Injecting Dependencies   180
Testing Dependencies   185
The Assembled Pipeline   187
Wrapping Up   190

10. **Implementation: Working with Errors** **191**
Using the Result Type to Make Errors Explicit   191
Working with Domain Errors   192
Chaining Result-Generating Functions   196
Using bind and map in Our Pipeline   203
Adapting Other Kinds of Functions to the Two-Track Model   205
Making Life Easier with Computation Expressions   209
Monads and More   217
Adding the Async Effect   218
Wrapping Up   220

11. **Serialization** **221**
Persistence vs. Serialization   221
Designing for Serialization   222
Connecting the Serialization Code to the Workflow   223
A Complete Serialization Example   224

How to Translate Domain Types to DTOs   229
Wrapping Up   238

12. Persistence   239
Pushing Persistence to the Edges   239
Command-Query Separation   244
Bounded Contexts Must Own Their Data Storage   248
Working with Document Databases   250
Working with Relational Databases   251
Transactions   262
Wrapping Up   263

13. Evolving a Design and Keeping It Clean   265
Change 1: Adding Shipping Charges   266
Change 2: Adding Support for VIP Customers   270
Change 3: Adding Support for Promotion Codes   273
Change 4: Adding a Business Hours Constraint   280
Dealing with Additional Requirements Changes   281
Wrapping Up   282
Wrapping Up the Book   283

Index   285

Preface

Many people think of functional programming as being all about mathematical abstractions and incomprehensible code. In this book, I aim to show that functional programming is in fact an excellent choice for domain modeling, producing designs that are both clear and concise.

Who Is This Book For?

This book is for experienced software developers who want to add some new tools to their programming tool belt. You should read this book if:

- You are curious to see how you can model and implement a domain using only types and functions.

- You want a simple introduction to domain-driven design and want to learn how it is different from object-oriented design or database-first design.

- You are an experienced domain-driven design practitioner who wants to learn why DDD is a great fit with functional programming.

- You want to learn about functional programming, but have been put off by too much theory and abstraction.

- You want to see how F# and functional programming can be applied to real-world domains.

You don't need to have prior knowledge of domain-driven design or functional programming in order to read this book. This is an introductory book and all the important concepts will be explained as we need them.

What's in This Book?

This book is divided into three parts:

- Understanding the domain
- Modeling the domain
- Implementing the model

Each part builds on the previous one, so it's best if you read them in order.

In the first part, Understanding the Domain, we'll look at the ideas behind domain-driven design and the importance of having a shared understanding of a domain. We'll have a brief look at techniques that help to build this shared understanding, such as Event Storming, and then we'll look at decomposing a large domain into smaller components that we can implement and evolve independently.

To be clear, this book is not meant to be a thorough exploration of domain-driven design. That's a large topic that many excellent books and websites cover in detail. Instead, the goal of this book is to introduce you to domain-driven design as a partner to functional domain modeling. We will cover the most important concepts of domain-driven design, of course, but rather than diving deeply into the subject, we'll stay at a high level and stress two things: (a) the importance of communication with domain experts and other non-technical team members and (b) the value of a shared domain model based on real-world concepts.

In the second part, Modeling the Domain, we'll take one workflow from the domain and model it in a functional way. We'll see how the functional decomposition of a workflow differs from an object-oriented approach, and we'll learn how to use types to capture requirements. By the end, we'll have written concise code that does double-duty: first as readable documentation of the domain but also as a compilable framework that the rest of the implementation can build upon.

In the third part, Implementing the Model, we'll take that same modeled workflow and implement it. In the process of doing that, we'll learn how to use common functional programming techniques such as composition, partial application, and the scary-sounding "monad."

This book is not intended to be a complete guide to functional programming. We'll cover just what we need in order to model and implement the domain, and we won't cover more advanced techniques. Nevertheless, by the end of Part III, you'll be familiar with all the most important functional programming concepts and you'll have acquired a toolkit of skills that you can apply to most programming situations.

As sure as the sun rises, requirements will change, so in the final chapter we'll look at some common directions in which the domain might evolve and how our design can adapt in response.

Other Approaches to Domain Modeling

This book focuses on the "mainstream" way of doing domain modeling, by defining data structures and the functions that act on them, but other approaches might be more applicable in some situations. I'll mention two of them here in case you want to explore them further.

- If the domain revolves around semistructured data, then the kinds of rigid models discussed in this book are not suitable and a better approach would be to use flexible structures such as maps (also known as dictionaries) to store key-value pairs. The Clojure community has many good practices here.

- If the emphasis of the domain is on combining elements together to make other elements, then it's often useful to focus on what these composition rules are (the so-called "algebra") before focusing on the data. Domains like this are widespread, from financial contracts to graphic design tools, and the principle of "composition everywhere" makes them especially suitable for being modeled with a functional approach. Unfortunately, due to space limitations, we will not be covering these kinds of domains here.

Working with the Code in This Book

This book will use the F# programming language to demonstrate the concepts and techniques of functional programming. The code has been tested with the latest version of F# as of June 2017, which is F# 4.1 (available in Visual Studio 2017 or installable separately). All the code will work with earlier versions of F# as well, and any important differences will be pointed out in the text.

One of the great features of F# is that it can be used like a scripting language. If you are playing with the example code in conjunction with reading this book, I suggest that you type it into a file and evaluate it interactively rather than compiling it. For how to do this, search the Internet for "F# scripting tips."

All the code in this book is available on this book's page on the Pragmatic Programmers website.[1]

---

1. https://pragprog.com/titles/swdddf/source_code

Getting Started with F#

If you are new to F#, here's some helpful information:

- F# is an open-source, cross-platform language. Details of how to download and install it are available at fsharp.org.[2]

- Many free development environments are available for F#. The most popular are Visual Studio[3] (for Windows and Mac) and Visual Studio Code with the Ionide plugin.[4] (all platforms)

- For help learning F#, there is StackOverflow (using the "F#" tag) as well as the Slack forums run by the F# Software Foundation.[5] The F# community is very friendly and will be happy to help if you have questions.

- For F# news, follow the "#fsharp" tag on Twitter and read the F# Weekly newsletter.[6]

This book uses only a small set of features from F#, and most of the syntax will be explained as we go. If you need a fuller overview of F# syntax, I suggest searching the Internet for "F# cheat sheet" or "F# syntax."

Questions or Suggestions?

I would love to get your feedback, so if you have questions or suggestions, please participate in the PragProg community forum for this book.[7] And if you find any specific problems with the text, please use the errata submission form there.

Credits

All diagrams were created by the author using Inkscape. The clipart is from openclipart.org. The script typeface ("KitType") used in the diagrams was created by Kenneth Lamug.[8]

---

2. http://fsharp.org/
3. https://code.visualstudio.com/
4. http://ionide.io/
5. http://fsharp.org/guides/slack/
6. https://sergeytihon.com/category/f-weekly/
7. https://forums.pragprog.com/forums/457
8. https://www.dafont.com/kittype.font

Acknowledgments

I'd like to thank the reviewers of this book for their very helpful comments and feedback: Gien Verschatse, Mathias Brandewinder, Jérémie Chassaing, Clément Boudereau, Brian Schau, Nick McGinness, Tibor Simic, Vikas Manchanda, Stephen Wolff, Colin Yates, Gabor Hajba, Jacob Chae, Nouran Mhmoud and the early access commenters on the book's forum page.

I'd also like to thank my editor, Brian MacDonald, for his editorial feedback and for keeping me on track, and the rest of the PragProg team for making the publishing process so smooth.

Finally, I'd like to thank you, dear reader, for devoting some of your precious time to this book. I hope you find it useful.

Part I

Understanding the Domain

In this first part, we'll look at the ideas behind domain-driven design and the importance of a shared understanding of a domain. We'll have a brief look at techniques that help to build this shared understanding, such as Event Storming, and then we'll look at decomposing a large domain into smaller components that we can implement and evolve independently.

CHAPTER 1

Introducing Domain-Driven Design

As a developer, you may think that your job is to write code.

I disagree. A developer's job is to solve a problem through software, and coding is just one aspect of software development. Good design and communication are just as important, if not more so.

If you think of software development as a pipeline with an input (requirements) and an output (the final deliverable), then the "garbage in, garbage out" rule applies. If the input is bad (unclear requirements or a bad design), then no amount of coding can create a good output.

In the first part of this book we'll look at how to minimize the "garbage in" part by using a design approach focused on clear communication and shared domain knowledge: *domain-driven design*, or *DDD*.

In this chapter, we'll start by discussing the principles of DDD and by showing how they can be applied to a particular domain. DDD is a large topic, so we won't be exploring it in detail (for more detailed information on DDD, visit dddcommunity.org[1]). However, by the end of this chapter you should at least have a good idea of how domain-driven design works and how it is different from database-driven design and object-oriented design.

Domain-driven design is not appropriate for all software development, of course. There are many types of software (systems software, games, and so on) that can be built using other approaches. However, it is particularly useful for business and enterprise software, where developers have to collaborate with other nontechnical teams, and that kind of software will be the focus of this book.

1.　http://dddcommunity.org

The Importance of a Shared Model

Before attempting to solve a problem it's important that we understand the problem correctly. Obviously, if our understanding of the problem is incomplete or distorted, then we won't to be able to provide a useful solution. And sadly, of course, it's the developers' understanding, not the domain experts' understanding, that gets released to production!

So how can we ensure that we, as developers, *do* understand the problem?

Some software development processes address this by using written specifications or requirements documents to try to capture all the details of a problem. Unfortunately, this approach often creates distance between the people who understand the problem best and the people who will implement the solution. We'll call the latter the "development team," by which we mean not just developers but also UX and UI designers, testers, and so on. And we'll call the former "domain experts." I won't attempt to define "domain expert" here—I think you'll know one when you see one!

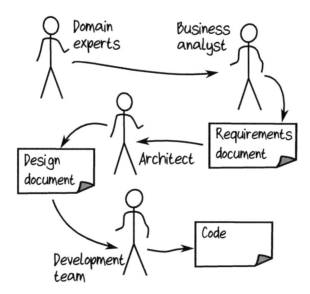

In a children's game called "Telephone," a message is whispered from person to person along a chain of people. With each retelling the message gets more and more distorted, with comic results.

It's not so funny in a real-world development project. A mismatch between the developer's understanding of the problem and the domain expert's understanding of the problem can be fatal to the success of the project.

A much better solution is to eliminate the intermediaries and encourage the domain experts to be intimately involved with the development process, introducing a feedback loop between the development team and the domain expert. The development team regularly delivers something to the domain expert, who can quickly correct any misunderstandings for the next iteration.

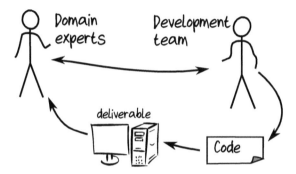

This kind of iterative process is at the core of "agile" development processes.

However, even this approach has its problems. The developer acts as a translator, translating the domain expert's mental model into code. But as in any translation, this process can result in distortion and loss of important subtleties. If the code doesn't quite correspond to the concepts in the domain, then future developers working on the codebase without input from a domain expert can easily misunderstand what's needed and introduce errors.

But there is a third approach. What if the domain experts, the development team, other stakeholders, and (most importantly) the source code itself all share the *same* model? In this case, there is no translation from the domain expert's requirements to the code. Rather, the code is designed to reflect the shared mental model directly.

And that is the goal of domain-driven design.

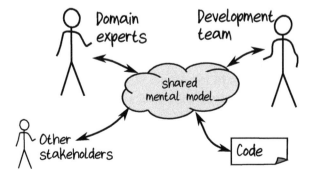

Aligning the software model with the business domain has a number of benefits:

- *Faster time to market.* When the developer and the codebase share the same model as the person who has the problem, the team is more likely to develop an appropriate solution quickly.

- *More business value.* A solution that is accurately aligned with the problem means happier customers and less chance of going offtrack.

- *Less waste.* Clearer requirements means less time wasted in misunderstanding and rework. Furthermore, this clarity often reveals which components are high value so that more development effort can be focused on them and less on the low-value components.

- *Easier maintenance and evolution.* When the model expressed by the code closely matches the domain expert's own model, making changes to the code is easier and less error-prone. Furthermore, new team members are able to come up to speed faster.

The Insanely Effective Delivery Machine

Dan North, the well-known developer and promoter of Behavior-Driven Development, described his experience with a shared mental model in his talk "Accelerating Agile." He joined a small team at a trading firm, which he described as the most insanely effective delivery machine he'd ever been a part of. In that firm, a handful of programmers produced state-of-the-art trading systems in weeks rather than months or years.

One of the reasons for the success of this team was that the developers were trained to be traders alongside the real traders. That is, they became domain experts themselves. This in turn meant that they could communicate very effectively with the traders, due to the shared mental model, and build exactly what their domain experts (the traders) wanted.

So we need to create a shared model. How can we do this? The domain-driven design community has developed some guidelines to help us here. They are as follows:

- Focus on business events and workflows rather than data structures.
- Partition the problem domain into smaller subdomains.
- Create a model of each subdomain in the solution.
- Develop a common language (known as the "Ubiquitous Language") that is shared between everyone involved in the project and is used everywhere in the code.

Let's look at these in turn.

Understanding the Domain Through Business Events

A DDD approach to gathering requirements will emphasize building a shared understanding between developers and domain experts. But where should we start in order to develop this understanding?

Our first guideline says to focus on business events rather than data structures. Why is that?

Well, a business doesn't just *have* data, it *transforms* it somehow. That is, you can think of a typical business process as a series of data or document transformations. The value of the business is created in this process of transformation, so it is critically important to understand how these transformations work and how they relate to each other.

Static data—data that is just sitting there unused—is not contributing anything. So what causes an employee (or automated process) to start working with that data and adding value? Often it's an outside trigger (a piece of mail arriving or your phone ringing), but it can also be a time-based trigger (you do something every day at 10 a.m.) or an observation (there are no more orders in the inbox to process, so do something else).

Whatever it is, it's important to capture it as part of the design. We call these things *Domain Events*.

Domain Events are the starting point for almost all of the business processes we want to model. For example, "new order form received" is a Domain Event that will kick off the order-taking process.

Domain Events are always written in the past tense—something happened—because it's a fact that can't be changed.

Using Event Storming to Discover the Domain

There are a number of ways to discover events in a domain, but one that is particularly suitable for a DDD approach is *Event Storming*, which is a collaborative process for discovering business events and their associated workflows.

In Event Storming, you bring together a variety of people (who understand different parts of the domain) for a facilitated workshop. The attendees should include not just developers and domain experts but all the other stakeholders who have an interest in the success of the project: as event stormers like to say, "anyone who has questions and anyone who has answers." The workshop should be held in a room that has a lot of wall space, and the walls should be covered with paper or whiteboard material so that the participants can post sticky notes or draw on them. At the end of a successful session, the walls will be covered with hundreds of these notes.

During the workshop, people write down business events on the sticky notes and post them on the wall. Other people may respond by posting notes summarizing the business workflows that are triggered by these events. These workflows, in turn, often lead to other business events being created. In addition, the notes can often be organized into a timeline, which may well trigger further discussion in the group. The idea is to get all the attendees to participate in posting what they know and asking questions about what they don't know. It's a highly interactive process that encourages everyone to be involved. For more detail on Event Storming in practice, see the *EventStorming* book by Alberto Brandolini,[2] the creator of this technique.

Discovering the Domain: An Order-Taking System

In this book, we'll take a realistic business problem—an order-taking system—and use it to explore design, domain modeling, and implementation.

Say that we are called in to help a small manufacturing company, Widgets Inc, to automate its order-taking workflow. Max, the manager at Widgets, explains:

> "We're a tiny company that manufactures parts for other companies: widgets, gizmos, and the like. We've been growing quite fast, and our current processes are not able to keep up. Right now, everything we do is paper-based, and we'd like to computerize all that so that our staff can handle larger volumes of orders. In particular, we'd like to have a self-service website so that customers can do some tasks themselves. Things like placing an order, checking order status, and so on."

Sounds good. So now what do we do? Where should we start?

The first guideline says "focus on business events," so let's use an event-storming session for that. Here's how one might start out at Widgets.

> You: "Someone start by posting a business event!"
>
> Ollie: "I'm Ollie from the order-taking department. Mostly we deal with orders and quotes coming in."
>
> You: "What triggers this kind of work?"
>
> Ollie: "When we get forms sent to us by the customer in the mail."
>
> You: "So the events would be something like 'Order form received' and 'Quote form received'?"

---

2.   http://eventstorming.com

Ollie: "Yes. Let me put those up on the wall then."

Sam: "I'm Sam from the shipping department. We fulfill those orders when they're signed off."

You: "And how do you know when to do that?"

Sam: "When we get an order from the order-taking department."

You: "What would you call that as an event?"

Sam: "How about 'Order available'?"

Ollie: "We call an order that's completed and ready to ship a 'Placed order.' Can we agree on using that term everywhere?"

Sam: "So 'Order placed' would be the event we care about, yes?"

You get the idea. After a while, we might have list of posted events like this:

- Order form received
- Order placed
- Order shipped
- Order change requested
- Order cancellation requested
- Return requested
- Quote form received
- Quote provided
- New customer request received
- New customer registered

Here's what the wall might look like at this point:

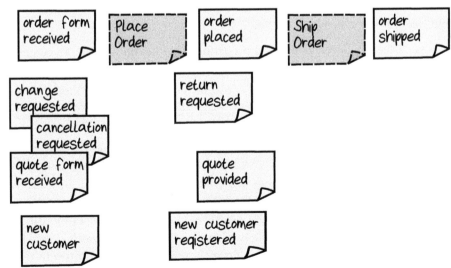

Some of the events have business workflows posted next to them, such as "Place order" and "Ship order," and we're beginning to see how the events connect up into larger workflows.

We can't cover a full event-storming session in detail, but let's look at some of the aspects of requirements gathering that Event Storming facilitates:

• *A shared model of the business*

As well as revealing the events, a key benefit of Event Storming is that the participants develop a shared understanding of the business, because everyone is seeing the same thing on the big wall. Just like DDD, Event Storming has an emphasis on communication and shared models and avoiding "us" vs. "them" thinking. Not only will attendees learn about unfamiliar aspects of the domain, but they might realize that their assumptions about other teams are wrong or perhaps even develop insights that can help the business improve.

• *Awareness of all the teams*

Sometimes it's easy to focus on just one aspect of the business—the one that you are involved in—and forget that other teams are involved and may need to consume data that you produce. If all the stakeholders are in the room, anyone who is being overlooked can speak out.

> "I'm Blake from the billing department. Don't forget about us. We need to know about completed orders too, so we can bill people and make money for the company! So we need to get an 'order placed' event as well."

• *Finding gaps in the requirements*

When the events are displayed on a wall in a timeline, missing requirements often become very clear:

> Max: "Ollie, when you've finished preparing an order, do you tell the customer? I don't see that on the wall."

> Ollie: "Oh, yes. I forgot. When the order has been placed successfully, we send an email to the customer saying that we got it and are about to ship it. That's another event, I suppose: 'Order acknowledgment sent to customer'."

If the question doesn't have a clear answer, then the question itself should be posted on the wall as a trigger for further discussion. And if a particular part of the process creates debate or disagreement, don't treat it as a problem, treat it as an opportunity! You'll learn a lot by drilling into these areas. It's common for the requirements to be fuzzy at the beginning of a project, so documenting the questions and debate in this visible way makes it clear more work needs to be done, and it discourages starting the development process prematurely.

- *Connections between teams*

The events can be grouped in a timeline, which often makes it clear that one team's output is another team's input.

For example, when the order-taking team has finished processing an order, they need to signal that a new order has been placed. This "Order placed" event becomes the input for the shipping and billing teams:

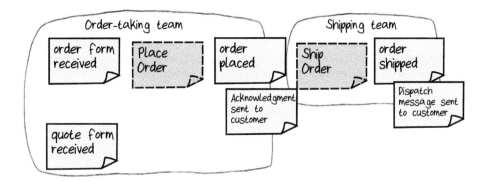

The technical details of *how* the teams are connected is not relevant at this stage. We want to focus on the domain, not the pros and cons of message queues vs. databases.

- *Awareness of reporting requirements*

It's easy to focus only on processes and transactions when trying to understand the domain. But any business needs to understand what happened in the past—reporting is always part of the domain! Make sure that reporting and other read-only models (such as view models for the UI) are included in the event-storming session.

Expanding the Events to the Edges

It is often useful to follow the chain of events out as far as you can, to the boundaries of the system. To start, you might ask if any events occur before the leftmost event.

You: "Ollie, what triggers the 'Order form received' event? Where does that come from?"

Ollie: "We open the mail every morning, and the customers send in order forms on paper, which we open up and classify as orders or quotes."

You: "So it looks like we need a 'Mail received' event as well?"

Workflows, Scenarios, and Use Cases

We have many different words to describe business activities: "workflows," "scenarios," "use cases," "processes," and so on. They're often used interchangeably; but in this book, we'll try to be a bit more precise.

- A *scenario* describes a goal that a customer (or other user) wants to achieve, such as placing an order. It is similar to a "story" in agile development. A *use case* is a more detailed version of a scenario, which describes in general terms the user interactions and other steps that the user needs to take to accomplish a goal. Both *scenario* and *use case* are user-centric concepts, focused on how interactions appear from the user's point of view.

- A *business process* describes a goal that the business (rather than an individual user) wants to achieve. It's similar to a scenario but has a business-centric focus rather than a user-centric focus.

- A *workflow* is a detailed description of part of a business process. That is, it lists the exact steps that an employee (or software component) needs to do to accomplish a business goal or subgoal. We'll limit a workflow to what a single person or team can do, so that when a business process is spread over multiple teams (as the ordering process is), we can divide the overall business process into a series of smaller workflows, which are then coordinated in some way.

In the same way, we might extend the events on the shipping side of the business.

> You: "Sam, are there any possible events *after* you ship the order to the customer?"

> Sam: "Well, if the order is "Signed for delivery," we'll get a notification from the courier service. So let me add a 'Shipment received by customer' event."

Extending the events out as far as you can in either direction is another great way of catching missing requirements. You might find that the chain of events ends up being longer than you expect.

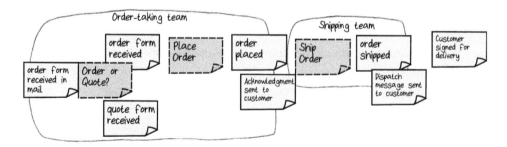

Notice that the domain expert is talking about paper forms and printed mail. The system that we want to replace this with will be computerized, but we can learn a lot by thinking about paper-based systems in terms of workflow, prioritization, edge cases, and so on. Let's focus on understanding the domain for now; only when we understand it thoroughly should we think about how to implement a digital equivalent.

Indeed, in many business processes the whole paper vs. digital distinction is irrelevant—understanding the high-level concepts of the domain does not depend on any particular implementation at all. The domain of accounting is a good example; the concepts and terminology have not changed for hundreds of years.

Also, when converting a paper-based system to a computerized system, there's often no need to convert all of it at once. We should look at the system as a whole and start by converting only the parts that would benefit most.

Documenting Commands

Once we have a number of these events on the wall, we might ask, "What made these Domain Events happen?" Somebody or something wanted an activity to happen. For example, the customer wanted us to receive an order form, or your boss asked you to do something.

We call these requests *commands* in DDD terminology (not be confused with the Command pattern used in OO programming). Commands are always written in the imperative: "Do this for me."

Of course, not all commands actually succeed—the order form might have gotten lost in the mail, or you're too busy with something more important to help your boss. But if the command does succeed, it will initiate a workflow that in turn will create corresponding Domain Events. Here are some examples:

- If the command was "Make X happen," then, if the workflow made X happen, the corresponding Domain Event would be "X happened."

- If the command was "Send an order form to Widgets Inc," then, if the workflow sent the order, the corresponding Domain Event would be "Order form sent."

- Command: "Place an order"; Domain Event: "Order placed."

- Command: "Send a shipment to customer ABC"; Domain Event: "Shipment sent."

In fact, we will try to model most business processes in this way. An event triggers a command, which initiates some business workflow. The output of the workflow is some more events. And then, of course, those events can trigger further commands.

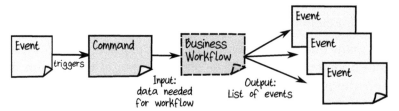

This way of thinking about business processes—a pipeline with an input and some outputs—is an excellent fit with the way that functional programming works, as we will see later.

Using this approach, then, the order-taking process looks like this:

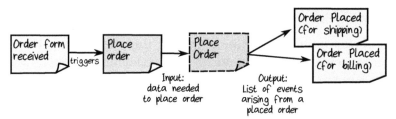

For now, we'll assume that every command succeeds and the corresponding event happens. Later on, in Chapter 10, *Implementation: Working with Errors*, on page 191, we'll see how to model failure—how to handle the cases when things go wrong and commands do not succeed.

By the way, not *all* events need be associated with a command. Some events might be triggered by a scheduler or monitoring system, such as MonthEndClose for an accounting system or OutOfStock for a warehouse system.

Partitioning the Domain into Subdomains

We now have a list of events and commands, and we have a good understanding of what the various business processes are. But the big picture is still quite chaotic. We'll have to tame it before we start writing any code.

This brings us to our second guideline: "Partition the problem domain into smaller subdomains." When faced with a large problem, it's natural to break it into smaller components that can be addressed separately. And so it is here. We have a large problem: organizing the events around order taking. Can we break it into smaller pieces?

Yes, we can. It's clear that various aspects of the "order-taking process" can be separated: the order taking, the shipping, the billing, and so on. As we know, the business already has separate departments for these areas, and that's a pretty strong hint that we can follow that same separation in our design. We will call each of these areas a *domain*.

Now *domain* is a word with many meanings, but in the world of domain-driven design, we can define a "domain" as "an area of coherent knowledge." Unfortunately that definition is too vague to be useful, so here's an alternative definition of a domain: a "domain" is just that which a "domain expert" is expert in! This is much more convenient in practice: rather than struggling to provide a dictionary definition of what "billing" means, we can just say that "billing" is what people in the billing department—the domain experts—do.

We all know what a "domain expert" is; as programmers we ourselves are often experts in a number of domains. For example, you could be an expert in the use of a particular programming language or in a particular area of programming, such as games or scientific programming. And you might have knowledge of areas such as security or networking or low-level optimizations. All these things are "domains."

Within a domain might be areas that are distinctive as well. We call these *sub-domains*—a smaller part of a larger domain that has its own specialized knowledge. For example, "web programming" is a subdomain of "general programming." And "JavaScript programming" is a subdomain of web programming (at least, it used to be).

Here's a diagram showing some programming-related domains:

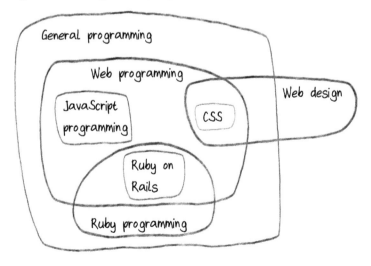

You can see that domains can overlap. For example, the "CSS" subdomain could be considered part of the "web programming" domain but also part of the "web design" domain. So we must be careful when partitioning a domain into smaller parts: it's tempting to want clear, crisp boundaries, but the real world is fuzzier than that.

If we apply this domain-partitioning approach to our order-taking system, we have something like this:

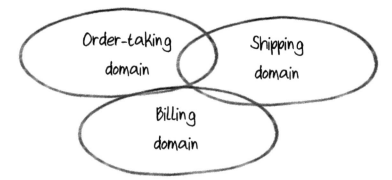

The domains overlap a little bit. An order-taker must know a little bit about how the billing and shipping departments work, a shipper must know a little bit about how the order-taking and billing departments work, and so on.

As we have stressed before, if you want be effective when developing a solution, you need become a bit of a domain expert yourself. That means that, as developers, we'll need to make an effort to understand the domains above more deeply than we have done so far.

But let's hold off on that for now and move on to the guidelines for creating a solution.

Creating a Solution Using Bounded Contexts

Understanding the problem doesn't mean that building a solution is easy. The solution can't possibly represent *all* the information in the original domain, nor would we want it to. We should only capture the information that is relevant to solving a particular problem. Everything else is irrelevant.

We therefore need to create a distinction between a "problem space" and a "solution space," and they must be treated as two different things. To build the solution we will create a *model* of the problem domain, extracting only the aspects of the domain that are relevant and then re-creating them in our solution space as shown in the figure on page 17.

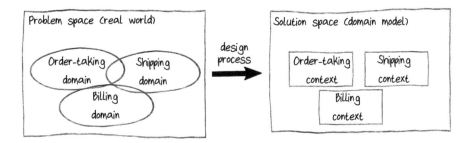

In the solution space, you can see that the domains and subdomains in the problem space are mapped to what DDD terminology calls *bounded contexts*—a kind of subsystem in our implementation. Each bounded context is a mini domain model in its own right. We use the phrase *bounded context* instead of something like *subsystem* because it helps us stay focused on what's important when we design a solution: being aware of the context and being aware of the boundaries.

Why *context*? Because each context represents some specialized knowledge in the solution. Within the context, we share a common language and the design is coherent and unified. But, just as in the real world, information taken out of context can be confusing or unusable.

Why *bounded*? In the real world, domains have fuzzy boundaries, but in the world of software we want to reduce coupling between separate subsystems so that they can evolve independently. We can do this using standard software practices, such as having explicit APIs between subsystems and avoiding dependencies such as shared code. This means, sadly, that our domain model will never be as rich as the real world, but we can tolerate this in exchange for less complexity and easier maintenance.

A domain in the problem space does not always have a one-to-one relationship to a context in the solution space. Sometimes, for various reasons, a single domain is broken into multiple bounded contexts—or more likely—multiple domains in the problem space are modeled by only one bounded context in the solution space. This is especially common when you need to integrate with a legacy software system.

For example, in an alternate world, Widgets Inc might already have installed a software package that did order taking and billing together in one system. If you needed to integrate with this legacy system, you would probably need to treat it as a single bounded context, even though it covers multiple domains as shown in the figure on page 18.

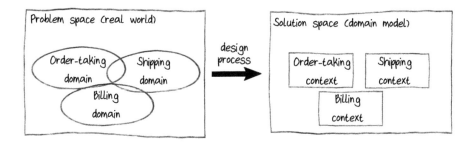

However you partition the domain, it's important that each bounded context have a clear responsibility, because when we come to implement the model, a bounded context will correspond exactly to some kind of software component. The component could be implemented as a separate DLL, or as a standalone service, or just as a simple namespace. The details don't matter right now, but getting the partitioning right is important.

Getting the Contexts Right

Defining these bounded contexts sounds straightforward, but it can be tricky in practice. Indeed, one of the most important challenges of a domain-driven design is to get these context boundaries right. This is an art, not a science, but here are some guidelines that can help:

- *Listen to the domain experts.* If they all share the same language and focus on the same issues, they are probably working in the same subdomain (which maps to a bounded context).

- *Pay attention to existing team and department boundaries.* These are strong clues to what the business considers to be domains and subdomains. Of course, this is not always true: sometimes people in the same department are working at odds with each other. Conversely, people in different departments may collaborate very closely, which in turn may mean they're working in the same domain.

- *Don't forget the "bounded" part of a bounded context.* Watch out for scope creep when setting boundaries. In a complex project with changing requirements, you need to be ruthless about preserving the "bounded" part of the bounded context. A boundary that is too big or too vague is no boundary at all. As the saying goes, "Good fences make good neighbors."

- *Design for autonomy.* If two groups contribute to the same bounded context, they might end up pulling the design in different directions as it evolves. Think of a three-legged race: two runners tied at the leg are much slower than two runners free to run independently. And so it is with a domain model. It's always better to have separate and autonomous bounded contexts that can evolve independently than one mega-context that tries to make everyone happy.

- *Design for friction-free business workflows.* If a workflow interacts with multiple bounded contexts and is often blocked or delayed by them, consider refactoring the contexts to make the workflow smoother, even if the design becomes "uglier." That is, always focus on business and customer value rather than any kind of "pure" design.

Finally, no design is static, and any model must need to evolve over time as the business requirements change. We will discuss this further in Chapter 13, *Evolving a Design and Keeping It Clean*, on page 265, where we will demonstrate various ways to adapt the order-taking domain to new demands.

Creating Context Maps

Once we have defined these contexts, we need a way to communicate the interactions between them—the big picture—without getting bogged down in the details of a design. In DDD terminology, these diagrams are called *Context Maps*.

Think of a route map used for traveling. A route map doesn't show you every detail: it focuses only on the main routes so that you can plan your journey. For example, here's a sketch of an airline route map:

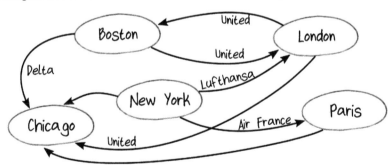

This diagram doesn't show the details of each city, just the available routes between each city. The map's only purpose is to help you plan your flights. If you want to do something different, such as drive around New York, you're going to need a different map (and some blood pressure pills).

In the same way, a context map shows the various bounded contexts and their relationships at a high level. The goal is not to capture every detail but to provide a view of the system as a whole. For example, this is what we have so far for the order-taking system as shown in the figure on page 20.

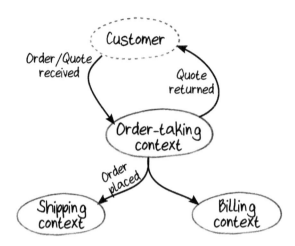

In making this map, we are not concerned with the internal structure of the shipping context, only that it receives data from the order-taking context. We say informally that the shipping context is *downstream* and the order-taking context is *upstream*.

Obviously the two contexts will need to agree on a shared format for the messages that they exchange. In general, the upstream context has more influence over the format, but sometimes the downstream context is inflexible (such as working with a legacy system); and either the upstream context must adapt to that, or some sort of translator component will be needed as an intermediary. (This is discussed further in *Contracts Between Bounded Contexts*, on page 48.)

Finally, it's worth pointing out that in our design we can fit everything into one map (so far). In more complex designs, you'd naturally want to create a series of smaller maps, each focusing on specific subsystems.

Focusing on the Most Important Bounded Contexts

We have a few obvious bounded contexts at this point, and we may find that we discover more as we work with the domain. But are they all equally important? Which ones should we focus on when we start development?

Generally, some domains *are* more important than others. These are the core domains—the ones that provide a business advantage, the ones that bring in the money.

Other domains may be required but are not core. These are called *supportive* domains, and if they are not unique to the business they are called *generic* domains.

For example, for Widgets Inc, the order-taking and shipping domains might be core, because their business advantage is their excellent customer service. The billing domain would be considered as supportive, and delivery of the shipments could be considered generic, which means they can safely outsource it.

Of course, reality is never as simple. Sometimes the core domain is not what you might expect. An e-commerce business might find that having items in stock and ready to ship is critical to customer satisfaction, in which case inventory management might become a core domain, just as important to the success of the business as an easy-to-use website.

Sometimes there's no consensus about what is the most important domain; each department may think that its domain is the most important. And sometimes, the core domain is simply whatever your client wants you to work on.

In all cases though, it is important to prioritize and not to attempt to implement all the bounded contexts at the same time—that often leads to failure. Focus instead on those bounded contexts that add the most value, and then expand from there.

Creating a Ubiquitous Language

We said earlier the code and the domain expert must share the same model.

That means that things in our design must represent real things in the domain expert's mental model. That is, if the domain expert calls something an "order," then we should have something called an Order in the code that corresponds to it and that behaves the same way.

And conversely, we should *not* have things in our design that do not represent something in the domain expert's model. That means no terms like OrderFactory, OrderManager, OrderHelper, and so forth. A domain expert wouldn't know what you meant by these words. Of course, some technical terms will have to occur in the codebase, but you should avoid exposing them as part of the *design*.

The set of concepts and vocabulary that is shared between everyone on the team is called the *Ubiquitous Language*—the "everywhere language." This is the language that defines the shared mental model for the business domain. And, as its name implies, this language should used *everywhere* in the project, not just in the requirements but in the design and, most importantly, in the source code.

The construction of the ubiquitous language is not a one-way process dictated by the domain expert, it is a collaboration between everyone on the team. Nor should you expect the ubiquitous language to be static: it's always a work in progress. As the design evolves, be prepared to discover new terms and new concepts, and let the ubiquitous language evolve correspondingly. We'll see this happen in the course of this book.

Finally, it's important to realize that you often cannot have a single Ubiquitous Language that covers *all* domains and contexts. Each context will have a "dialect" of the Ubiquitous Language, and the same word can mean different things in different dialects. For example, "class" means one thing in the object-oriented programming domain but a completely different thing in the CSS domain. Trying to make a word like "Customer" or "Product" mean the same in different contexts can lead to complex requirements at best, and serious design errors at worst.

Indeed, our event-storming session demonstrates this exact issue. All the attendees used the word "order" when describing events. But we might well find that the shipping department's definition of "order" is subtly different definition than the billing department's definition. The shipping department probably cares about inventory levels, the quantity of items, and so on, while the billing department probably cares more about prices and money. If we use the same word "order" everywhere *without* specifying the context for its use, we might well run into some painful misunderstandings.

Summarizing the Concepts of Domain-Driven Design

We've been introduced to a lot of new concepts and terminology, so let's quickly summarize them in one place before moving on.

- A *domain* is an area of knowledge associated with the problem we are trying to solve, or simply, that which a "domain expert" is expert in.

- A *Domain Model* is a set of simplifications that represent those aspects of a domain that are relevant to a particular problem. The domain model is part of the solution space, while the domain that it represents is part of the problem space.

- The *Ubiquitous Language* is a set of concepts and vocabulary that is associated with the domain and is shared by both the team members and the source code.

- A *bounded context* is a subsystem in the solution space with clear boundaries that distinguish it from other subsystems. A bounded context often corresponds to a subdomain in the problem space. A bounded context also has its own set of concepts and vocabulary, its own dialect of the Ubiquitous Language.

- A *Context Map* is a high-level diagram showing a collection of bounded contexts and the relationships between them.

- A *Domain Event* is a record of something that happened in the system. It's always described in the past tense. An event often triggers additional activity.

- A *Command* is a request for some process to happen and is triggered by a person or another event. If the process succeeds, the state of the system changes and one or more Domain Events are recorded.

Wrapping Up

At the beginning of the chapter, we emphasized the importance of creating a shared model of the domain and solution—a model that is the same for the development team and the domain experts.

We then discussed four guidelines to help us do that:

- Focus on events and processes rather than data.
- Partition the problem domain into smaller subdomains.
- Create a model of each subdomain in the solution.
- Develop an "everywhere language" that can be shared between everyone involved in the project.

Let's see how we applied them to the order-taking domain.

Events and Processes

The event-storming session quickly revealed all the major *Domain Events* in the domain. For example, we learned that the order-taking process is triggered by receiving an order form in the mail, and that there are workflows for processing a quote, for registering a new customer, and so on.

We also learned that when the order-taking team finished processing an order, that event triggered the shipping department to start the shipping process and the billing department to start the billing process.

Many more events and processes could be documented, but we'll focus primarily on this one workflow for the rest of this book.

Subdomains and Bounded Contexts

It appears that we have discovered three *subdomains* so far: "Order Taking," "Shipping," and "Billing." Let's check our sense of this by using our "a domain is what a domain expert is expert in" rule.

You: "Hey Ollie, do you know how the billing process works?"

Ollie: "A little bit, but you should really ask the billing team if you want the details."

Billing is a separate domain? Confirmed!

We then defined three *bounded contexts* to correspond with these subdomains and created a *context map* that shows how these three contexts interact.

Which one is the *core* domain that we should focus on? We should really consult with Max the manager to decide where automation can add the most value, but for now, let's assume that we will implement the order-taking domain first. If needed, the output of the domain can be converted to paper documents so that the other teams can continue with their existing processes without interruption.

The Ubiquitous Language

So far we have terms like "order form," "quote," and "order," and no doubt we will discover more as we drill into the design. To help maintain a shared understanding, it would be a good idea to create a living document or wiki page that lists these terms and their definitions. This will help keep everyone aligned and help new team members get up to speed quickly.

What's Next?

We now have an overview of the problem and an outline of a solution, but we still have many questions that need answering before we can create a low-level design or start coding.

What happens, exactly, in the order-processing workflow? What are the inputs and outputs? Are there any other contexts that this workflow interacts with? How does the shipping team's concept of an "order" differ from the billing team's? And so on.

In the next chapter, we'll dive deeply into the order-placing workflow and attempt to answer these questions.

CHAPTER 2

Understanding the Domain

In the previous chapter, we looked at the big picture—an overview of the domain and the key business events—and we divided the solution space into a number of bounded contexts. Along the way, we learned about domain-driven design and the importance of a shared model.

In this chapter, we're going to take one particular workflow and try to understand it deeply. What exactly triggers it? What data is needed? What other bounded contexts does it need to collaborate with?

We'll see that careful listening is a key skill in this process. We want to avoid imposing our own mental model on the domain.

Interview with a Domain Expert

In order to get the understanding we want, let's do an in-depth interview with a domain expert: Ollie from the order-taking department.

Now, domain experts tend to be busy and generally can't spend too much time with developers. But one nice thing about the commands/events approach is that rather than needing all-day meetings, we can have a series of short interviews, each focusing on only one workflow, so a domain expert is more likely to be able to make time for this.

In the first part of the interview, we want to stay at a high level and focus only on the inputs and outputs of the workflow. This will help us avoid getting swamped with details that are not (yet) relevant to the design.

> You: "Ollie, let's talk about just one workflow, the order-placing process. What information do you need to start this process?"

> Ollie: "Well, it all starts with this piece of paper: the order form that customers fill out and send us in the mail. In the computerized version, we want the customer to fill out this form online."

Ollie shows you something that looks like this:

Order Form

Customer Name: ----------------------------.

Billing Address: *Shipping Address:*

----------------------------.   ----------------------------.

----------------------------.   ----------------------------.

----------------------------.   ----------------------------.

Order: ☐   Quote: ☐   Express Delivery: ☐

Product Code	Quantity	Cost
	Subtotal	
	Shipping	
	Total	

At this point you might think that this is a typical e-commerce model.

> You: "I see. So the customers will browse the product pages on the website, then click to add items to the shopping cart, and then check out?"

> Ollie: "No, of course not. Our customers already know exactly what they want to order. We just want a simple form where they can type in the product codes and quantities. They might order two or three hundred items at once, so clicking around in product pages to find each item first would be terribly slow."

This is an important lesson. You're supposed to be learning about the domain, so resist the urge to jump to conclusions about anything, such as (in this case) how the customers will use the system. Good interviewing means doing lots of listening! The best way to learn about a domain is to pretend you're an anthropologist and avoid having any preconceived notions. Ideally, we would do in-depth research (such as observing people at work, usability testing, and so on) before we commit to a design. In this case, though, we'll take the risk and skip these steps, trusting that Ollie understands the customer's needs well enough to represent them to us.

Understanding the Non-functional Requirements

This would be a good time to take a step back and discuss the context and scale of the workflow.

> You: "Sorry, I misunderstood who the customer was. Let me get some more background information. For example, who uses this process and how often?"

> Ollie: "We're a B2B company,[1] so our customers are other businesses. We have about 1000 customers, and they typically place an order every week."

> You: "So about two hundred orders per business day. Does it ever get much busier than that, say in the holiday season?"

> Ollie: "No. It's pretty consistent all year."

This is good—we know that we don't need to design for massive scale, nor do we have to design for spiky traffic. Now, what about customer expectations of the system?

> You: "And you say that the customers are experts?"

> Ollie: "They spend all day purchasing things, so yes, they are experts in that domain. They know what they want; they just need an efficient way to get it."

This information affects how we think about the design. A system designed for beginners will often be quite different from a system designed for experts. If the customers are experts, then we don't want to put barriers in their way or anything else that will slow them down.

> You: "What about latency? How quickly do they need a response?"

> Ollie: "They need an acknowledgment by the end of the business day. For our business, speed is less important than consistency. Our customers want to know that we will respond and deliver in a predictable way."

These are typical requirements for a B2B application: needs like predictability, robust data handling, and an audit trail of everything that happens in case there are any questions or disputes.

Understanding the Rest of the Workflow

Let's keep going with the interview.

> You: "OK, what do you do with each form?"

> Ollie: "First we check that the product codes are correct. Sometimes there are typos or the product doesn't exist."

> You: "How you know if a product doesn't exist?"

---

1. https://en.wikipedia.org/wiki/Business-to-business

> Ollie: "I look it up in the product catalog. It's a leaflet listing all the products and their prices. A new one is published every month. Look, here's the latest one sitting on my desk."

The product catalog sounds like another bounded context. We'll make a note to revisit it in detail later. For now, we'll skip it and just keep track of what this workflow needs from that context: the list of products and their prices.

> You: "And then?"

> Ollie: "Then we add up the cost of the items, write that into the Total field at the bottom, and then make two copies: one for the shipping department and one for the billing department. We keep the original in our files."

> You: "And then?"

> Ollie: "Then we scan the order and email it to the customer so that they can see the prices and the amount due. We call this an 'order acknowledgment.'"

OK, that makes sense so far. At some point you will want to go deeper into understanding how the validation is done and how the orders are transmitted to the other departments. One more question, though.

> You: "What are those boxes marked 'Quote' and 'Order' for?"

> Ollie: "If the 'Order' box is checked, then it's an order and if the 'Quote' box is checked, then it's a quote. Obviously."

> You: "So what's the difference between a quote and an order?"

> Ollie: "A quote is when the customer just wants us to calculate the prices but not actually dispatch the items. With a quote, we just add prices to the form and send it back to the customer. We don't send copies to the shipping and billing departments because there's nothing for them to do."

> You: "I see. Orders and quotes are similar enough that you use the same order form for both, but they have different workflows associated with them."

Thinking About Inputs and Outputs

Let's pause to document what we've learned about the inputs and outputs of the workflow so far.

First, the input is clearly an order form (the exact definition of which we need to flesh out soon).

But what's the output? We've seen the concept of a "completed order" (based on the input but validated and with prices calculated). But that can't be the output, because we don't do anything with it directly. What about the "order acknowledgment" then? Could that be the output? Probably not. Sending the order acknowledgment is a side effect of the order-placing workflow, not an output.

The output of a workflow should always be the events that it generates, the things that trigger actions in other bounded contexts. In our case, the output of the workflow would be something like an "OrderPlaced" event, which is then sent to the shipping and billing contexts. (How the event actually gets to those departments is a discussion for later; it's not relevant to the design right now.)

Let's diagram the "Place Order" workflow with its inputs and outputs:

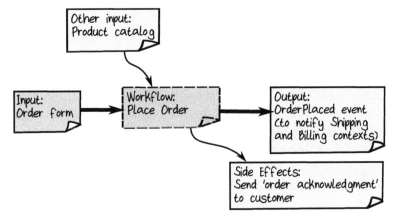

Fighting the Impulse to Do Database-Driven Design

At this point, if you are like most developers, you can't help but start sketching out a low-level design and implementation immediately.

For example, you might look at that order form and see that it consists of customer information, some addresses, a list of order lines, and so on.

If you have a lot of database experience, your first instinct might be to think about tables and the relationships between them. You might envision an Order table, an OrderLine table, and Customer, Address, and Product tables. And then you'll probably want to describe the relationships between them as shown in the figure.

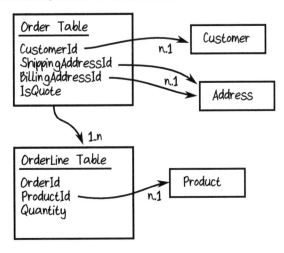

But if you do this, you are making a mistake. In domain-driven design we let the *domain* drive the design, not a database schema.

It's better to work from the domain and to model it without respect to any particular storage implementation. After all, in a real-world, paper-based system, there is no database. The concept of a "database" is certainly not part of the ubiquitous language. The users do not care about how data is persisted.

In DDD terminology this is called *persistence ignorance*. It is an important principle because it forces you to focus on modeling the domain accurately, without worrying about the representation of the data in a database.

Why is this important? Well, if you design from the database point of view all the time, you often end up distorting the design to fit a database model.

As an example of the distortion that a database-driven model brings, we have already ignored the difference between an order and a quote in the diagram above. Sure, in the database we can have a flag to distinguish them, but the business rules and validation rules are different. For example, we might later learn that an Order must have a billing address but a Quote doesn't. This is hard to model with a foreign key. This subtlety has been lost in database design because the same foreign key does dual duty for both types of relationships.

Of course, the design can be corrected to deal with it, and in the chapter on persistence on page 239, we'll see how to persist a domain-driven design into a relational database. But for now we really want to concentrate on listening to the requirements without prejudice.

Fighting the Impulse to Do Class-Driven Design

If you're an experienced object-oriented developer, then the idea of not being biased to a particular database model will be familiar, Indeed, object-oriented techniques such as dependency injection encourage you to separate the database implementation from the business logic.

But you, too, may end up introducing bias into the design if you think in terms of objects rather than the domain.

For example, as Ollie is talking, you may be creating classes in your head, like the figure on page 31.

Letting classes drive the design can be just as dangerous as letting a database drive the design—again, you're not really listening to the requirements.

In the preliminary design above we have separated orders and quotes, but we have introduced an artificial base class, OrderBase, that doesn't exist in the real world. This is a distortion of the domain. Try asking the domain expert what an OrderBase is!

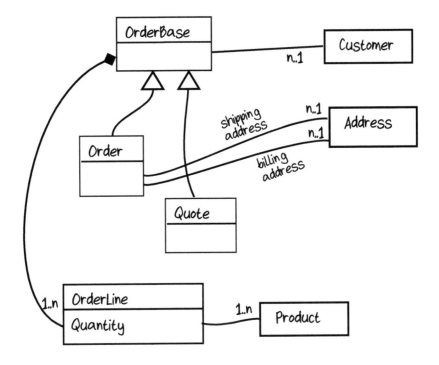

The lesson here is that we should keep our minds open during requirements gathering and not impose our own technical ideas on the domain.

Documenting the Domain

OK, we want to avoid biasing ourselves with technical implementations, but then how *should* we record these requirements?

We could use visual diagrams (such as UML), but these are often hard to work with and not detailed enough to capture some of the subtleties of the domain.

Later in this book we'll see how to create an accurate domain model in code, but for now, let's just create a simple text-based language that we can use to capture the domain model:

- For workflows, we'll document the inputs and outputs and then just use some simple pseudocode for the business logic.

- For data structures, we'll use AND to mean that both parts are required, such as in Name AND Address. And we'll use OR to mean that either part is required, such as in Email OR PhoneNumber.

Using this mini-language, then, we can document the Place Order workflow like this:

```
Bounded context: Order-Taking

Workflow: "Place order"
    triggered by:
        "Order form received" event (when Quote is not checked)
    primary input:
        An order form
    other input:
        Product catalog
    output events:
        "Order Placed" event
    side-effects:
        An acknowledgment is sent to the customer,
        along with the placed order
```

And we can document the data structures associated with the workflow like this:

```
bounded context: Order-Taking

data Order =
    CustomerInfo
    AND ShippingAddress
    AND BillingAddress
    AND list of OrderLines
    AND AmountToBill

data OrderLine =
    Product
    AND Quantity
    AND Price

data CustomerInfo = ???    // don't know yet
data BillingAddress = ??? // don't know yet
```

The Provide Quote workflow and its associated data structures can be documented in a similar way.

Note that we have not attempted to create a class hierarchy or database tables or anything else. We have just tried to capture the domain in a slightly structured way.

The advantage of this kind of text-based design is that it's not scary to non-programmers, which means it can be shown to the domain expert and worked on together.

The big question is whether can we make our code look as simple as this, too. In a following chapter, *Domain Modeling with Types*, we'll try to do just that.

Diving Deeper into the Order-Taking Workflow

We've got the inputs and outputs documented, so let's move on to understanding the order-taking workflow in detail.

> You: "Ollie, could you go into detail on how you work with an order form?"
>
> Ollie: "When we get the mail in the morning, the first thing I do is sort it. Order forms are put on one pile, and other correspondence is put on another pile. Then, for each form, I look at whether the Quote box has been checked; if so, I put the form on the Quotes pile to be handled later."
>
> You: "Why is that?"
>
> Ollie: "Because orders are always more important. We make money on orders. We don't make money on quotes."

Ollie has mentioned something very important when gathering requirements. As developers, we tend to focus on technical issues and treat all requirements as equal. Businesses do not think that way. Making money (or saving money) is almost always the driver behind a development project. If you are in doubt as to what the most important priority is, follow the money! In this case, then, we need to design the system so that (money-making) orders are prioritized over quotes.

Moving on...

> You: "What's the first thing you do when processing an order form?"
>
> Ollie: "The first thing I do is check that the customer's name, email, shipping address, and billing address are valid."

After further discussion with Ollie, we learn that addresses are checked using a special application on Ollie's computer. Ollie types in the addresses, and the computer looks up whether they exist or not. It also puts them into a standard format that the delivery service likes.

We learned something new again. The workflow requires communication outside the context to some third-party address checking service. We missed that in the Event Storming, so we'll have to make a note of that.

If the name and addresses are not valid, Ollie marks the problems on the form with a red pen and puts it on the pile of invalid forms. Later on, Ollie will call the customer and ask to correct that information.

We are now aware of *three* piles: incoming order forms (from the mail), incoming quotes (to be processed later), and invalid order forms (also to be processed later).

Piles of paper are a very important part of most business processes. And let's reiterate that some piles are more important than other piles; we must not forget to capture this in our design. When we come to the implementation phase, a "pile of paper" corresponds nicely with a queue, but again we have to remind ourselves to stay away from technical details right now.

> Ollie: "After that, I check the product codes on the form. Sometimes they are obviously wrong."
>
> You: "How can you tell?"
>
> Ollie: "Because the codes have certain formats. The codes for widgets start with a *W* and then four digits. The codes for gizmos start with a *G* and then three digits."
>
> You: "Are there any other types of product codes? Or likely to be soon?"
>
> Ollie: "No. The product code formats haven't changed in years."
>
> You: "What about product codes that look right? Do you check that they are real products?"
>
> Ollie: "Yes. I look them up in my copy of the product catalog. If any codes are not there, I mark the form with the errors and put it in the pile of invalid orders."

Let's pause and look at what's going on with the product codes here:

- First, Ollie looks at the format of the code: does it start with a *W* or a *G*, and so on. In programming terms, this is a purely syntactic check. We don't need access to a product catalog to do that.

- Next, Ollie checks to see that the code exists in the product catalog. In Ollie's case, this involves looking something up in a book. In a software system, this would be a database lookup.

> You: "Here's a silly question. Let's say that someone on the product team could respond instantly to all your questions. Would you still need your own copy of the product catalog?"
>
> Ollie: "But what if they are busy? Or the phones were down? It's not really about speed, it's about control. I don't want my job to be interrupted because somebody else isn't available. If I have my own copy of the product catalog, I can process almost every order form without being dependent on the product team."

So this is really about dependency management, not performance. We discussed the importance of *autonomy* in relation to bounded contexts earlier (*Getting the Contexts Right*, on page 18). This may be important to model in the domain—or not—but either way you should be aware of the requirement for the departments to work independently.

You: "OK, now say that all the product codes are good. What next?"

Ollie: "I check the quantities."

You: "Are the quantities integers or floats?"

Ollie: "Float? Like in water?"

Ubiquitous language time! Pro tip: Domain experts do not use programming terms like "float."

You: "What do you call those numbers then?"

Ollie: "I call them 'order quantities,' duh!"

OK, we can see that OrderQuantity will need to be a word in the ubiquitous language, along with ProductCode, AmountToBill, and so on.

Let's try again:

You: "Do the order quantities have decimals, or are they just whole numbers?"

Ollie: "It depends."

"It depends." When you hear that, you know things are going to get complicated.

You: "It depends on what?"

Ollie: "It depends on what the product is. Widgets are sold by the unit, but gizmos are sold by the kilogram. If someone has asked for 1.5 widgets, then of course that's a mistake."

You scribble some notes down furiously.

You: "OK, say that all the product codes and order quantities are good. What next?"

Ollie: "Next, I write in the prices for each line on the order and then sum them up to calculate the total amount to bill. Next, as I said earlier, I make two copies of the order form. I file the original and I put one copy in the shipping outbox and a second copy in the billing outbox. Finally, I scan the original, attach it to a standard acknowledgment letter, and email it back to the customer."

You: "One last question. You have all these order forms lying around. Do you ever accidentally mix up ones you have processed with ones that are still unvalidated?"

Ollie: "No. Every time I do something with them I mark them somehow. For example, when a form has been validated, I put a mark up here in the corner, so I know I've done that. I can tell when I've calculated the prices because the "total" box is filled out. Doing this means I can always tell order forms at different stages apart."

This is a good point to stop and digest what we've learned.

Representing Complexity in Our Domain Model

As we have drilled down into this one workflow, the domain model has become a lot more complicated. That's good. Better to spend time on understanding complexity now rather than later, when we are in the middle of coding. "A few weeks of programming can save you hours of planning," as they say.

Here's a diagram of the workflow now:

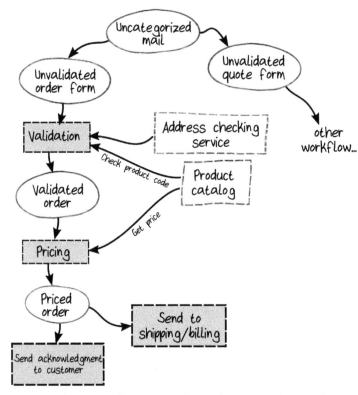

But this diagram doesn't reflect everything that we've learned. Let's see if we can do better and capture all this new information in our text-based language.

Representing Constraints

We'll start with the most primitive values first: the product codes and quantities, which we've learned are not just simple strings and integers but are constrained in various ways.

```
context: Order-Taking

data WidgetCode = string starting with "W" then 4 digits
data GizmoCode = string starting with "G" then 3 digits
data ProductCode = WidgetCode OR GizmoCode
```

In the fragment above, the words that Ollie used (such as WidgetCode) have also been used for the design, and we are treating them as part of the Ubiquitous Language. Furthermore, we have documented the constraints on Widget-Code and GizmoCode and then defined a ProductCode as a choice between those two types.

But isn't that being too strict? What happens if a new type of product needs to be handled? This is a problem we frequently run into. If we are too strict, we make things harder to change. But if we have too much freedom, we don't have a design at all.

The right answer depends on the context, as always. Generally though, it's important to capture the design from the domain expert's point of view. Checking the different kinds of codes is an important part of the validation process, and so it should be reflected in the design of the domain, which aims to be self-documenting. And if we didn't document the different kinds of product codes here, as part of the model, we'd have to document them somewhere else anyway.

Also, if the requirements *do* change, our model is very easy to change; adding a new kind of product code would only require an extra line.

Finally, remember that just because the design is strict doesn't mean that the implementation has to be strict. For example, an automated version of the validation process might just flag a strange code for human approval, rather than rejecting the whole order outright.

Now, what about documenting the requirements for the quantities? Here's the proposed design:

```
data OrderQuantity = UnitQuantity OR KilogramQuantity

data UnitQuantity = integer between 1 and ?
data KilogramQuantity = decimal between ? and ?
```

Just as we did with product codes, we'll define OrderQuantity as a choice—in this case between UnitQuantity and KilogramQuantity.

Writing this down, though, we realize that we don't have upper bounds for UnitQuantity and KilogramQuantity. Surely UnitQuantity can't be allowed to be in the billions?

Let's check with the domain expert. Ollie gives us the limits we need:

- The largest number of units allowed for an order quantity is 1000.
- The lowest weight is 0.05 kg and the highest is 100 kg.

These kinds of constraints are important to capture. We never want a situation in production where the units are accidentally negative, or the weight is hundreds of kilotons. Here is the updated spec, with these constraints documented:

```
data UnitQuantity = integer between 1 and 1000
data KilogramQuantity = decimal between 0.05 and 100.00
```

Representing the Life Cycle of an Order

Now let's move on to the Order. In our earlier design sketch, we had a simple definition for Order:

```
data Order =
    CustomerInfo
    AND ShippingAddress
    AND BillingAddress
    AND list of OrderLines
    AND AmountToBill
```

But now it's clear that this design is too simplistic and doesn't capture how Ollie thinks of orders. In Ollie's mental model, orders have a life cycle. They start off as unvalidated (straight from the mail), then they get "validated," and then they get "priced."

In the beginning, an order doesn't have a price, but by the end it does. The simple Order definition above erases that distinction.

With the paper forms, Ollie distinguishes between these phases by putting marks on the order after each phase, so an unvalidated order is immediately distinguishable from a validated one, and a validated one from a priced one.

We need to capture these same phases in our domain model, not just for documentation but to make it clear that (for example) an unpriced order should not be sent to the shipping department.

The easiest way to do that is by creating new names for each phase: UnvalidatedOrder, ValidatedOrder, and so on. It does mean that the design becomes longer and more tedious to write out, but the advantage is that everything is crystal clear.

Let's start with the initial unvalidated orders and quotes that arrive. We can document them like this:

```
data UnvalidatedOrder =
    UnvalidatedCustomerInfo
    AND UnvalidatedShippingAddress
    AND UnvalidatedBillingAddress
    AND list of UnvalidatedOrderLine
```

```
data UnvalidatedOrderLine =
    UnvalidatedProductCode
    AND UnvalidatedOrderQuantity
```

This documentation makes it explicit that at the beginning of the workflow, the CustomerInfo is not yet validated, the ShippingAddress is not yet validated, and so on.

The next stage is when the order has been validated. We can document it like this:

```
data ValidatedOrder =
    ValidatedCustomerInfo
    AND ValidatedShippingAddress
    AND ValidatedBillingAddress
    AND list of ValidatedOrderLine

data ValidatedOrderLine =
    ValidatedProductCode
    AND ValidatedOrderQuantity
```

This shows that all the components have now been checked and are valid.

The next stage is to price the order. A Priced Order is just like a validated order except for the following:

- Each line now has a price associated with it. That is, a PricedOrderLine is a ValidatedOrderLine plus a LinePrice.

- The order as a whole has an AmountToBill associated with it, calculated as the sum of the line prices.

Here's the model for this:

```
data PricedOrder =
    ValidatedCustomerInfo
    AND ValidatedShippingAddress
    AND ValidatedBillingAddress
    AND list of PricedOrderLine   // different from ValidatedOrderLine
    AND AmountToBill              // new

data PricedOrderLine =
    ValidatedOrderLine
    AND LinePrice                 // new
```

The final stage is to create the order acknowledgment.

```
data PlacedOrderAcknowledgment =
    PricedOrder
    AND AcknowledgmentLetter
```

You can see now that we've captured quite a lot of the business logic in this design already—rules such as these:

- An unvalidated order does not have a price.
- All the lines in a validated order must be validated, not just some of them.

The model is a lot more complicated than we originally thought. But we are just reflecting the way that the business works. If our model wasn't this complicated, we wouldn't be capturing the requirements properly.

Now if we can preserve these distinctions in our code as well, then our code will reflect the domain accurately and we will have a proper "domain-driven" design.

Fleshing out the Steps in the Workflow

It should be apparent that the workflow can be broken down into smaller steps: validation, pricing, and so on. Let's apply the same input/output approach to each of these steps.

First, the output of the overall workflow is a little more complicated than we thought earlier. Originally the only output was a "Order placed" event, but now the possible outcomes for the workflow are as follows:

- We send a "Order placed" event to shipping/billing, OR
- We add the order form to the invalid order pile and skip the rest of the steps.

Let's document the whole workflow in pseudocode, with steps like ValidateOrder broken out into separate substeps:

```
workflow "Place Order" =
    input: OrderForm
    output:
        OrderPlaced event (put on a pile to send to other teams)
        OR InvalidOrder (put on appropriate pile)

    // step 1
    do ValidateOrder
    If order is invalid then:
        add InvalidOrder to pile
        stop

    // step 2
    do PriceOrder

    // step 3
    do SendAcknowledgmentToCustomer

    // step 4
    return OrderPlaced event (if no errors)
```

With the overall flow documented, we can now add the extra details for each substep.

For example, the substep that validates the form takes an UnvalidatedOrder as input, and its output is either a ValidatedOrder or a ValidationError. We will also document the dependencies for the substep: it needs input from the product catalog (we'll call this the CheckProductCodeExists dependency) and the external address checking service (the CheckAddressExists dependency).

```
substep "ValidateOrder" =
    input: UnvalidatedOrder
    output: ValidatedOrder OR ValidationError
    dependencies: CheckProductCodeExists, CheckAddressExists

    validate the customer name
    check that the shipping and billing address exist
    for each line:
        check product code syntax
        check that product code exists in ProductCatalog

    if everything is OK, then:
        return ValidatedOrder
    else:
        return ValidationError
```

The substep that calculates the prices takes a ValidatedOrder as input and has a dependency on the product catalog (which we'll call GetProductPrice). The output is a PricedOrder.

```
substep "PriceOrder" =
    input: ValidatedOrder
    output: PricedOrder
    dependencies: GetProductPrice

    for each line:
        get the price for the product
        set the price for the line
    set the amount to bill ( = sum of the line prices)
```

Finally, the last substep takes a PricedOrder as input and then creates and sends the acknowledgment.

```
substep "SendAcknowledgmentToCustomer" =
    input: PricedOrder
    output: None

    create acknowledgment letter and send it
    and the priced order to the customer
```

This documentation of the requirements is looking a lot more like code now, but it can still be read and checked by a domain expert.

Wrapping Up

We'll stop gathering requirements now, as we'll have plenty to work with when we move to the modeling phase in the second part of this book. But first let's review what we've learned in this chapter.

We saw that it's important not to dive into implementation details while doing design: DDD is neither database-driven nor class-driven. Instead, we focused on capturing the domain without assumptions and without assuming any particular way of coding.

And we saw that listening to the domain expert carefully reveals a lot of complexity, even in a relatively simple system like this. For example, we originally thought that there would be a single "Order," but more investigation uncovered many variants of an order throughout its life cycle, each with slightly different data and behavior.

What's Next

We'll be looking shortly at how we can model this order-taking workflow using the F# type system. But before we do that, let's step back and look at the big picture again and discuss how to translate a complete system into a software architecture. That will be the topic of the next chapter.

CHAPTER 3

A Functional Architecture

Here's our next challenge: how should we translate our understanding of the domain into a software architecture, especially one that is based on functional programming principles?

We really shouldn't be doing too much thinking about architecture at this point, because we still don't really understand the system yet—we are at the peak of our ignorance! The best use of our time is to do things that reduce this ignorance: Event Storming, interviews, and all the other best practices around requirements gathering.

On the other hand, it's good to have a rough idea of how we are going to implement our domain model as software. In a fast-paced development cycle, we often need to start implementing some of the domain before we have understood the rest of it, so we'll need to have some plan for fitting the various components together even before they're built. And there's a lot to be said for creating a crude prototype—a "walking skeleton"—that demonstrates how the system will work as a whole. Early feedback on a concrete implementation is a great way to discover gaps in your knowledge.

In this chapter we'll take a brief look at a typical software architecture for a functionally oriented domain model. We'll look at how DDD concepts such as *bounded contexts* and *Domain Events* might be translated into software, and we'll sketch out the approach to implementation that we'll use in the rest of this book.

Software architecture is a domain in its own right, of course, so let's follow our own advice and use a "ubiquitous language" when talking about it. We'll use the terminology from Simon Brown's "C4" approach,[1] whereby a software architecture consists of four levels that can be described as follows:

---

1.   http://static.codingthearchitecture.com/c4.pdf

- The "system context" is the top level, representing the entire system.

- The system context comprises a number of "containers," which are deployable units such as a website, a web service, a database, and so on.

- Each container in turn comprises a number of "components," which are the major structural building blocks in the code.

- Finally, each component comprises a number of "classes" (or in a functional architecture, "modules") that contain a set of low-level methods or functions.

One of the goals of a good architecture is to define the various boundaries between containers, components, and modules, such that when new requirements arise, as they will, the "cost of change" is minimized.

Bounded Contexts as Autonomous Software Components

Let's start with the concept of a "bounded context" and how it relates to an architecture. As we saw earlier, it's important that a context is an *autonomous* subsystem with a *well-defined boundary*. Even with those constraints, though, we have a number of common architectural styles to choose from.

If the entire system is implemented as a single monolithic deployable (a single container using the C4 terminology above), a bounded context could be as simple as a separate module with a well-defined interface, or preferably, a more distinct component such as a .NET assembly. Alternatively, each bounded context could be deployed separately in its own container—a classic service-oriented architecture. Or we could go even more fine-grained and make each individual *workflow* into a standalone deployable container—a microservice architecture.

At this early stage, however, we do not need to commit to a particular approach. The translation from the *logical* design to the *deployable* equivalent is not critical, as long as we ensure that the bounded contexts stay decoupled and autonomous.

We stressed earlier that it's important to get the boundaries right, but of course, this is hard to do at the beginning of a project, and we should expect that the boundaries will change as we learn more about the domain. It's a lot easier to refactor a monolith, so a good practice is to build the system as a monolith initially and refactor to decoupled containers only as needed. There's no need to jump straight to microservices and pay the "microservice premium"[2]

---

2.   https://www.martinfowler.com/bliki/MicroservicePremium.html

(the extra burden on operations) unless you are sure the benefits outweigh the drawbacks. It's tricky to create a truly decoupled microservice architecture: if you switch one of the microservices off and anything else breaks, you don't really have a microservice architecture, you just have a distributed monolith!

Communicating Between Bounded Contexts

How do bounded contexts communicate with each other? For example, when the order-taking context has finished processing the order, how does it tell the shipping context to actually ship it? As we've seen earlier, the answer is to use events. For example, the implementation might look like this:

- The Place-Order workflow in the order-taking context emits an OrderPlaced event.
- The OrderPlaced event is put on a queue or otherwise published.
- The shipping context listens for OrderPlaced events.
- When an event is received, a ShipOrder command is created.
- The ShipOrder command initiates the Ship-Order workflow.
- When the Ship-Order workflow finishes successfully, it emits an OrderShipped event.

Here's a diagram for this example:

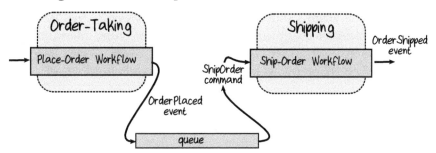

You can see that this is a completely decoupled design: the upstream component (the order-taking subsystem) and the downstream component (the shipping subsystem) are not aware of each other and are communicating only through events. This kind of decoupling is critical if we want to have truly autonomous components.

The exact mechanism for transmitting events between contexts depends on the architecture we choose. Queues are great for buffered asynchronous communication and so would be the first choice for an implementation with microservices or agents. In a monolithic system, we can use the same queuing approach internally, or just use a simple direct linkage between the upstream component and the downstream component via a function call. As always, we don't need to choose right now, as long as we design the components to be decoupled.

As for the handler that translates events (such as OrderPlaced) to commands (such as ShipOrder), it can be part of the downstream context (living at the boundary of the context), or it can be done by a separate router[3] or process manager[4] running as part of the infrastructure, depending on your architecture and where you want to do the coupling between events and commands.

Transferring Data Between Bounded Contexts

In general, an event used for communication between contexts will not be just a simple signal but will also contain all the data that the downstream components need to process the event. For example, the OrderPlaced event might contain the complete order that was placed. That gives the shipping context all the information it needs to construct a corresponding ShipOrder command. (If the data is too large to be contained in the event, some sort of reference to a shared data storage location can be transmitted instead.)

The data objects that are passed around may be superficially similar to the objects defined inside the bounded context (which we'll call *domain objects*), but they are *not* the same; they are specifically designed to be serialized and shared as part of the intercontext infrastructure. We will call these objects *Data Transfer Objects* or DTOs (although that term originated outside of DDD,[5] and I am using it slightly differently here). In other words, the OrderDTO contained in an OrderPlaced event will contain most of the same information as an Order domain object, but it will be structured differently to suit its purpose. (The *Serialization* chapter goes into detail on how to define DTOs.)

At the boundaries of the upstream context then, the domain objects are converted into DTOs, which are in turn serialized into JSON, XML, or some other serialization format:

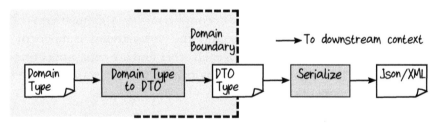

At the downstream context, the process is repeated in the other direction: the JSON or XML is deserialized into a DTO, which in turn is converted into a domain object as shown in the figure on page 47.

---

3.   http://www.enterpriseintegrationpatterns.com/patterns/messaging/MessageRouter.html

4.   https://www.slideshare.net/BerndRuecker/long-running-processes-in-ddd

5.   https://martinfowler.com/eaaCatalog/dataTransferObject.html

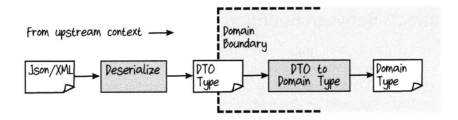

In practice, the top-level DTOs that are serialized are typically event DTOs, which in turn contain child DTOs, such as a DTO for Order, which in turn contains additional child DTOs (such as a list of DTOs representing OrderLines).

Trust Boundaries and Validation

The perimeter of a bounded context acts as a "trust boundary." Anything inside the bounded context will be trusted and valid, while anything outside the bounded context will be untrusted and might be invalid. Therefore, we will add "gates" at the beginning and end of the workflow that act as intermediaries between the trusted domain and the untrusted outside world.

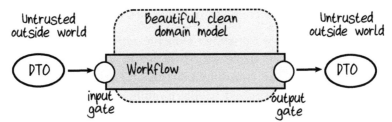

At the input gate, we will *always* validate the input to make sure that it conforms to the constraints of the domain model. For example, say that a certain property of an Order must be non-null and less than fifty characters. The incoming OrderDTO will have no such constraints and could contain anything, but after validation at the input gate, we can be sure that the Order domain object is valid. If the validation fails, then the rest of the workflow is bypassed and an error is generated. (The *Serialization* chapter covers this kind of DTO validation.)

The job of the output gate is different. Its job is to ensure that private information doesn't leak out of the bounded context, both to avoid accidental coupling between contexts and for security reasons. For example, there's no need for the shipping context to know the credit card number used to pay for an order. In order to do this, the output gate will often deliberately "lose" information (such as the card number) in the process of converting domain objects to DTOs.

Contracts Between Bounded Contexts

We want to reduce coupling between bounded contexts as much as possible, but a shared communication format always induces some coupling: the events and related DTOs form a kind of contract between bounded contexts. The two contexts will need to agree on a common format for them in order for communication to be successful.

So who gets to decide the contract? There are various relationships between the contexts, and the DDD community has developed some terms for the common ones:

- A *Shared Kernel* relationship is where two contexts share some common domain design, so the teams involved must collaborate. In our domain, for example, we might say that the order-taking and shipping contexts must use the same design for a delivery address: the order-taking context accepts an address and validates it, while the shipping context uses the same address to ship the package. In this relationship, changing the definition of an event or a DTO must be done only in consultation with the owners of the other contexts that are affected.

- A *Customer/Supplier* or *Consumer Driven Contract*[6] relationship is where the downstream context defines the contract that they want the upstream context to provide. The two domains can still evolve independently, as long as the upstream context fulfills its obligations under the contract. In our domain, the billing context might define the contract ("this is what I need in order to bill a customer") and then the order-taking context provides only that information and no more.

- A *Conformist* relationship is the opposite of consumer-driven. The downstream context accepts the contract provided by the upstream context and adapts its own domain model to match. In our domain, the order-taking context might just accept the contract defined by the product catalog and adapt its code to use it as is.

Anti-Corruption Layers

Often when communicating with an external system, the interface that is available does not match our domain model at all. In this case, the interactions and data need to be transformed into something more suitable for use inside

---

6.   https://www.infoq.com/articles/consumer-driven-contracts

the bounded context, otherwise our domain model will become "corrupted" by trying to adapt to the external system's model.

This extra level of decoupling between contexts is called an *Anti-Corruption Layer* in DDD terminology, often abbreviated as "ACL." In the diagram above, the "input gate" often plays the role of the ACL—it prevents the internal, pure domain model from being "corrupted" by knowledge of the outside world.

That is, the Anti-Corruption Layer is not primarily about performing validation or preventing data corruption, but instead acts as a translator between two different languages—the language used in the upstream context and the language used in the downstream context. In our order-taking example, then, we might have an Anti-Corruption Layer that translates from "order-taking" vocabulary to "shipping" vocabulary, allowing the two contexts, each with their own vocabulary, to evolve independently.

A Context Map with Relationships

Let's say that we have progressed with our design and have now decided what the relationships between our contexts are:

- The relationship between the order-taking and shipping contexts will be a "Shared Kernel," meaning that they will jointly own the communications contract.

- The relationship between order-taking and billing will be a "Consumer-Driven Contract" one, meaning that the billing context determines the contract and the order-taking system will supply the billing context with exactly the data it needs.

- The relationship between order-taking and the product catalog will be a "Conformist" one, meaning that the order-taking context will submit to using the same model as the product catalog.

- Finally, the external address checking service has a model that's not at all similar to our domain, so we'll insert an explicit Anti-Corruption Layer into our interactions with it. This is a common pattern when using a third-party component. It helps us avoid vendor lock-in and lets us swap to a different service later.

A context map of our domain showing these kinds of intercontext relationships is shown in the figure on page 50.

You can see that the context map is no longer just showing purely technical relationships between contexts, but is now also showing the relationships between the *teams* that own the contexts and how we expect them to

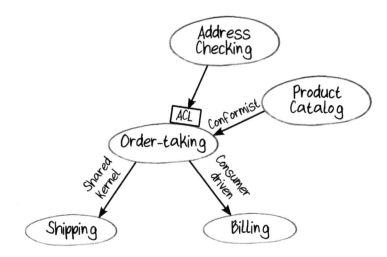

collaborate (or not!). Deciding on how the domains interact is often just as much an organizational challenge as it is a technical one, and some teams have used the so-called "inverse Conway maneuver"[7] to ensure that the organization structure is aligned with the architecture.

Workflows Within a Bounded Context

In our discovery process, we treated business workflows as a mini-process initiated by a command, which generated one or more Domain Events. In our functional architecture, each of these workflows will be mapped to a single function, where the input is a command object and the output is a list of event objects.

When we create diagrams of the design, we represent workflows as little pipes with an input and output. Public workflows (those that are triggered from outside the bounded context) are shown as "sticking out" a little over the boundary as shown in the figure on page 51.

A workflow is always contained within a single bounded context and never implements a scenario "end-to-end" through multiple contexts. The *Modeling Workflows as Pipelines* chapter goes into detail on how to model workflows.

Workflow Inputs and Outputs

The input to a workflow is always the data associated with a command, and the output is always a set of events to communicate to other contexts. In our order-placing workflow, for example, the input is the data associated with a PlaceOrder command and the output is a set of events such as the OrderPlaced event.

---

7.   http://bit.ly/InverseConwayManeuver

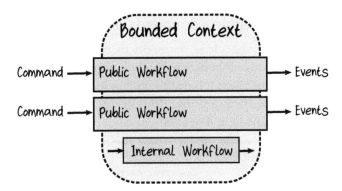

But remember that we have now determined that there is a "customer/supplier" relationship with the billing context. That means that, rather than sending a generic OrderPlaced event to the billing context, we need to send *only* the information that billing needs and no more. For example, this might just be the billing address and the total amount to bill but not the shipping address or the list of items.

This means we will need to emit a new event (BillableOrderPlaced say) from our workflow, with a structure that might look something like this:

```
data BillableOrderPlaced =
    OrderId
    AND BillingAddress
    AND AmountToBill
```

We might also want to emit an OrderAcknowledgmentSent event as well. With these changes, our earlier diagram of the workflow on page 29 is misleading and we need to update it:

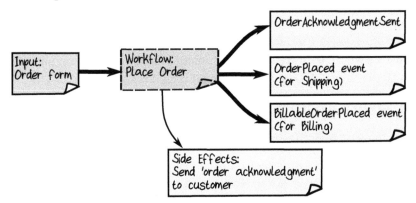

In the preceding diagram, it's important to note that a workflow function does not "publish" Domain Events—it simply returns them. How they get published is a separate concern.

Avoid Domain Events Within a Bounded Context

In an object-oriented design, it is common to have Domain Events raised internally within a bounded context. In that approach, a workflow object raises an OrderPlaced event. Next a handler listens for that event and sends the order acknowledgment, then another handler generates a BillableOrderPlaced event, and so on. It might look like this:

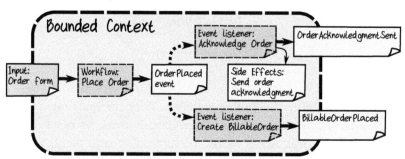

In a functional design, we prefer not to use this approach because it creates hidden dependencies. Instead, if we need a "listener" for an event, we just append it to the end of workflow like this:

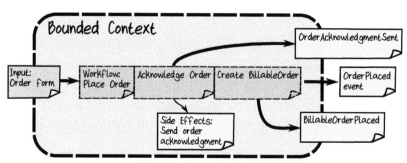

This approach is more explicit—there are no global event managers with mutable state—and therefore it's easier to understand and maintain. We'll see how this works in practice in the Implementation chapter on page 161 and also in the Evolving A Design chapter on page 265.

Code Structure Within a Bounded Context

Now let's look at how the code is structured within a bounded context.

In a traditional "layered approach," the code is divided into layers: a core domain or business logic layer, a database layer, a services layer, and an API or user interface layer (or some variant of these). A workflow will start at the top layer, work its way down to the database layer, and then return back to the top as shown in the figure on page 53.

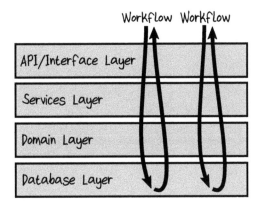

This approach has many problems, however. One particular issue is that it breaks the important design principle of "code that changes together belongs together." Because the layers are assembled "horizontally," a change to the way that the workflow works means that you need to touch every layer. A better way is to switch to "vertical" slices, where each workflow contains all the code it needs to get its job done, and when the requirements change for a workflow, only the code in that particular vertical slice needs to change as shown in the figure.

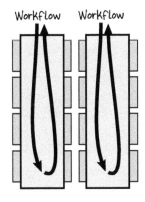

This is still not ideal, though. To see this, let's stretch a workflow into a horizontal pipe and look at the layers in that way.

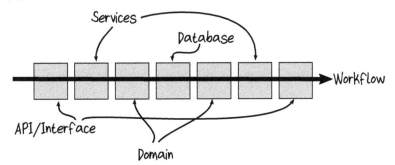

It's clear that the layers are intermingled in a way that makes understanding the logic (and testing it) unnecessarily complicated.

The Onion Architecture

Let's instead put the domain code at the center and then have the other aspects be assembled around it using the rule that each layer can only depend on inner layers, not on layers further out. That is, *all dependencies must point inward.* This is called the "Onion Architecture."[8]

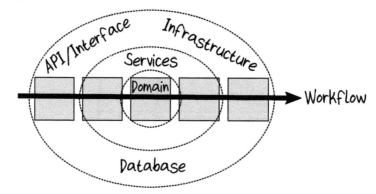

Other similar approaches exist, such as the Hexagonal Architecture[9] and the Clean Architecture.[10]

In order to ensure that all dependencies point inward, we will have to use the functional equivalent of dependency injection, which is discussed in *Implementation: Composing a Pipeline.*

Keep I/O at the Edges

A major aim of functional programming is to work with functions that are predictable and easy to reason about without having to look inside them. In order to do this, we will try to work with immutable data wherever possible and try to ensure that our functions have *explicit* dependencies instead of hidden dependencies. Most importantly, we will try to avoid side effects in our functions, including randomness, mutation of variables outside the function, and most importantly, any kind of I/O.

For example, a function that reads or writes to a database or file system would be considered "impure," so we would try to avoid these kinds of functions in our core domain.

But then how *do* we read or write data? The answer is to push any I/O to the edges of the onion—to access a database, say, only at the start or end of a workflow, not inside the workflow. This has the additional benefit of forcing us to separate different concerns: the core domain model is concerned only with business logic, while persistence and other I/O is an infrastructural concern.

---

8.   http://jeffreypalermo.com/blog/the-onion-architecture-part-1/
9.   http://alistair.cockburn.us/Hexagonal+architecture
10. https://8thlight.com/blog/uncle-bob/2012/08/13/the-clean-architecture.html

In fact, the practice of shifting I/O and database access to the edges combines very nicely with the concept of *persistence ignorance* that we introduced in the previous chapter. You can't model your domain using a database if you can't even access the database from inside the workflow! (The *Persistence* chapter discusses the use of databases in more detail.)

Wrapping Up

We've been introduced to a few more DDD-related concepts and terminology in this chapter, so let's summarize them in one place:

- A *Domain Object* is an object designed for use only within the boundaries of a context, as opposed to a Data Transfer Object.

- A *Data Transfer Object*, or *DTO*, is an object designed to be serialized and shared between contexts.

- *Shared Kernel*, *Customer/Supplier*, and *Conformist* are different kinds of relationships between bounded contexts.

- An *Anti-Corruption Layer*, or *ACL*, is a component that translates concepts from one domain to another in order to reduce coupling and allow domains to evolve independently.

- *Persistence Ignorance* means that the domain model should be based only on the concepts in the domain itself and should not contain any awareness of databases or other persistence mechanisms.

What's Next

We've now got an understanding of the domain and a general approach to designing a solution for it, so we can move on to the challenge of modeling and implementing the individual workflows. In the next few chapters, we'll be using the F# type system to define a workflow and the data that it uses, creating compilable code that is still understandable by domain experts and non-developers.

To start with, though, we need to understand what *type* means to functional programmers and how it is different from *class* in object-oriented design. That's the topic of the next chapter.

Part II

Modeling the Domain

In this second part, we'll take one workflow from the domain and model it in a functional way. We'll see how the functional decomposition of a domain differs from an object-oriented approach, and we'll learn how to use types to capture requirements. By the end of this part, you'll know how to write concise code that does double-duty: first as readable documentation of the domain but also as a compilable framework that the rest of the implementation can build upon.

CHAPTER 4

Understanding Types

In the second chapter, we captured the domain-driven requirements for a single workflow of the order-taking system. The next challenge is to convert those informal requirements into compilable code.

The approach we are going to take is to represent the requirements using F#'s "algebraic type system." In this chapter we'll learn what algebraic types are, how they are defined and used, and how they can represent a domain model. Then, in the next chapter, we'll use what we've learned to accurately model the order-placing workflow.

Understanding Functions

Before we can understand types, we need to understand the most basic concept in functional programming—a function.

If you remember your high-school mathematics, a function is a kind of black box with an input and an output. You can imagine it as a bit of railroad track, with a Tunnel of Transformation sitting on it. Something goes in, is transformed somehow, and comes out the other side.

For example, let's say that this particular function turns apples into bananas. We describe a function by writing down the input and output, separated by an arrow, as shown in the figure on page 60.

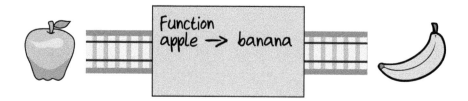

Type Signatures

The `apple -> banana` description is called a *type signature* (also known as a function signature). This particular signature is simple, but type signatures can get very complicated. Understanding and using type signatures is a critical part of coding with F#, so let's make sure we understand how they work.

Here are two functions: `add1` adds 1 to its single input `x`, and `add` adds its two inputs, `x` and `y`:

```
let add1 x = x + 1    // signature is: int -> int
let add x y = x + y  // signature is: int -> int -> int
```

As you can see, the `let` keyword is used to define a function. The parameters are separated by spaces, without parentheses or commas. Unlike C# or Java, there is no `return` keyword. The last expression in the function definition is the output of the function.

Even though F# cares about the types of the inputs and outputs, you rarely need to explicitly declare what they are, because in most cases the compiler will infer the types for you automatically.[1]

- For `add1`, the inferred type of `x` (before the arrow) is `int` and the inferred type of the output (after the arrow) is also `int`, so the type signature is `int -> int`.

- For `add`, the inferred type of `x` and `y` is `int` and the inferred type of the output (after the last arrow) is also `int`. `add` has two parameters, and each parameter is separated by an arrow, so the type signature is `int -> int -> int`.

If you are using an IDE such as Visual Studio, hovering over the definition of a function will show you its type signature, but since this is a book, we'll put the type signature in a comment above the definition when we need to make it clear. It's just a comment and isn't used by the compiler.

Functions that consist of more than one line are written with an indent (like Python). There are no curly braces. Here's an example:

---

1. https://fsharpforfunandprofit.com/posts/type-inference/

```
// squarePlusOne : int -> int
let squarePlusOne x =
  let square = x * x
  square + 1
```

This example also shows that you can define subfunctions within a function (let square = ...) and again, that the last line (square + 1) is the return value.

Functions with Generic Types

If the function will work with *any* type, then the compiler will automatically infer a *generic* type, as in this areEqual function.

```
// areEqual : 'a -> 'a -> bool
let areEqual x y =
  (x = y)
```

For areEqual the inferred type of x and y is 'a. A tick-then-letter is F#'s way of indicating a generic type. And it's true, since x and y could be *any* type as long as they are the *same* type.

And by the way, this code shows that the equality test is = in F#, not == like in C-like languages. For comparison, the code for areEqual in C#, using generics, might look something like this:

```
static bool AreEqual<T>(T x, T y)
{
    return (x == y);
}
```

Types and Functions

In a programming language like F#, types play a key role, so let's look at what a functional programmer means by *type*.

A *type* in functional programming is not the same as a *class* in object-oriented programming. It's much simpler. In fact, a type is just the name given to the set of possible values that can be used as inputs or outputs of a function:

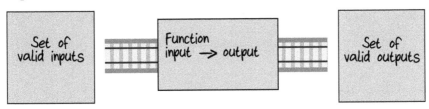

For example, we might take the set of numbers in the range -32768 to +32767 and give them the label int16. There is no special meaning or behavior to a type beyond that.

Here is an example of a function with an int16 input:

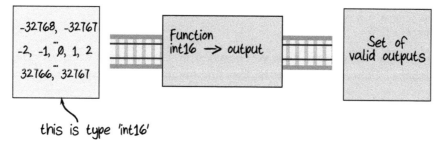

this is type 'int16'

The type is what determines the function's signature, so the signature for this function might look like this:

```
int16 -> someOutputType
```

Here is an example of a function with an output consisting of the set of all possible strings, which we will call the string type:

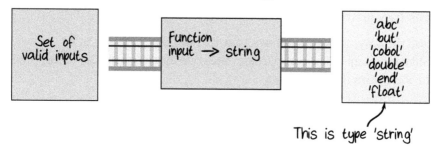

This is type 'string'

The signature for this function would be this:

```
someInputType -> string
```

The set of things in a type do not have to be primitive objects. For example, we may have a function that works with a set of objects that collectively we call Person:

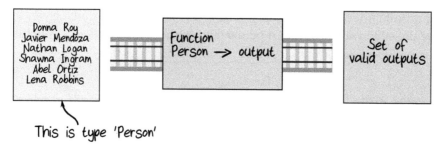

This is type 'Person'

From a conceptual point of view, the things in the type can be *any* kind of thing, real or virtual. The figure on page 63 shows a function that works with "Fruit." Whether these are real fruit or a virtual representation isn't important right now.

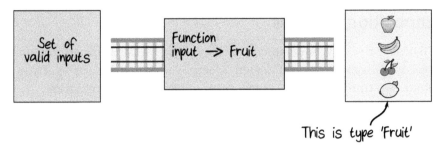

This is type 'Fruit'

And finally, functions are things too, so we can use sets of functions as a type as well. The function below outputs something that is a Fruit-to-Fruit function:

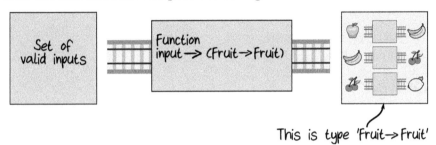

This is type 'Fruit→Fruit'

Each element in the output set is a Fruit -> Fruit function, so the signature of the function as a whole is this:

```
someInputType -> (Fruit -> Fruit)
```

Jargon Alert: "Values" vs. "Objects" vs. "Variables"

In a functional programming language, most things are called "values." In an object-oriented language, most things are called "objects." So what is the difference between a "value" and an "object"?

A value is just a member of a type, something that can be used as an input or an output. For example, 1 is a value of type int, "abc" is a value of type string, and so on.

Functions can be values too. If we define a simple function such as let add1 x = x + 1, then add1 is a (function) value of type int->int.

Values are immutable (which is why they are not called "variables"). And values do not have any behavior attached to them, they are just data.

In contrast, an object is an encapsulation of a data structure *and* its associated behavior (methods). In general, objects are expected to have state (that is, be mutable), and all operations that change the internal state must be provided by the object itself (via "dot" notation).

So in the world of functional programming (where objects don't exist), you should use the term "value" rather than "variable" or "object."

Composition of Types

You'll hear the word "composition" used a lot in functional programming—it's the foundation of functional design. Composition just means that you can combine two things to make a bigger thing, like using Lego blocks.

In the functional programming world, we use composition to build new functions from smaller functions and new types from smaller types. We'll talk about composition of types right now, and we'll talk about function composition later, in Chapter 8, *Understanding Functions*, on page 147.

In F#, new types are built from smaller types in two ways:

- By _AND_ing them together
- By _OR_ing them together

"AND" Types

Let's start with building types using *AND*. For example, we might say that to make fruit salad you need an apple *and* a banana *and* some cherries:

In F# this kind of type is called a *record*. Here's how the definition of a FruitSalad record type would be written in F#:

```
type FruitSalad = {
  Apple: AppleVariety
  Banana: BananaVariety
  Cherries: CherryVariety
}
```

The curly braces indicate that it is a record type, and the three fields are Apple, Banana, and Cherries.

"OR" Types

The other way of building new types is by using *OR*. For example, we might say that for a fruit snack you need an apple *or* a banana *or* some cherries:

These kinds of "choice" types will be incredibly useful for modeling (as we will see throughout this book). Here is the definition of a FruitSnack using a choice type:

```
type FruitSnack =
  | Apple of AppleVariety
  | Banana of BananaVariety
  | Cherries of CherryVariety
```

A choice type like this is called a *discriminated union* in F#. It can be read like this:

- A FruitSnack is either an AppleVariety (tagged with Apple) *or* a BananaVariety (tagged with Banana) *or* a CherryVariety (tagged with Cherries).

The vertical bar separates each choice, and the tags (such as Apple and Banana) are needed because sometimes the two or more choices may have the same type and so tags are needed to distinguish them.

The varieties of fruit are themselves defined as *OR* types, which in this case is used similarly to an enum in other languages.

```
type AppleVariety =
  | GoldenDelicious
  | GrannySmith
  | Fuji
type BananaVariety =
  | Cavendish
  | GrosMichel
  | Manzano
type CherryVariety =
  | Montmorency
  | Bing
```

This can be read as:

- An AppleVariety is either a GoldenDelicious *or* a GrannySmith *or* a Fuji,

and so on.

Jargon Alert: "Product Types" and "Sum Types"

The types that are built using *AND* are called *product types*.

The types that are built using *OR* are called *sum types* or *tagged unions* or, in F# terminology, *discriminated unions*. In this book I will often call them *choice types*, because I think that best describes their role in domain modeling.

Simple Types

We will often define a choice type with only *one* choice, such as this:

```
type ProductCode =
  | ProductCode of string
```

This type is almost always simplified to this:

```
type ProductCode = ProductCode of string
```

Why would we create such a type? Because it's an easy way to create a "wrapper"—a type that contains a primitive (such as a string or int) as an inner value.

We'll be seeing a lot of these kinds of types when we do domain modeling. In this book I will label these single-case unions as "simple types," as opposed to compound types like records and discriminated unions. More discussion of them is available in the section on Simple Types on page 79.

Algebraic Type Systems

Now we can define what we mean by an "algebraic type system." It's not as scary as it sounds—an algebraic type system is simply one where every compound type is composed from smaller types by *AND*-ing or *OR*-ing them together. F#, like most functional languages (but unlike OO languages), has a built-in algebraic type system.

Using *AND* and *OR* to build new data types should feel familiar—we used the same kind of *AND* and *OR* to document our domain. We'll see shortly that an algebraic type system is indeed an excellent tool for domain modeling.

Working with F# Types

In F#, the way that types are defined and the way that they are constructed are very similar.

For example, to define a record type, we use curly braces and then name:type definitions for each field, like this:

```
type Person = {First:string; Last:string}
```

To construct a value of this type, we use the same curly braces but use = to assign a value to a field, like this:

```
let aPerson = {First="Alex"; Last="Adams"}
```

And to deconstruct a value of this type using pattern matching, we use the same syntax but this time on the *left* side of the equation, like this:

```
let {First=first; Last=last} = aPerson
```

This code says that the values first and last will be set to the corresponding fields in the record. With records, we can also use the more familiar dot syntax as well. So the code above is equivalent to this:

```
let first = aPerson.First
let last = aPerson.Last
```

The symmetry between construction and deconstruction applies to discriminated unions as well. To define a choice type, we use the vertical bar to separate each choice, with each choice defined as caseLabel of type, like this:

```
type OrderQuantity =
  | UnitQuantity of int
  | KilogramQuantity of decimal
```

A choice type is constructed by using any one of the case labels as a constructor function, with the associated information passed in as a parameter, like this:

```
let anOrderQtyInUnits = UnitQuantity 10
let anOrderQtyInKg = KilogramQuantity 2.5
```

Cases are *not* the same as subclasses—UnitQuantity and KilogramQuantity are not types themselves, just distinct cases of the OrderQuantity type. In the example above, both these values have the *same* type: OrderQuantity.

To deconstruct a choice type, we must use pattern matching (the match..with syntax) with a test for each case, like this:

```
let printQuantity aOrderQty =
  match aOrderQty with
  | UnitQuantity uQty ->
    printfn "%i units" uQty
  | KilogramQuantity kgQty ->
    printfn "%g kg" kgQty
```

As part of the matching process, any data associated with a particular case is also made available. In the example above, the uQty value will be set if the input matches the UnitQuantity case.

Here's the result of the pattern matching when we pass in the two values we defined above:

```
printQuantity anOrderQtyInUnits // "10 units"
printQuantity anOrderQtyInKg    // "2.5 kg"
```

Building a Domain Model by Composing Types

A composable type system is a great aid in doing domain-driven design because we can quickly create a complex model simply by mixing types together in different combinations. For example, say that we want to track payments for an e-commerce site. Let's see how this might be sketched out in code during a design session.

First, we start with some wrappers for the primitive types, such as CheckNumber. These are the "simple types" we discussed above. Doing this gives them meaningful names and makes the rest of the domain easier to understand.

```
type CheckNumber = CheckNumber of int
type CardNumber = CardNumber of string
```

Next, we build up some low-level types. A CardType is an *OR* type—a choice between Visa *or* Mastercard, while CreditCardInfo is an *AND* type, a record containing a CardType *and* a CardNumber:

```
type CardType =
  Visa | Mastercard        // 'OR' type

type CreditCardInfo = {    // 'AND' type (record)
  CardType : CardType
  CardNumber : CardNumber
  }
```

We then define another *OR* type, PaymentMethod, as a choice between Cash or Check or Card. This is no longer a simple "enum" because some of the choices have data associated with them: the Check case has a CheckNumber and the Card case has CreditCardInfo:

```
type PaymentMethod =
  | Cash
  | Check of CheckNumber
  | Card of CreditCardInfo
```

We can define a few more basic types, such as PaymentAmount and Currency:

```
type PaymentAmount = PaymentAmount of decimal
type Currency = EUR | USD
```

And finally, the top-level type, Payment, is a record containing a PaymentAmount *and* a Currency *and* a PaymentMethod:

```
type Payment = {
  Amount : PaymentAmount
  Currency:  Currency
  Method:  PaymentMethod
  }
```

So there you go. In about 25 lines of code, we have defined a pretty useful set of types already.

Of course, there is no behavior directly associated with these types because this is a functional model, not an object-oriented model. To document the actions that can be taken, we instead define types that represent functions.

So, for example, if we want to show there is a way to use a Payment type to pay for an unpaid invoice, where the final result is a paid invoice, we could define a function type that looks like this:

```
type PayInvoice =
  UnpaidInvoice -> Payment -> PaidInvoice
```

Which means this: Given an UnpaidInvoice and then a Payment, we can create a PaidInvoice.

Or, to convert a payment from one currency to another:

```
type ConvertPaymentCurrency =
  Payment -> Currency -> Payment
```

where the first Payment is the input, the second parameter (Currency) is the currency to convert to, and the second Payment—the output—is the result after the conversion.

Modeling Optional Values, Errors, and Collections

While we are discussing domain modeling, let's talk about some common situations and how to represent them with the F# type system, namely:

- Optional or missing values
- Errors
- Functions that return no value
- Collections

Modeling Optional Values

The types that we have used so far—records and choice types—are not allowed to be null in F#. That means that every time we reference a type in a domain model, it's a *required* value.

So how can we model missing or optional data?

The answer is to think about what missing data means: it's either present or absent. There's something there, or nothing there. We can model this with a choice type called Option, defined like this:

```
type Option<'a> =
  | Some of 'a
  | None
```

The Some case means that there is data stored in the associated value 'a. The None case means there is no data. Again, the tick in 'a is F#'s way of indicating a generic type—that is, the Option type can be used to wrap *any* other type. The C# or Java equivalent would be something like Option<T>.

You don't need to define the Option type yourself. It's part of the standard F# library, and it has a rich set of helper functions that work with it.

To indicate optional data in the domain model then, we wrap the type in Option<..>, just as we would in C# or Java. For example, if we have a PersonalName type and the first and last names are required but the middle initial is optional, we could model it like this:

```
type PersonalName = {
  FirstName : string
  MiddleInitial: Option<string>  // optional
  LastName : string
  }
```

F# also supports using the option label *after* the type, which is easier to read and more commonly used:

```
type PersonalName = {
  FirstName : string
  MiddleInitial: string option
  LastName : string
  }
```

Modeling Errors

Let's say we have a process with a possible failure: "The payment was made successfully, or it failed because the card has expired." How should we model this? F# does support throwing exceptions, but we'll often want to *explicitly* document in the type signature the fact that a failure can happen. This calls out for a choice type with two cases, so let's define a type Result:

```
type Result<'Success,'Failure> =
  | Ok of 'Success
  | Error of 'Failure
```

We'll use the Ok case to hold the value when the function succeeds and the Error case to hold the error data when the function fails. And of course we want this type to be able to contain any kind of data, hence the use of generic types in the definition.

If you are using F# 4.1 and above (or Visual Studio 2017), then you don't need to define the Result type yourself, since it's part of the standard F# library. If you are using an earlier version of F#, you can easily define it and its helper functions in a few lines.

To indicate that a function can fail, we wrap the output with a Result type. For example, if the PayInvoice function could fail, then we might define it like this:

```
type PayInvoice =
  UnpaidInvoice -> Payment -> Result<PaidInvoice,PaymentError>
```

This shows that the type associated with the Ok case is PaidInvoice and the type associated with the Error case is PaymentError. We could then define PaymentError as a choice type with a case for each possible error:

```
type PaymentError =
  | CardTypeNotRecognized
  | PaymentRejected
  | PaymentProviderOffline
```

This approach to documenting errors will be covered in detail in Chapter 10, *Implementation: Working with Errors*, on page 191.

Modeling No Value at All

Most programming languages have a concept of void, used when a function or method returns nothing.

In a functional language like F#, every function must return *something*, so we can't use void. Instead we use a special built-in type called unit. There is only one value for unit, written as a pair of parentheses: ().

Let's say that you have a function that updates a customer record in a database. The input is a customer record, but there's no useful output. In F#, we would write the type signature using unit as the output type, like this:

```
type SaveCustomer = Customer -> unit
```

(In practice it would be more complex than this, of course! See Chapter 12, *Persistence*, on page 239, for a detailed discussion of working with databases.)

Alternatively, let's say you have a function that has no input yet returns something useful, such as a function that generates random numbers. In F#, you would indicate "no input" with unit as well, like this:

```
type NextRandom = unit -> int
```

When you see the unit type in a signature, that's a strong indication that there are side effects. Something somewhere is changing state, but it's hidden from you. Generally, functional programmers try to avoid side effects, or at least limit them to restricted areas of code.

Modeling Lists and Collections

F# supports a number of different collection types in the standard libraries:

- list is a fixed-size immutable collection (implemented as a linked list).

- array is a fixed-size mutable collection, where individual elements can be fetched and assigned to by index.

- ResizeArray is a variable size array. That is, items can be added or removed from the array. It is the F# alias for the C# List<T> type.

- seq is a lazy collection, where each element is returned on demand. It is the F# alias for the C# IEnumerable<T> type.

- There are also built-in types for Map (similar to Dictionary) and Set, but these are rarely used directly in a domain model.

For domain modeling, I suggest always using the list type. Just like option, it can be used as a suffix after a type (which makes it very readable), like this:

```
type Order = {
  OrderId : OrderId
  Lines : OrderLine list // a collection
  }
```

To create a list, you can use a list literal, with square brackets and semicolons (not commas!) as separators:

```
let aList = [1; 2; 3]
```

or you can prepend a value to an existing list using the :: (also known as "cons") operator:

```
let aNewList = 0 :: aList   // new list is [0;1;2;3]
```

To deconstruct a list in order to access elements in it, you use similar patterns. You can match against list literals like this:

```
let printList1 aList =
  // matching against list literals
  match aList with
  | [] ->
    printfn "list is empty"
  | [x] ->
    printfn "list has one element: %A" x
  | [x;y] ->        // match using list literal
    printfn "list has two elements: %A and %A" x y
  | longerList ->  // match anything else
    printfn "list has more than two elements"
```

Or you can match using the "cons" operator, like this:

```
let printList2 aList =
  // matching against "cons"
  match aList with
  | [] ->
    printfn "list is empty"
  | first::rest ->
    printfn "list is non-empty with the first element being: %A" first
```

Organizing Types in Files and Projects

There's one last thing you should know. F# has strict rules about the order of declarations. A type higher in a file cannot reference another type further down in a file. And a file earlier in the compilation order cannot reference a file later in the compilation order. This means that when you are coding your types, you have to think about how you organize them.

A standard approach is to put all the domain types in one file, say Types.fs or Domain.fs, and then have the functions that depend on them be put later in the compilation order. If you have a lot of types and you need to split them across multiple files, put the shared ones first and the subdomain-specific ones after. Your file list might look something like this:

```
Common.Types.fs
Common.Functions.fs
OrderTaking.Types.fs
OrderTaking.Functions.fs
Shipping.Types.fs
Shipping.Functions.fs
```

Within a file, that rule means you need to put the simple types at the top and the more complex types (that depend on them) further down, in dependency order:

```
module Payments =
  // simple types at the top of the file
  type CheckNumber = CheckNumber of int

  // domain types in the middle of the file
  type PaymentMethod =
    | Cash
    | Check of CheckNumber // defined above
    | Card of ...

  // top-level types at the bottom of the file
  type Payment = {
    Amount: ...
    Currency: ...
    Method: PaymentMethod  // defined above
    }
```

When you are developing a model from the top down, the dependency order constraint can sometimes be inconvenient, because you often will want to write the lower-level types below the higher-level types. In F# 4.1 you can use the "rec" keyword at the module or namespace level to solve this. The rec keyword allows types to reference each other anywhere in the module.

```
module rec Payments =
  type Payment = {
    Amount: ...
    Currency: ...
    Method: PaymentMethod  // defined BELOW
    }

  type PaymentMethod =
    | Cash
    | Check of CheckNumber // defined BELOW
    | Card of ...

  type CheckNumber = CheckNumber of int
```

For earlier versions of F# you can use the "and" keyword to allow a type definition to reference a type directly underneath it.

```
type Payment = {
    Amount: ...
    Currency:  ...
    Method:  PaymentMethod // defined BELOW
    }
and PaymentMethod =
  | Cash
  | Check of CheckNumber    // defined BELOW
  | Card of ...
and CheckNumber = CheckNumber of int
```

This out-of-order approach is fine for sketching, but once the design has settled and is ready for production, it's generally better to put the types in the correct dependency order. This makes it consistent with other F# code and makes it easier for other developers to read.

For a real-world example of how to organize types in a project, see the code repository for this book.

Wrapping Up

In this chapter, we looked at the concept of *type* and how it relates to functional programming, and we also saw how the composition of types could be used to create larger types from smaller types using F#'s algebraic type system. We were introduced to record types, built by *AND*-ing data together, and choice types (also known as discriminated unions), built by *OR*-ing data together, as well as other common types based on these, such as Option and Result.

Now that we understand how types work, we can revisit our requirements and document them using what we've learned.

CHAPTER 5

Domain Modeling with Types

In the first chapter, when we were talking about the importance of a shared mental model, we emphasized that the code must also reflect this shared model and that a developer should not have to do lossy translations between the domain model and the source code. Ideally, we would like the source code to also act as documentation, which means that the domain expert and other non-developers should be able to review the code and check on the design.

Is that a realistic goal? Can we use the source code directly like this and avoid the need for UML diagrams and the like?

The answer is yes. In this chapter you'll learn how to use the F# type system to capture the domain model accurately enough for code but also in a way that can be read and understood by domain experts and other non-developers. We'll see that types can replace most documentation, and that ability has a powerful benefit: the implementation can never get out of sync with the design because the design is represented in code itself.

Reviewing the Domain Model

Let's review the domain model that we created previously on page 36:

```
context: Order-Taking

// ----------------------
// Simple types
// ----------------------

// Product codes
data ProductCode = WidgetCode OR GizmoCode
data WidgetCode = string starting with "W" then 4 digits
data GizmoCode = ...
```

```
// Order Quantity
data OrderQuantity = UnitQuantity OR KilogramQuantity
data UnitQuantity = ...
data KilogramQuantity = ...

// ---------------------
// Order life cycle
// ---------------------

// ----- unvalidated state -----
data UnvalidatedOrder =
    UnvalidatedCustomerInfo
    AND UnvalidatedShippingAddress
    AND UnvalidatedBillingAddress
    AND list of UnvalidatedOrderLine

data UnvalidatedOrderLine =
    UnvalidatedProductCode
    AND UnvalidatedOrderQuantity

// ----- validated state -----
data ValidatedOrder = ...
data ValidatedOrderLine =  ...

// ----- priced state -----
data PricedOrder = ...
data PricedOrderLine = ...

// ----- output events -----
data OrderAcknowledgmentSent = ...
data OrderPlaced = ...
data BillableOrderPlaced = ...

// ---------------------
// Workflows
// ---------------------

workflow "Place Order" =
    input: UnvalidatedOrder
    output (on success):
        OrderAcknowledgmentSent
        AND OrderPlaced (to send to shipping)
        AND BillableOrderPlaced (to send to billing)
    output (on error):
        InvalidOrder

// etc
```

The goal of this chapter is to turn this model into code.

Seeing Patterns in a Domain Model

Although each domain model is different, many patterns occur repeatedly.

Let's look at some of the patterns of a typical domain and see how we can relate components of our model to them.

- *Simple values*. These are the basic building blocks represented by primitive types such as strings and integers. But note that they are *not* actually strings or integers. A domain expert does not think in terms of int and string, but instead thinks in terms of OrderId and ProductCode—concepts that are part of the ubiquitous language.

- *Combinations of values with* AND. These are groups of closely linked data. In a paper-based world, these are typically documents or subcomponents of a document: names, addresses, orders, and so forth.

- *Choices with* OR. We have things that represent a choice in our domain: an Order *or* a Quote, a UnitQuantity *or* a KilogramQuantity.

- *Workflows*. Finally, we have business processes that have inputs and outputs.

In the next few sections, we'll look at how we can represent these different patterns using F# types.

Modeling Simple Values

Let's first look at the building blocks of a domain: simple values.

As we found out when we gathered the requirements on page 33, a domain expert does not generally think in terms of int and string but instead in terms of domain concepts such as OrderId and ProductCode. Furthermore, it's important that OrderIds and ProductCodes don't get mixed up. Just because they're both represented by ints, say, doesn't mean that they are interchangeable. So to make it clear that these types are distinct, we'll create a "wrapper type"—a type that wraps the primitive representation.

As we mentioned earlier, the easiest way to create a wrapper type in F# is to create a "single-case" union type, a choice type with only one choice.

Here's an example:

```
type CustomerId =
  | CustomerId of int
```

Since there's only one case, we invariably write the whole type definition on one line, like this:

```
type CustomerId = CustomerId of int
```

We'll call these kinds of wrapper types "simple types" to distinguish them both from compound types (such as records) and the raw primitive types (such as string and int) that they contain.

In our domain, the simple types would be modeled this way:

```
type WidgetCode = WidgetCode of string
type UnitQuantity = UnitQuantity of int
type KilogramQuantity = KilogramQuantity of decimal
```

The definition of a single case union has two parts: the name of the type and the "case" label:

```
type CustomerId = CustomerId of int
//    ^type name    ^case label
```

As you can see from the examples above, the label of the (single) case is typically the same as the name of the type. This means that when using the type, you can also use the same name for constructing and deconstructing it, as we'll see next.

Working with Single Case Unions

To create a value of a single case union, we use the case name as a constructor function. That is, we've defined a simple type like this:

```
type CustomerId = CustomerId of int
//                      ^this case name will be the constructor function
```

Now we can create it by using the case name as a constructor function:

```
let customerId = CustomerId 42
//                      ^this is a function with an int parameter
```

Creating simple types like this ensures that we can't confuse different types by accident. For example, if we create a CustomerId and an OrderId and try to compare them, we get a compiler error:

```
// define some types
type CustomerId = CustomerId of int
type OrderId = OrderId of int

// define some values
let customerId = CustomerId 42
let orderId = OrderId 42

// try to compare them -- compiler error!
printfn "%b" (orderId = customerId)
//                      ^ This expression was expected to
//                        have type 'OrderId'
```

Or if we have defined a function that takes a CustomerId as input, then trying to pass it an OrderId is another compiler error:

```
// define a function using a CustomerId
let processCustomerId (id:CustomerId) = ...

// call it with an OrderId -- compiler error!
processCustomerId orderId
//                ^ This expression was expected to
//                  have type 'CustomerId' but here has
//                  type 'OrderId'
```

To deconstruct or unwrap a single case union, we can pattern-match using the case label:

```
// construct
let customerId = CustomerId 42

// deconstruct
let (CustomerId innerValue) = customerId
//                ^ innerValue is set to 42

printfn "%i" innerValue  // prints "42"
```

It's very common to deconstruct directly in the parameter of a function definition. When we do this, we not only can access the inner value immediately but the F# compiler will also infer the correct type for us. For example, in the code below, the compiler infers the input parameter is a CustomerId:

```
// deconstruct
let processCustomerId (CustomerId innerValue) =
  printfn "innerValue is %i" innerValue

// function signature
// val processCustomerId: CustomerId -> unit
```

Constrained Values

Almost always, the simple types are constrained in some way, such as having to be in a certain range or match a certain pattern. It's very rare to have an unbounded integer or string in a real-world domain.

We'll discuss how to enforce these constraints in the next chapter (*The Integrity of Simple Values*, on page 104).

Avoiding Performance Issues with Simple Types

Wrapping primitive types into simple types is a great way to ensure type-safety and prevent many errors at compile time. However, it does come at a cost in memory usage and efficiency. For typical business applications a small decrease in performance shouldn't be a problem, but for domains that require high performance, such as scientific or real-time domains, you might want to be more careful. For example, looping over a large array of UnitQuantity values will be slower than looping over an array of raw ints.

But there are a couple of ways you can have your cake and eat it too.

First, you can use type aliases instead of simple types to document the domain. This has no overhead, but it does mean a loss of type-safety.

```
type UnitQuantity = int
```

Next, as of F# 4.1, you can use a value type (a struct) rather than a reference type. You'll still have overhead from the wrapper, but when you store them in arrays the memory usage will be contiguous and thus more cache-friendly.

```
[<Struct>]
type UnitQuantity = UnitQuantity of int
```

Finally, if you are working with large arrays, consider defining the entire collection of primitive values as a single type rather than having a collection of simple types:

```
type UnitQuantities = UnitQuantities of int[]
```

This will give you the best of both worlds. You can work efficiently with the raw data (such as for matrix multiplication) while preserving type-safety at a high level. Extending this approach further leads you to data-oriented design,[1] as used in modern game development.

You might even find that there is a word in the ubiquitous language for these kinds of collections that are treated as a unit, such as "DataSample" or "Measurements." If so, use it!

As always, performance is a complex topic and depends on your specific code and environment. It's generally best to model your domain in the most straightforward way first and only then work on tuning and optimization.

Modeling Complex Data

When we documented our domain on page 31, we used *AND* and *OR* to represent more complex models. In *Understanding Types*, we learned about F#'s algebraic type system and saw that it also used *AND* and *OR* to create complex types from simple ones.

Let's now take the obvious step and use the algebraic type system to model our domain.

---

1. https://en.wikipedia.org/wiki/Data-oriented_design

Modeling with Record Types

In our domain, we saw that many data structures were built from *AND* relationships. For example, our original, simple Order was defined like this:

```
data Order =
    CustomerInfo
    AND ShippingAddress
    AND BillingAddress
    AND list of OrderLines
    AND AmountToBill
```

This translates directly to an F# record structure, like this:

```
type Order = {
  CustomerInfo : CustomerInfo
  ShippingAddress : ShippingAddress
  BillingAddress : BillingAddress
  OrderLines : OrderLine list
  AmountToBill : ...
  }
```

We have given each field a name ("CustomerInfo," "ShippingAddress") and a type (CustomerInfo, ShippingAddress).

Doing this shows a lot of still-unanswered questions about the domain—we don't know what these types actually are right now. Is ShippingAddress the same type as BillingAddress? What type should we use to represent "AmountToBill"?

Ideally, we can ask our domain experts to help with this. For example, if your experts talk about billing addresses and shipping addresses as different things, it's better to keep these logically separate, even if they have the same structure. They may evolve in different directions as your domain understanding improves or as requirements change.

Modeling Unknown Types

During the early stages of the design process, you often won't have definitive answers to some modeling questions. For example, you'll know the names of types that you need to model, thanks to the ubiquitous language, but not their internal structure.

This isn't a problem—you can represent types of unknown structure with best guesses, or alternatively you can model them as a type that's *explicitly* undefined, one that acts as a placeholder, until you have a better understanding later in the design process.

If you want to represent an undefined type in F#, you can use the exception type exn and alias it to Undefined:

```
type Undefined = exn
```

You can then use the Undefined alias in your design model, like this:

```
type CustomerInfo = Undefined
type ShippingAddress = Undefined
type BillingAddress = Undefined
type OrderLine = Undefined
type BillingAmount = Undefined

type Order = {
  CustomerInfo : CustomerInfo
  ShippingAddress : ShippingAddress
  BillingAddress : BillingAddress
  OrderLines : OrderLine list
  AmountToBill : BillingAmount
  }
```

This approach means that you can keep modeling the domain with types and compile the code. But when you try to write the functions that process the types, you will be forced to replace Undefined with something a bit better.

Modeling with Choice Types

In our domain, we also saw many things that were choices between other things, such as these:

```
data ProductCode =
    WidgetCode
    OR GizmoCode

data OrderQuantity =
    UnitQuantity
    OR KilogramQuantity
```

How can we represent these choices with the F# type system? With choice types, obviously!

```
type ProductCode =
    | Widget of WidgetCode
    | Gizmo of GizmoCode

type OrderQuantity =
    | Unit of UnitQuantity
    | Kilogram of KilogramQuantity
```

Again, for each case we need to create two parts: the "tag" or case label (before the "of") and the type of the data that is associated with that case. The example above shows that the case label (such as Widget) doesn't have to be the same as the name of the type (WidgetCode) associated with it.

Modeling Workflows with Functions

We've now got a way to model all the data structures—the "nouns" of the ubiquitous language. But what about the "verbs," the business processes? In this book, we will model workflows and other processes as function types. For example, if we have a workflow step that validates an order form, we might document it like this:

```
type ValidateOrder = UnvalidatedOrder-> ValidatedOrder
```

It's clear from this code that the ValidateOrder process transforms an unvalidated order into a validated one.

Working with Complex Inputs and Outputs

Every function has only one input and one output, but some workflows might have multiple inputs and outputs. How can we model that? We'll start with the outputs. If a workflow has an outputA *and* an outputB, then we can create a record type to store them both. We saw this with the order-placing workflow: the output needs to be three different events, so let's create a compound type to store them as one record:

```
type PlaceOrderEvents = {
  AcknowledgmentSent : AcknowledgmentSent
  OrderPlaced : OrderPlaced
  BillableOrderPlaced : BillableOrderPlaced
  }
```

Using this approach, the order-placing workflow can be written as a function type, starting with the raw UnvalidatedOrder as input and returning the PlaceOrderEvents record:

```
type PlaceOrder = UnvalidatedOrder -> PlaceOrderEvents
```

On the other hand, if a workflow has an outputA *or* an outputB, then we can create a choice type to store them both. For example, we briefly talked about categorizing the inbound mail as quotes or orders on page 33. That process had at least two different choices for outputs:

```
workflow "Categorize Inbound Mail" =
    input: Envelope contents
    output:
        QuoteForm (put on appropriate pile)
        OR OrderForm (put on appropriate pile)
        OR ...
```

It's easy to model this workflow: just create a new type, say CategorizedMail, to represent the choices, and then have CategorizeInboundMail return that type. Our model might then look like this:

```
type EnvelopeContents = EnvelopeContents of string
type CategorizedMail =
  | Quote of QuoteForm
  | Order of OrderForm
  // etc

type CategorizeInboundMail = EnvelopeContents -> CategorizedMail
```

Now let's look at modeling inputs. If a workflow has a choice of different inputs (*OR*), then we can create a choice type. But if a process has multiple inputs that are all required (*AND*), such as "Calculate Prices" (below), we can choose between two possible approaches.

```
"Calculate Prices" =
    input: OrderForm, ProductCatalog
    output: PricedOrder
```

The first and simplest approach is just to pass each input as a separate parameter, like this:

```
type CalculatePrices = OrderForm -> ProductCatalog -> PricedOrder
```

Alternatively, we could create a new record type to contain them both, such as this CalculatePricesInput type:

```
type CalculatePricesInput = {
  OrderForm : OrderForm
  ProductCatalog : ProductCatalog
  }
```

And now the function looks like this:

```
type CalculatePrices = CalculatePricesInput -> PricedOrder
```

Which approach is better? In the cases above, where the ProductCatalog is a dependency rather than a "real" input, we want to use the separate parameter approach. This lets us use the functional equivalent of dependency injection. We'll discuss this in detail in *Injecting Dependencies*, on page 180, when we implement the order-processing pipeline.

On the other hand, if both inputs are always required and are strongly connected with each other, then a record type will make that clear. (In some situations, you can use tuples as an alternative to simple record types, but it's generally better to use a named type.)

Documenting Effects in the Function Signature

We just saw that the ValidateOrder process could be written like this:

```
type ValidateOrder = UnvalidatedOrder -> ValidatedOrder
```

But that assumes that the validation always works and a ValidatedOrder is always returned. In practice, of course, this would not be true, so it would better to indicate this situation by returning a Result type (introduced on page 70) in the function signature:

```
type ValidateOrder =
  UnvalidatedOrder -> Result<ValidatedOrder,ValidationError list>

and ValidationError = {
  FieldName : string
  ErrorDescription : string
  }
```

This signature shows us that the input is an UnvalidatedOrder and, if successful, the output is a ValidatedOrder. But if validation failed, the result is a list of ValidationError, which in turn contains a description of the error and which field it applies to.

Functional programming people use the term *effects* to describe things that a function does in addition to its primary output. By using Result here, we've now documented that ValidateOrder might have "error effects." This makes it clear in the type signature that we can't assume the function will always succeed and that we should be prepared to handle errors.

Similarly, we might want to document that a process is asynchronous—it will not return immediately. How can we do that? With another type of course!

In F#, we use the Async type to show that a function will have "asynchronous effects." So if ValidateOrder had async effects as well as error effects, then we would write the function type like this:

```
type ValidateOrder =
  UnvalidatedOrder -> Async<Result<ValidatedOrder,ValidationError list>>
```

This type signature now documents (a) when we attempt to fetch the contents of the return value, the code won't return immediately and (b) when it does return, the result might be an error.

Listing all the effects explicitly like this is useful, but it does make the type signature ugly and complicated, so we would typically create a type alias for this to make it look nicer.

```
type ValidationResponse<'a> = Async<Result<'a,ValidationError list>>
```

Then the function could be documented like this:

```
type ValidateOrder =
  UnvalidatedOrder -> ValidationResponse<ValidatedOrder>
```

A Question of Identity: Value Objects

We've now got a basic understanding of how to model the domain types and workflows, so let's move on and look at an important way of classifying data types based on whether they have a persistent identity or not.

In DDD terminology, objects with a persistent identity are called *Entities* and objects without a persistent identity are called *Value Objects*. Let's start by discussing Value Objects first.

In many cases, the data objects we're dealing with have no identity—they're interchangeable. For example, one instance of a WidgetCode with value "W1234" is the same as any other WidgetCode with value "W1234." We don't need to keep track of which one is which—they're equal to each other.

In F# we might demonstrate this as follows:

```
let widgetCode1 = WidgetCode "W1234"
let widgetCode2 = WidgetCode "W1234"
printfn "%b" (widgetCode1 = widgetCode2)  // prints "true"
```

The concept of "values without identity" shows up frequently in a domain model, and for complex types as well as simple types. For example, a Personal-Name record type might have two fields—FirstName and LastName— so it's more complex than a simple string; but it's also a *Value Object*, because two personal names with the same fields are interchangeable. We can see that with the following F# code:

```
let name1 = {FirstName="Alex"; LastName="Adams"}
let name2 = {FirstName="Alex"; LastName="Adams"}
printfn "%b" (name1 = name2)  // prints "true"
```

An "address" type is also a Value Object. If two values have the same street address, city, and zip code, they are the same address:

```
let address1 = {StreetAddress="123 Main St"; City="New York"; Zip="90001"}
let address2 = {StreetAddress="123 Main St"; City="New York"; Zip="90001"}
printfn "%b" (address1 = address2)  // prints "true"
```

You can tell that these are Value Objects in the domain because when discussing them, you would say something like, "Chris has the same name as me." That is, even though Chris and I are different people, our *names* are the same. They don't have a unique identity. Similarly, "Pat has the same postal address as me" means that my address and Pat's address have the same content and are thus equal.

Implementing Equality for Value Objects

When we model the domain using the F# algebraic type system, the types we create will implement this kind of field-based equality testing by default. We don't need to write any special equality code ourselves, which is nice.

To be precise, two record values (of the same type) are equal in F# if all their fields are equal, and two choice types are equal if they have the same choice case and the data associated with that case is also equal. This is called *structural equality*.

A Question of Identity: Entities

However, we often model things that, in the real world, *do* have a unique identity, even as their components change. For example, even if I change my name or my address, I am still the same person.

In DDD terminology, we call such things *Entities*.

In a business context, Entities are often a document of some kind: orders, quotes, invoices, customer profiles, product sheets, and so on. They have a *life cycle* and are transformed from one state to another by various business processes.

The distinction between "Value Object" and "Entity" is context-dependent. For example, consider the life cycle of a cell phone. During manufacturing, each phone is given a unique serial number—a unique identity—so in that context, the phone would be modeled as an Entity. When they're being sold, however, the serial number isn't relevant—all phones with the same specs are interchangeable—and they can be modeled as Value Objects. But once a particular phone is sold to a particular customer, identity becomes relevant again and it should be modeled as an Entity: the customer thinks of it as the same phone even after replacing the screen or battery.

Identifiers for Entities

Entities need to have a stable identity despite any changes. Therefore, when modeling them we need to give them a unique identifier or key, such as an "Order ID" or "Customer ID."

For example, the Contact type below has a ContactId that stays the same even if the PhoneNumber or EmailAddress fields change:

```
type ContactId = ContactId of int

type Contact = {
  ContactId : ContactId
  PhoneNumber : ...
  EmailAddress: ...
  }
```

Where do these identifiers come from? Sometimes the identifier is provided by the real-world domain itself—paper orders and invoices have always had some kind of reference written on them—but sometimes we'll need to create an artificial identifier ourselves using techniques such as UUIDs, an auto-incrementing database table, or an ID-generating service. This is a complex topic, so in this book we'll just assume that any identifiers have been provided to us by the client.

Adding Identifiers to Data Definitions

Given that we have identified a domain object as an Entity, how do we add an identifier to its definition?

Adding an identifier to a record type is straightforward—just add a field—but what about adding an identifier to a choice type? Should we put the identifier *inside* (associated with each case) or *outside* (not associated with any of the cases)?

For example, say that we have two choices for an 'Invoice': paid and unpaid. If we model it using the "outside" approach, we'll have a record containing the 'InvoiceId', and then within that record we'll have a choice type 'InvoiceInfo' that has information for each type of invoice. The code will look something like this:

```
// Info for the unpaid case (without id)
type UnpaidInvoiceInfo = ...

// Info for the paid case (without id)
type PaidInvoiceInfo = ...

// Combined information (without id)
type InvoiceInfo =
  | Unpaid of UnpaidInvoiceInfo
  | Paid of PaidInvoiceInfo

// Id for invoice
type InvoiceId = ...

// Top level invoice type
type Invoice = {
  InvoiceId : InvoiceId // "outside" the two child cases
  InvoiceInfo : InvoiceInfo
  }
```

The problem with this approach is that it's hard to work with the data for one case easily because it's spread between different components.

In practice, it's more common to store the ID using the "inside" approach, where each case has a copy of the identifier. Applied to our example, we would create two separate types, one for each case (UnpaidInvoice and PaidInvoice), both of which have their own InvoiceId, and then a top-level Invoice type, which is a choice between them. The code will look something like this:

```
type UnpaidInvoice = {
  InvoiceId : InvoiceId // id stored "inside"
  // and other info for the unpaid case
  }
type PaidInvoice = {
  InvoiceId : InvoiceId // id stored "inside"
  // and other info for the paid case
  }
// top level invoice type
type Invoice =
  | Unpaid of UnpaidInvoice
  | Paid of PaidInvoice
```

The benefit of this approach is that now, when we do our pattern matching, we have all the data accessible in one place, including the ID:

```
let invoice = Paid {InvoiceId = ...}

match invoice with
  | Unpaid unpaidInvoice ->
    printfn "The unpaid invoiceId is %A" unpaidInvoice.InvoiceId
  | Paid paidInvoice ->
    printfn "The paid invoiceId is %A" paidInvoice.InvoiceId
```

Implementing Equality for Entities

We saw earlier that, by default, equality testing in F# uses *all* the fields of a record. But when we compare Entities we want to use only one field, the identifier. That means that in order to model Entities correctly in F#, we must change the default behavior.

One way of doing this is to override the equality test so that only the identifier is used. To change the default we have to do the following:

1. Override the Equals method

2. Override the GetHashCode method

3. Add the CustomEquality and NoComparison attributes to the type to tell the compiler that we want to change the default behavior

When we do all this to the Contact type, we get this result:

```
[<CustomEquality; NoComparison>]
type Contact = {
  ContactId : ContactId
  PhoneNumber : PhoneNumber
  EmailAddress: EmailAddress
  }
  with
  override this.Equals(obj) =
    match obj with
    | :? Contact as c -> this.ContactId = c.ContactId
    | _ -> false
  override this.GetHashCode() =
    hash this.ContactId
```

 This is a new kind of syntax we haven't seen yet: F#'s object-oriented syntax. We are only using it here to demonstrate equality overriding, but object-oriented F# is out of scope, so we won't use it elsewhere in the book.

With the type defined, we can create one contact:

```
let contactId = ContactId 1

let contact1 = {
  ContactId = contactId
  PhoneNumber = PhoneNumber "123-456-7890"
  EmailAddress = EmailAddress "bob@example.com"
  }
```

And create a different contact with the same ContactId:

```
// same contact, different email address
let contact2 = {
  ContactId = contactId
  PhoneNumber = PhoneNumber "123-456-7890"
  EmailAddress = EmailAddress "robert@example.com"
  }
```

Finally, when we compare them using =, the result is true:

```
// true even though the email addresses are different
printfn "%b" (contact1 = contact2)
```

This is a common approach in object-oriented designs, but by changing the default equality behavior silently it can trip you up on occasion. Therefore, an (often preferable) alternative is to disallow equality testing on the object altogether by adding a NoEquality type annotation like this:

```
[<NoEquality; NoComparison>]
type Contact = {
  ContactId : ContactId
  PhoneNumber : PhoneNumber
  EmailAddress: EmailAddress
  }
```

Now when we attempt to compare values with this annotation, we get a compiler error:

```
// compiler error!
printfn "%b" (contact1 = contact2)
//              ^ the Contact type does not
//                support equality
```

Of course we can still compare the ContactId fields directly, like this:

```
// no compiler error
printfn "%b" (contact1.ContactId = contact2.ContactId) // true
```

The benefit of the "NoEquality" approach is that it removes any ambiguity about what equality means at the object level and forces us to be explicit.

Finally, in some situations, you might have multiple fields that are used for testing equality. In this case, you can easily expose a synthetic Key property that combines them:

```
[<NoEquality;NoComparison>]
type OrderLine = {
  OrderId : OrderId
  ProductId : ProductId
  Qty : int
  }
  with
  member this.Key =
    (this.OrderId,this.ProductId)
```

And then, when you need to do a comparison, you can use the Key field, like this:

```
printfn "%b" (line1.Key = line2.Key)
```

Immutability and Identity

As we saw in *Understanding Types*, values in functional programming languages like F# are immutable by default, which means that none of the objects defined so far can be changed after being initialized.

How does this affect our design?

- For *Value Objects*, immutability is required. Think of how we use them in common speech: if we change any part of a personal name, say, we call it a *new*, distinct name, not the same name with different data.

- For *Entities*, it's a different matter. We expect the data associated with Entities to change over time; that's the whole point of having a constant identifier. So how can immutable data structures be made to work this way? The answer is that we make a *copy* of the Entity with the changed data while preserving the identity. All this copying might seem like a lot of extra work but isn't an issue in practice. In fact, throughout this book we will be using immutable data everywhere, and you will see that immutability is rarely a problem.

Here's an example of how an Entity can be updated in F#. First, we'll start with an initial value:

```
let initialPerson = {PersonId=PersonId 42; Name="Joseph"}
```

To make a copy of the record while changing only some fields, F# uses the with keyword, like this:

```
let updatedPerson = {initialPerson with Name="Joe"}
```

After this copy, the updatedPerson value has a different Name but the same PersonId as the initialPerson value.

A benefit of using immutable data structures is that any changes have to be made explicit in the type signature. For example, if we want to write a function that changes the Name field in a Person, we can't use a function with a signature, like this:

```
type UpdateName = Person -> Name -> unit
```

That function has no output, which implies that nothing changed (or that the Person was mutated as a side effect). Instead, our function must have a signature with the Person type as the output, like this:

```
type UpdateName = Person -> Name -> Person
```

This clearly indicates that, given a Person and a Name, some kind of variant of the original Person is being returned.

Aggregates

Let's take a closer look at two data types that are especially relevant to our design: Order and OrderLine.

First, is Order an Entity or a Value Object? Obviously it's an Entity—the details of the order may change over time, but it's the same order.

What about an OrderLine, though? If we change the quantity of a particular order line, for example, is it still the same order line? In most designs, it would make sense to say yes, it *is* still the same order line, even though the quantity or price has changed over time. So OrderLine is an Entity too, with its own identifier.

But now here's a question: if you change an order line, have you also changed the order that it belongs to?

In this case, it's clear that the answer is yes: changing a line also changes the entire order. In fact, having immutable data structures makes this unavoidable. If I have an immutable Order containing immutable OrderLines, then just making a copy of one of the order lines *does not* also make a copy of the Order as well. In order to make a change to an OrderLine contained in an Order, I need to make the change at the level of the Order, not at the level of the OrderLine.

For example, here's some pseudocode for updating the price of an order line:

```
/// We pass in three parameters:
/// * the top-level order
/// * the id of the order line we want to change
/// * the new price
let changeOrderLinePrice order orderLineId newPrice =

  // 1. find the line to change using the orderLineId
  let orderLine = order.OrderLines |> findOrderLine orderLineId

  // 2. make a new version of the OrderLine with the new price
  let newOrderLine = {orderLine with Price = newPrice}

  // 3. create a new list of lines, replacing
  //    the old line with the new line
  let newOrderLines =
    order.OrderLines |> replaceOrderLine orderLineId newOrderLine

  // 4. make a new version of the entire order, replacing
  //    all the old lines with the new lines
  let newOrder = {order with OrderLines = newOrderLines}

  // 5. return the new order
  newOrder
```

The final result, the output of the function, is a new Order containing a new list of lines, where one of the lines has a new price. You can see that immutability causes a ripple effect in a data structure, whereby changing one low-level component can force changes to higher-level components too.

Therefore, even though we're just changing one of its "subentities" (an OrderLine), we always have to work at the level of the Order itself.

This is a very common situation: we have a collection of Entities, each with their own ID and also some "top-level" Entity that contains them. In DDD terminology, a collection of Entities like this is called an *aggregate*, and the top-level Entity is called the *aggregate root*. In this case, the aggregate comprises both the Order and the collection of OrderLines, and the aggregate root is the Order itself.

Aggregates Enforce Consistency and Invariants

An aggregate plays an important role when data is updated. The aggregate acts as the consistency boundary: when one part of the aggregate is updated, other parts might also need to be updated to ensure consistency.

For example, we might extend this design to have an additional "total price" stored in the top-level Order. Obviously, if one of the lines changes price, the total must also be updated in order to keep the data consistent. This would be done in the changeOrderLinePrice function above. It's clear that the only component that "knows" how to preserve consistency is the top-level Order—the aggregate root—so this is another reason for doing all updates at the order level rather than at the line level.

The aggregate is also where any invariants are enforced. Say that you have a rule that every order has at least one order line. Then if you try to delete multiple order lines, the aggregate ensures there is an error when there's only one line left.

We'll discuss this further in Chapter 6, *Integrity and Consistency in the Domain*, on page 103.

Aggregate References

Let's say we need information about the customer to be associated with an Order. The temptation might be to add the Customer as a field of an Order, like this:

```
type Order = {
  OrderId : OrderId
  Customer : Customer  // info about associated customer
  OrderLines : OrderLine list
  // etc
  }
```

But think about the ripple effect of immutability. If I change any part of the customer, I must also change the order as well. Is that really what we want?

A much better design is just to store a *reference* to the customer, not the whole customer record itself. That is, we would just store the CustomerId in the Order type, like this:

```
type Order = {
  OrderId : OrderId
  CustomerId : CustomerId  // reference to associated customer
  OrderLines : OrderLine list
  // etc
  }
```

In this approach, when we need the full information about the customer, we would get the CustomerId from the Order and then load the relevant customer data from the database separately, rather than loading it as part of the order.

In other words, the Customer and the Order are *distinct* and *independent* aggregates. They each are responsible for their own internal consistency, and the only connection between them is via the identifiers of their root objects.

This leads to another important aspect of aggregates: they are the basic unit of persistence. If you want to load or save objects from a database, you should load or save whole aggregates. Each database transaction should work with a *single* aggregate and not include multiple aggregates or cross aggregate boundaries. See *Transactions*, on page 262, for more information.

Similarly, if you want to serialize an object to send it down the wire, you always send whole aggregates, not parts of them.

Just to be clear, an aggregate is not just any collection of Entities. For example, a list of Customers is a collection of Entities, but it's not a DDD "aggregate," because it doesn't have a top-level Entity as a root and it isn't trying to be a consistency boundary.

Here's a summary of the important role of aggregates in the domain model:

- An aggregate is a collection of domain objects that can be treated as a single unit, with the top-level Entity acting as the "root."

- All of the changes to objects inside an aggregate must be applied via the top level to the root, and the aggregate acts as a consistency boundary to ensure that all of the data inside the aggregate is updated correctly at the same time.

- An aggregate is the atomic unit of persistence, database transactions, and data transfer.

As you can see, defining the aggregates is an important part of the design process. Sometimes Entities that are used together are part of the same aggregate (OrderLine and Order) and sometimes they're not (Customer and Order). This is where collaborating with domain experts is critical: only they can help you understand the relationships between Entities and the consistency boundaries.

We'll be seeing lots of aggregates in the course of this modeling process, so we'll be using this terminology from now on.

More Domain-Driven Design Vocabulary

Here are the new DDD terms that we've introduced in this chapter:

- A *Value Object* is a domain object without identity. Two Value Objects containing the same data are considered identical. Value Objects must be immutable: if any part changes, it becomes a different Value Object. Examples of Value Objects are names, addresses, locations, money, and dates.

- An *Entity* is a domain object that has an intrinsic identity that persists even as its properties change. Entity objects generally have an ID or key field, and two Entities with the same ID/key are considered to be the same object. Entities typically represent domain objects that have a life-span and a history of changes, such as a document. Examples of Entities are customers, orders, products, and invoices.

- An *aggregate* is a collection of related objects that are treated as a single component both to ensure consistency in the domain and to be used as an atomic unit in data transactions. Other Entities should only reference the aggregate by its identifier, which is the ID of the "top-level" member of the aggregate, known as the "root."

Putting It All Together

We've created a lot of types in the chapter, so let's step back and look at how they fit together as a whole, as a complete domain model.

First, we put all these types in a namespace called OrderTaking.Domain, which is used to keep these types separate from other namespaces. In other words, we're using a namespace in F# to indicate a DDD bounded context, at least for now.

```
namespace OrderTaking.Domain

// types follow
```

Then let's add the simple types.

```
// Product code related
type WidgetCode = WidgetCode of string
  // constraint: starting with "W" then 4 digits
type GizmoCode = GizmoCode of string
  // constraint: starting with "G" then 3 digits
type ProductCode =
  | Widget of WidgetCode
  | Gizmo of GizmoCode

// Order Quantity related
type UnitQuantity = UnitQuantity of int
type KilogramQuantity = KilogramQuantity of decimal
type OrderQuantity =
  | Unit of UnitQuantity
  | Kilos of KilogramQuantity
```

These are all Value Objects and don't need an identifier.

The order, on the other hand, has an identity that's maintained as it changes—it's an Entity—so we must model it with an ID. We don't know whether the ID is a string or an int or a Guid, but we know we need it, so let's use Undefined for now. We'll treat other identifiers the same way.

```
type OrderId = Undefined
type OrderLineId = Undefined
type CustomerId = Undefined
```

The order and its components can be sketched out now:

```
type CustomerInfo = Undefined
type ShippingAddress = Undefined
type BillingAddress = Undefined
type Price = Undefined
type BillingAmount = Undefined

type Order = {
  Id : OrderId              // id for entity
  CustomerId : CustomerId   // customer reference
  ShippingAddress : ShippingAddress
  BillingAddress : BillingAddress
  OrderLines : OrderLine list
  AmountToBill : BillingAmount
  }

and OrderLine = {
  Id : OrderLineId  // id for entity
  OrderId : OrderId
  ProductCode : ProductCode
  OrderQuantity : OrderQuantity
  Price : Price
  }
```

In the snippet above, we're using the and keyword to allow forward references to undeclared types. See the explanation in *Organizing Types in Files and Projects*, on page 73.

Let's now conclude with the workflow itself. The input for the workflow, the UnvalidatedOrder, will be built from the order form "as is," so it will contain only primitive types such as int and string.

```
type UnvalidatedOrder = {
  OrderId : string
  CustomerInfo : ...
  ShippingAddress : ...
  ...
  }
```

We need two types for the output of the workflow. The first is the events type for when the workflow is successful:

```
type PlaceOrderEvents = {
  AcknowledgmentSent : ...
  OrderPlaced : ...
  BillableOrderPlaced : ...
  }
```

The second is the error type for when the workflow fails:

```
type PlaceOrderError =
  | ValidationError of ValidationError list
  | ...  // other errors

and ValidationError = {
    FieldName : string
    ErrorDescription : string
    }
```

Finally, we can define the top-level function that represents the order-placing workflow:

```
/// The "Place Order" process
type PlaceOrder =
  UnvalidatedOrder -> Result<PlaceOrderEvents,PlaceOrderError>
```

Obviously, lots of details still need to be fleshed out, but the process for doing that should now be clear.

Our model of the order-taking workflow isn't complete, though. For example, how are we going to model the different states of the order: validated, priced, and so on?

The Challenge Revisited: Can Types Replace Documentation?

At the beginning of this chapter, we gave ourselves a challenge: could we capture the domain requirements in the type system and in such a way that it can be reviewed by domain experts and other non-developers?

Well, if we look at the domain model listed above, we should be pleased. We have a complete domain model, documented as F# types rather than as text, but the types that we have designed look almost identical to the domain documentation that we developed earlier using *AND* and *OR* notation.

Imagine that you are a non-developer. What would you have to learn in order to understand this code as documentation? You'd have to understand the syntax for simple types (single-case unions), *AND* types (records with curly braces), *OR* types (choices with vertical bars), and "processes" (input, output, and arrows), but not much more. It certainly is more readable than a conventional programming language such as C# or Java.

Wrapping Up

In this chapter, we learned how to use the F# type system to model the domain using simple types, record types, and choice types. Throughout, we used the ubiquitous language of the domain, such as `ProductCode` and `OrderQuantity`, rather than developer-centric words such as `string` and `int`. Not once did we define a `Manager` or `Handler` type!

We also learned about different kinds of identity and how to model the DDD concepts of Value Object and Entity using types. And we were introduced to the concept of an "aggregate" as a way to ensure consistency.

We then created a set of types that looked very similar to the textual documentation at the beginning of this chapter. The big difference is that all these type definitions are *compilable code* and can be included with the rest of the code for the application. This in turn means that the application code is *always* in sync with the domain definitions, and if any domain definition changes, the application will fail to compile. We don't need to try to keep the design in sync with the code—the design *is* the code!

This approach, using types as documentation, is very general, and it should be clear how you can apply it to other domains as well. Because there's no implementation at this point, it's a great way to try ideas out quickly when you are collaborating with domain experts. And of course, because it is just text, domain experts can review it easily without needing special tools, and maybe even write some types themselves!

We haven't yet addressed a few aspects of the design, though. How do we ensure that simple types are always constrained correctly? How can we enforce the integrity of aggregates? How are we going to model the different states of the order? These topics will be addressed in the next chapter.

CHAPTER 6

Integrity and Consistency in the Domain

In the previous chapter, we looked at the basics of domain modeling using the F# type system. We built up a rich set of types that represented the domain but were also compilable and could be used to guide the implementation.

Since we've gone to this trouble to model the domain properly, we should take some precautions to make sure that any data in this domain is valid and consistent. The goal is to create a bounded context that always contains data we can trust as distinct from the untrusted outside world. If we can be sure that all data values are always valid, the implementation can stay clean and we can avoid having to do defensive coding.

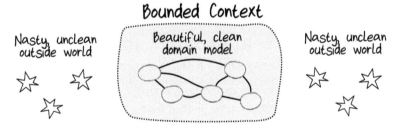

In this chapter, we'll look at modeling two aspects of a trusted domain: *integrity* and *consistency*.

Integrity (or validity) in this context means that a piece of data follows the correct business rules. For example:

- We said that a UnitQuantity is between 1 and 1000. Do we have to check this multiple times in our code, or can we rely on this to always be true?

- An order must always have at least one order line.

- An order must have a validated shipping address before being sent to the shipping department.

Consistency here means that different parts of the domain model agree about facts. Here are some examples:

- The total amount to bill for an order should be the sum of the individual lines. If the total differs, the data is inconsistent.

- When an order is placed, a corresponding invoice must be created. If the order exists but the invoice doesn't, the data is inconsistent.

- If a discount voucher code is used with an order, the voucher code must be marked as used so it can't be used again. If the order references that voucher but the voucher is not marked as used, the data is inconsistent.

How can we ensure this kind of data integrity and consistency? These are the kinds of questions we'll look at in this chapter. As always, the more information we can capture in the type system, the less documentation is needed and the more likely the code will be implemented correctly.

The Integrity of Simple Values

In the earlier discussion on modeling simple values on page 79, we saw that they should not be represented by string or int but by domain-focused types such as WidgetCode or UnitQuantity.

But we shouldn't stop there, because it's very rare to have an unbounded integer or string in a real-world domain. Almost always, these values are constrained in some way:

- An OrderQuantity might be represented by a signed integer, but it's very unlikely that the business wants it to be negative, or four billion.

- A CustomerName may be represented by a string, but that doesn't mean that it should contain tab characters or line feeds.

In our domain, we've seen some of these constrained types already. WidgetCode strings had to start with a specific letter, and UnitQuantity had to be between 1 and 1000. Here's how we've defined them so far, with a comment for the constraint.

```
type WidgetCode = WidgetCode of string    // starting with "W" then 4 digits
type UnitQuantity = UnitQuantity of int   // between 1 and 1000
type KilogramQuantity = KilogramQuantity of decimal // between 0.05 and 100.00
```

Rather than having the user of these types read the comments, we want to ensure that values of these types cannot be created unless they satisfy the constraints. Thereafter, because the data is immutable, the inner value never needs to be checked again. You can confidently use a WidgetCode or a UnitQuantity everywhere without ever needing to do any kind of defensive coding.

Sounds great. So how do we ensure that the constraints are enforced?

Answer: The same way we would in any programming language—make the constructor private and have a separate function that creates valid values and rejects invalid values, returning an error instead. In FP communities, this is sometimes called the *smart constructor* approach. Here's an example of this approach applied to UnitQuantity:

```
type UnitQuantity = private UnitQuantity of int
//                          ^ private constructor
```

So now a UnitQuantity value can't be created from outside the containing module due to the private constructor. However, if we write code in the same module that contains the type definition above, then we *can* access the constructor.

Let's use this fact to define some functions that will help us manipulate the type. We'll start by creating a submodule with exactly the same name (UnitQuantity); and within that, we'll define a create function that accepts an int and returns a Result type (as discussed in *Modeling Errors*) to return a success or a failure. These two possibilities are made explicit in its function signature: int -> Result<UnitQuantity,string>.

```
// define a module with the same name as the type
module UnitQuantity =

  /// Define a "smart constructor" for UnitQuantity
  /// int -> Result<UnitQuantity,string>
  let create qty =
    if qty < 1 then
      // failure
      Error "UnitQuantity can not be negative"
    else if qty > 1000 then
      // failure
      Error "UnitQuantity can not be more than 1000"
    else
      // success -- construct the return value
      Ok (UnitQuantity qty)
```

Compatibility with Older Versions of F#

Modules with the same name as a non-generic type will cause an error in versions of F# before v4.1 (VS2017), so you'll need to change the module definition to include a CompilationRepresentation attribute like this:

```
type UnitQuantity = ...

[<CompilationRepresentation(CompilationRepresentationFlags.ModuleSuffix)>]
module UnitQuantity =
  ...
```

One downside of a private constructor is that you can no longer use it to pattern-match and extract the wrapped data. One workaround for this is to define a separate value function, also in the UnitQuantity module, that extracts the inner value.

```
/// Return the wrapped value
let value (UnitQuantity qty) = qty
```

Let's see how this all works in practice. First, if we try to create a UnitQuantity directly, we get a compiler error:

```
let unitQty = UnitQuantity 1
//               ^ The union cases of the type 'UnitQuantity'
//                 are not accessible
```

But if we use the UnitQuantity.create function instead, it works and we get back a Result, which we can then match against:

```
let unitQtyResult = UnitQuantity.create 1

match unitQtyResult with
| Error msg ->
  printfn "Failure, Message is %s" msg
| Ok uQty ->
  printfn "Success. Value is %A" uQty
  let innerValue = UnitQuantity.value uQty
  printfn "innerValue is %i" innerValue
```

If you have many constrained types like this, you can reduce repetition by using a helper module that contains the common code for the constructors. We don't have space to show that here, but there's an example in the Domain.SimpleTypes.fs file in the sample code for this book.

Finally, it's worth saying that using private is not the only way to hide constructors in F#. There are other techniques, such as using signature files, but we won't discuss them here.

Units of Measure

For numeric values, another way of documenting the requirements while ensuring type-safety is to use *units of measure*. With a units of measure approach, numeric values are annotated with a custom "measure." For example, we might define some units of measure for kg (kilogram) and m (meter) like this:

```
[<Measure>]
type kg

[<Measure>]
type m
```

And then we annotate some values with those units of measure like this:

```
let fiveKilos = 5.0<kg>
let fiveMeters = 5.0<m>
```

 You don't need to define measure types for all the SI units. They are available in the Microsoft.FSharp.Data.UnitSystems.SI namespace.

Once this is done, the compiler will enforce compatibility between units of measure and present an error if they don't match.

```
// compiler error
fiveKilos = fiveMeters
//          ^ Expecting a float<kg> but given a float<m>

let listOfWeights = [
  fiveKilos
  fiveMeters  // <-- compiler error
  //              The unit of measure 'kg'
  //              does not match the unit of measure 'm'
  ]
```

In our domain, we could use units of measure to enforce that KilogramQuantity really *was* kilos, so that you couldn't accidentally initialize it with a value in pounds. We could encode this in the type like this:

```
type KilogramQuantity = KilogramQuantity of decimal<kg>
```

We've now got *two* checks: <kg> ensures that the number has the right unit, and KilogramQuantity enforces the constraints on the maximum and minimum values. This is probably design overkill for our particular domain, but it might be useful in other situations.

Units of measure need not just be used for physical units. You could use them to document the correct unit for timeouts (to avoid mixing up seconds and milliseconds) or for spatial dimensions (to avoid mixing up *x*- and *y*-axes), or for currency, and so on.

There's no performance hit from using units of measure. They're only used by the F# compiler and have no overhead at runtime.

Enforcing Invariants with the Type System

An *invariant* is a condition that stays true no matter what else happens. For example, at the beginning of the chapter, we said that a UnitQuantity must always be between 1 and 1000. That's an example of an invariant.

We also said that there must always be at least one order line in an order. Unlike the UnitQuantity case, this is an example of an invariant that can be captured directly in the type system. To make sure that a list isn't empty, we just need to define a NonEmptyList type. It's not built into F#, but it's easy to define yourself:

```
type NonEmptyList<'a> = {
  First: 'a
  Rest: 'a list
  }
```

The definition itself requires that there must always be at least one element, so a NonEmptyList is guaranteed never to be empty.

Of course, you'll also need some helper functions, such as add, remove, and so on. You can define these yourself or use one of the third-party libraries that provide this type, such as FSharpx.Collections.[1]

The Order type can now be rewritten to use this type instead of the normal list type:

```
type Order = {
  ...
  OrderLines : NonEmptyList<OrderLine>
  ...
  }
```

With this change, the constraint that "there is always at least one order line in an order" is now enforced automatically. Self-documenting code, and we've just eliminated any need to write unit tests for the requirement.

Capturing Business Rules in the Type System

Let's look at another modeling challenge: can we document business rules using just the type system? That is, we'd like to use the F# type system to represent what is valid or invalid so that the compiler can check it for us, instead of relying on runtime checks or code comments to ensure the rules are maintained.

Here's a real-world example. Suppose our company, Widgets Inc, stores email addresses for its customers. But let's also suppose not all email addresses should be treated the same way. Some email addresses have been *verified*—that is, the customer got a verification email and clicked on the verification link—while other email addresses aren't verified and we can't be sure they're valid. Furthermore, say some business rules are based on this difference, such as these:

---

1.   https://fsprojects.github.io/FSharpx.Collections/

- You should only send verification emails to *unverified* email addresses (to avoid spamming existing customers).

- You should only send password-reset emails to *verified* email addresses (to prevent a security breach).

Now, how can we represent the two different situations in the design? A standard approach is to use a flag to indicate whether verification happened, like this:

```
type CustomerEmail = {
  EmailAddress : EmailAddress
  IsVerified : bool
  }
```

But this approach has a number of serious problems. First, it's not clear when or why the IsVerified flag should be set or unset. For example, if the customer's email address changes, it should be set back to false (because the new email is not yet verified). However, nothing in the design makes that rule explicit. It would be easy for a developer to accidentally forget to do this when the email is changed, or worse, be unaware of the rule altogether (because it's buried in some comments somewhere).

There's also the possibility of a security breach. A developer could write code that accidentally set the flag to true, even for an unverified email, which would allow password reset emails to be sent to unverified addresses.

So, what's a better way of modeling this?

The answer is, as always, to pay attention to the domain. When domain experts talk about "verified" and "unverified" emails, you should model them as separate things. In this case, when a domain expert says "a customer's email is either verified or unverified," we should model that as a choice between two types, like this:

```
type CustomerEmail =
  | Unverified of EmailAddress
  | Verified of EmailAddress
```

But that still doesn't prevent us from accidentally creating the Verified case by passing in an unverified EmailAddress. To solve that problem, we'll do what we always do and create a new type! In particular, we'll create a type VerifiedEmailAddress, which is different from the normal EmailAddress type. Now our choice looks like this:

```
type CustomerEmail =
  | Unverified of EmailAddress
  | Verified of VerifiedEmailAddress // different from normal EmailAddress
```

Here's the clever part: we can give VerifiedEmailAddress a *private* constructor so normal code can't create a value of that type—only the verification service can create it.

That means that if I have a new email address, I *have* to construct a Customer-Email using the Unverified case because I don't have a VerifiedEmailAddress. The only way I can construct the Verified case is if I have a VerifiedEmailAddress, and the only way I can get a VerifiedEmailAddress is from the email verification service itself.

This is an example of the important design guideline, "Make illegal states unrepresentable." We're trying to capture business rules in the type system. If we do this properly, invalid situations can't ever exist in the code and we never need to write unit tests for them. Instead, we have "compile-time" unit tests.

Another important benefit of this approach is that it actually documents the domain better. Rather than having a simplistic EmailAddress that tries to serve two roles, we have two distinct types with different rules around them. And typically, once we have created these more fine-grained types, we immediately find uses for them.

For example, I can now explicitly document that the workflow that sends a password-reset message *must* take a VerifiedEmailAddress parameter as input rather than a normal email address.

```
type SendPasswordResetEmail = VerifiedEmailAddress -> ...
```

With this definition, we don't have to worry about someone accidentally passing in a normal EmailAddress and breaking the business rule because they haven't read the documentation.

Here's another example. Let's say we have a business rule that we need some way of contacting a customer:

• "A customer must have an email or a postal address."

How should we represent this? The obvious approach is just to create a record with both an Email and an Address property, like this:

```
type Contact = {
  Name: Name
  Email: EmailContactInfo
  Address: PostalContactInfo
  }
```

But this is an incorrect design. It implies both Email and Address are required. So let's make them optional:

```
type Contact = {
  Name: Name
  Email: EmailContactInfo option
  Address: PostalContactInfo option
  }
```

But this isn't correct either. As it stands, `Email` and `Address` could both be missing, and that would break the business rule.

Now, of course, we could add special runtime validation checks to make sure that this couldn't happen. But can we do better and represent this in the type system? Yes, we can!

The trick is to look at the rule closely. It implies that a customer has the following:

- An email address only
- A postal address only
- Both an email address and a postal address

That's only three possibilities. How can we represent these three? With a choice type, of course!

```
type BothContactMethods = {
  Email: EmailContactInfo
  Address : PostalContactInfo
  }

type ContactInfo =
    | EmailOnly of EmailContactInfo
    | AddrOnly of PostalContactInfo
    | EmailAndAddr of BothContactMethods
```

And then we can use this choice type in the main `Contact` type, like this:

```
type Contact = {
  Name: Name
  ContactInfo : ContactInfo
  }
```

Again what we've done is good for developers (we can't accidentally have no contact information—one less test to write), but it's also good for the design. The design makes it very clear that only three cases are possible and exactly what those three cases are. We don't need to look at documentation; we can just look at the code itself.

Making Illegal States Unrepresentable in Our Domain

Are there any places in our design where we can put this approach into practice?

I can think of one aspect of the design that is very similar to the email valida-tion example. In the validation process, we documented that there were unvalidated postal addresses (such as UnvalidatedAddress) and validated postal addresses (ValidatedAddress).

We could ensure that we never mix up these two cases and also ensure that we use the validation function properly by doing the following:

- Create two distinct types: UnvalidatedAddress and ValidatedAddress
- Give the ValidatedAddress a private constructor and then ensure that it can only be created by the address validation service.

```
type UnvalidatedAddress = ...

type ValidatedAddress = private ...
```

The validation service takes an UnvalidatedAddress and returns an optional Vali-datedAddress (optional to show that validation might fail).

```
type AddressValidationService =
  UnvalidatedAddress -> ValidatedAddress option
```

To enforce the rule that an order must have a validated shipping address before being sent to the shipping department, we'll create two more distinct types (UnvalidatedOrder and ValidatedOrder) and require that a ValidatedOrder record contain a shipping address that is a ValidatedAddress.

```
type UnvalidatedOrder = {
  ...
  ShippingAddress : UnvalidatedAddress
  ...
  }
type ValidatedOrder = {
  ...
  ShippingAddress : ValidatedAddress
  ...
  }
```

And now we can guarantee, without ever writing a test, that addresses in a ValidatedOrder have been processed by the address validation service.

Consistency

So far in this chapter we've looked at ways to enforce the integrity of the data in the domain, so now let's finish up by taking a look at the related concept of *consistency*.

We saw some examples of consistency requirements at the beginning of the chapter:

- The total amount for an order should be the sum of the individual lines. If the total differs, the data is inconsistent.

- When an order is placed, a corresponding invoice must be created. If the order exists but the invoice doesn't, the data is inconsistent.

- If a discount voucher code is used with an order, the voucher code must be marked as used so it can't be used again. If the order references that voucher but the voucher is not marked as used, the data is inconsistent.

As described here, consistency is a business term, not a technical one, and what consistency means is always context-dependent. For example, if a product price changes, should any unshipped orders be immediately updated to use the new price? What if the default address of a customer changes? Should any unshipped orders be immediately updated with the new address? There's no right answer to these questions—it depends on what the business needs.

Consistency places a large burden on the design, though, and can be costly, so we want to avoid the need for it if we can. Often during requirements gathering, a product owner will ask for a level of consistency that is undesirable and impractical. In many cases, however, the need for consistency can be avoided or delayed.

Finally, it's important to recognize that consistency and atomicity of persistence are linked. There's no point, for example, in ensuring that an order is internally consistent if the order is not going to be persisted atomically. If different parts of the order are persisted separately and then one part fails to be saved, then anyone loading the order later will be loading an order that is not internally consistent.

Consistency Within a Single Aggregate

In *Domain Modeling with Types*, we introduced the concept of an aggregate and noted that it acts both as a consistency boundary and as a unit of persistence. Let's see how this works in practice.

Let's say that we require that the total amount for an order should be the sum of the individual lines. The easiest way to ensure consistency is simply to calculate information from the raw data rather than storing it. In this case then, we could just sum the order lines every time we need the total, either in memory or using a SQL query.

If we do need to persist the extra data (say an additional AmountToBill stored in the top-level Order), then we need to ensure that it stays in sync. In this case then, if one of the lines is updated, the total must also be updated in order to keep the data consistent. It's clear that the only component that "knows" how to preserve consistency is the top-level Order. This is a good reason for doing all updates at the order level rather that at the line level—the order is the aggregate that enforces a consistency boundary. Here's some code that demonstrates how this might work:

```
/// We pass in three parameters:
/// * the top-level order
/// * the id of the order line we want to change
/// * the new price
let changeOrderLinePrice order orderLineId newPrice =

  // find orderLine in order.OrderLines using orderLineId
  let orderLine = order.OrderLines |> findOrderLine orderLineId

  // make a new version of the OrderLine with new price
  let newOrderLine = {orderLine with Price = newPrice}

  // create new list of lines, replacing old line with new line
  let newOrderLines =
    order.OrderLines |> replaceOrderLine orderLineId newOrderLine

  // make a new AmountToBill
  let newAmountToBill = newOrderLines |> List.sumBy (fun line -> line.Price)

  // make a new version of the order with the new lines
  let newOrder = {
      order with
        OrderLines = newOrderLines
        AmountToBill = newAmountToBill
      }

  // return the new order
  newOrder
```

Aggregates are also the unit of atomicity, so if we save this order to a relational database, say, we must ensure that the order header and the order lines are all inserted or updated in the same transaction.

Consistency Between Different Contexts

What if we need to coordinate between different contexts? Let's look at the second example on the list above:

- When an order is placed, a corresponding invoice must be created. If the order exists but the invoice doesn't, the data is inconsistent.

Invoicing is part of the billing domain, not the order-taking domain. Does that mean we need to reach into the other domain and manipulate its objects? No, of course not. We must keep each bounded context isolated and decoupled.

What about using the billing context's public API, like this:

```
Ask billing context to create invoice
If successfully created:
    create order in order-taking context
```

This approach is much trickier than it might seem, because you need to handle either update failing. There are ways to synchronize updates across separate systems properly (such as a two-phase commit), but in practice it's rare to need this. In his article "Starbucks Does Not Use Two-Phase Commit,"[2] Gregor Hohpe points out that in the real world businesses generally do not require that every process move in lockstep, waiting for all subsystems to finish one stage before moving to the next stage. Instead, coordination is done asynchronously using messages. Occasionally, things will go wrong, but the cost of dealing with rare errors is often much less than the cost of keeping everything in sync.

For example, let's say that instead of requiring an invoice be created immediately, we just send a message (or an event) to the billing domain and then continue with the rest of the order processing.

So now what happens if that message gets lost and no invoice is created?

- One option is to do nothing. Then the customer gets free stuff and the business has to write off the cost. That might be a perfectly adequate solution if errors are rare and the costs are small (as in a coffee shop).

- Another option is to detect that the message was lost and resend it. This is basically what a reconciliation process does: compare the two sets of data, and if they don't match up, fix the error.

- A third option is to create a *compensating action* that "undoes" the previous action or fixes the error. In an order-taking scenario, this would be equivalent to cancelling the order and asking the customer to send the items back! More realistically, a compensating action might be used to do things such as correct mistakes in an order or issue refunds.

In all three cases, there's no need for rigid coordination between the bounded contexts.

If we have a requirement for consistency, then we need to implement the second or third option. But this kind of consistency won't take effect immediately. Instead, the system will become consistent only after some time has passed—"eventual consistency." Eventual consistency is not "optional consistency": it's still very important that the system be consistent at some point in the future.

---

2. http://www.enterpriseintegrationpatterns.com/ramblings/18_starbucks.html

Here's an example. Let's say that if a product price has changed, we want to update the price for all orders that haven't shipped yet. If we need immediate consistency, then when we update the price in the product record, we also have to update all affected orders and do all this within the same transaction. This could take some time. But if we don't require instant consistency when a product price has changed, we might instead create a `PriceChanged` event that in turn triggers a series of `UpdateOrderWithChangedPrice` commands to update the outstanding orders. These commands will be processed some time after the price in the product record has changed, perhaps seconds later, perhaps hours later. Eventually the orders will be updated and the system will be consistent.

Consistency Between Aggregates in the Same Context

What about ensuring consistency between aggregates in the *same* bounded context? Let's say that two aggregates need to be consistent with each other. Should we update them together in the same transaction or update them separately using eventual consistency? Which approach should we take?

As always, the answer is that it depends. In general, a useful guideline is "only update one aggregate per transaction." If more than one aggregate is involved, we should use messages and eventual consistency as described above, even though both aggregates are within the same bounded context. But sometimes—and especially if the workflow is considered by the business to be a single transaction—it might be worth including all affected entities in the transaction. A classic example is transferring money between two accounts, where one account increases and the other decreases.

```
Start transaction
Add X amount to accountA
Remove X amount from accountB
Commit transaction
```

If the accounts are represented by an `Account` aggregate, then we would be updating two different aggregates in the same transaction. That's not necessarily a problem, but it might be a clue that you can refactor to get deeper insights into the domain. In cases like this, for example, the transaction often has its own identifier, which implies that it's a DDD Entity in its own right. In that case, why not model it as such?

```
type MoneyTransfer = {
  Id: MoneyTransferId
  ToAccount : AccountId
  FromAccount : AccountId
  Amount: Money
  }
```

After this change, the Account entities would still exist, but they would no longer be directly responsible for adding or removing money. Instead the current balance for an Account would now be calculated by iterating over the MoneyTransfer records that reference it. We've not only refactored the design, but we've also learned something about the domain.

This also shows that you shouldn't feel obligated to reuse aggregates if it doesn't make sense to do so. If you need to define a new aggregate just for one use case, go ahead.

Multiple Aggregates Acting on the Same Data

We stressed earlier that aggregates act to enforce integrity constraints, so how can we ensure that the constraints are enforced consistently if we have multiple aggregates that act on the same data? For example, we might have an Account aggregate and a MoneyTransfer aggregate that are both acting on account balances and both needing to ensure that a balance doesn't become negative.

In many cases constraints can be shared between multiple aggregates if they are modeled using types. For example, the requirement that an account balance never be below zero could be modeled with a NonNegativeMoney type. If this is not applicable, then you can use shared validation functions. This is one advantage of functional models over object-oriented models: validation functions are not attached to any particular object and don't rely on global state, so they can easily be reused in different workflows.

Wrapping Up

In this chapter, we learned how to ensure that data inside our domain could be trusted.

We saw that the combination of "smart constructors" for simple types, and "making illegal states unrepresentable" for more complex types, meant that we could enforce many kinds of integrity rules using the type system itself, leading to more self-documenting code and less need for unit tests.

We also looked at maintaining consistent data within one bounded context and between bounded contexts, concluding that, unless you are working within a single aggregate, you should design for eventual consistency rather that immediate consistency.

In the next chapter, we'll put all this into practice as we model our order-placing workflow.

CHAPTER 7

Modeling Workflows as Pipelines

In the previous two chapters, we saw how we could use types to do domain modeling in a general way. In this chapter, we'll apply what we've learned there to our order-placing workflow. Along the way, we'll look at a number of techniques that are useful for modeling *any* workflow. The goal, as always, is to have something that is readable by a domain expert.

So let's revisit the steps in the Place Order workflow on page 40. Here's the summary of what we need to model:

```
workflow "Place Order" =
    input: UnvalidatedOrder
    output (on success):
        OrderAcknowledgmentSent
        AND OrderPlaced (to send to shipping)
        AND BillableOrderPlaced (to send to billing)
    output (on error):
        ValidationError

    // step 1
    do ValidateOrder
    If order is invalid then:
        return with ValidationError

    // step 2
    do PriceOrder

    // step 3
    do AcknowledgeOrder

    // step 4
    create and return the events
```

Clearly the workflow consists of a series of substeps: `ValidateOrder`, `PriceOrder`, and so on. This is extremely common, of course. Many business processes can be thought of as a series of document transformations, and we will see that we can model the workflow in the same way. We'll create a "pipeline" to represent the business process, which in turn will be built from a series of smaller "pipes." Each smaller pipe will do one transformation, and then we'll glue the smaller pipes together to make a bigger pipeline. This style of programming is sometimes called "transformation-oriented programming."

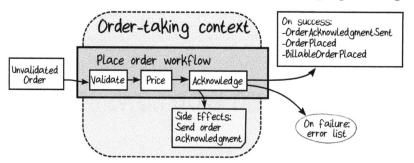

Following functional programming principles, we'll ensure each step in the pipeline is designed to be stateless and without side effects, which means each step can be tested and understood independently. Once we have designed the pieces of the pipeline, we'll just need to implement and assemble them.

The Workflow Input

Let's start by looking at the input of the workflow.

The input to a workflow should always be a domain object (we'll assume the input has been deserialized from a Data Transfer Object already). In our case, the object is the UnvalidatedOrder type, which we modeled earlier:

```
type UnvalidatedOrder = {
  OrderId : string
  CustomerInfo : UnvalidatedCustomerInfo
  ShippingAddress : UnvalidatedAddress
  ...
  }
```

Commands as Input

We saw at the beginning of the book on page 13 that a workflow is associated with the command that initiates it. In some sense then, the *real* input for the workflow is not actually the order form but the command.

For the order-placing workflow, let's call this command PlaceOrder. The command should contain everything that the workflow needs to process the request, which in this case is the UnvalidatedOrder above. We probably also want to track who created the command, the timestamp, and other metadata for logging and auditing, so the command type might end up looking like this:

```
type PlaceOrder = {
  OrderForm : UnvalidatedOrder
  Timestamp: DateTime
  UserId: string
  // etc
  }
```

Sharing Common Structures Using Generics

This isn't the only command we'll be modeling, of course. Each command will have the data needed for its own workflow, but it'll also share fields in common with all the other commands, such as UserId and Timestamp. Do we really need to implement the same fields over and over? Isn't there some way of sharing them?

If we were doing object-oriented design, the obvious solution would be to use a base class containing the common fields and then have each particular command inherit from it.

In the functional world, we can achieve the same goal by using generics. We first define a Command type that contains the common fields and a slot for the command-specific data (which we'll call Data), like this:

```
type Command<'data> = {
  Data : 'data
  Timestamp: DateTime
  UserId: string
  // etc
  }
```

Then we can create a workflow-specific command just by specifying what type goes in the Data slot:

```
type PlaceOrder = Command<UnvalidatedOrder>
```

Combining Multiple Commands in One Type

In some cases, all the commands for a bounded context will be sent on the same input channel (such as a message queue), so we need some way of unifying them into one data structure that can be serialized.

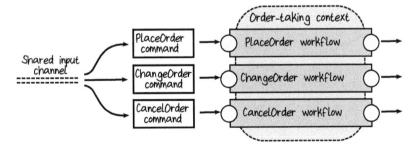

The solution is clear: just create a choice type containing all the commands. For example, if we need to choose from PlaceOrder, ChangeOrder, and CancelOrder, we could create a type like this:

```
type OrderTakingCommand =
    | Place of PlaceOrder
    | Change of ChangeOrder
    | Cancel of CancelOrder
```

Note that each case has a command type associated with it. We've already defined the PlaceOrder type, and ChangeOrder and CancelOrder would be defined in the same way, containing the information needed to execute the command.

This choice type would be mapped to a DTO and serialized and deserialized on the input channel. We just need to add a new "routing" or "dispatching" input stage at the edge of the bounded context (the "infrastructure" ring of the Onion Architecture on page 53).

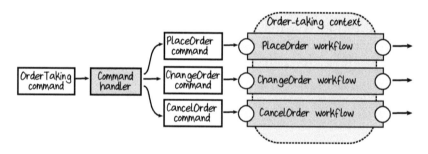

Modeling an Order as a Set of States

Now let's move on to the steps in the workflow pipeline. It's clear from our previous understanding of the workflow that the Order isn't just a static document but actually transitions through a series of different states:

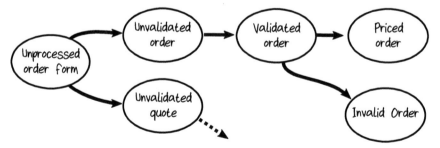

How should we model these states? A naïve approach would be to create a single record type that captures all the different states with flags, like this:

```
type Order = {
  OrderId : OrderId
  ...
  IsValidated : bool  // set when validated
  IsPriced : bool     // set when priced
  AmountToBill : decimal option // also set when priced
  }
```

But this approach has lots of problems:

- The system clearly has states, indicated by the various flags, but the states are implicit and would require lots of conditional code in order to be handled.

- Some states have data that is not needed in other states, and putting them all in one record complicates the design. For example, AmountToBill is only needed in the "priced" state, but because it doesn't exist in other states, we have to make the field optional.

- It's not clear which fields go with which flags. AmountToBill is required to be set when IsPriced is set, but the design does not enforce that, and we have to rely on the comment to remind us to keep the data consistent.

A much better way to model the domain is to create a new type for each state of the order. This allows us to eliminate implicit states and conditional fields.

The types can be defined directly from the domain documentation we created earlier. For example, here's the domain documentation for ValidatedOrder:

```
data ValidatedOrder =
    ValidatedCustomerInfo
    AND ValidatedShippingAddress
    AND ValidatedBillingAddress
    AND list of ValidatedOrderLine
```

And here's the corresponding type definition for ValidatedOrder. It's a straightforward translation (with the addition of OrderId, needed because the order identity must be maintained throughout the workflow):

```
type ValidatedOrder = {
  OrderId : OrderId
  CustomerInfo : CustomerInfo
  ShippingAddress : Address
  BillingAddress : Address
  OrderLines : ValidatedOrderLine list
  }
```

We can create a type for PricedOrder in the same way, with extra fields for the price information.

```
type PricedOrder = {
  OrderId : ...
  CustomerInfo : CustomerInfo
  ShippingAddress : Address
  BillingAddress : Address
  // different from ValidatedOrder
  OrderLines : PricedOrderLine list
  AmountToBill : BillingAmount
  }
```

Finally, we can create a top-level type that's a choice between all the states:

```
type Order =
  | Unvalidated of UnvalidatedOrder
  | Validated of ValidatedOrder
  | Priced of PricedOrder
  // etc
```

This is the object that represents the order at any time in its life cycle. And this is the type that can be persisted to storage or communicated to other contexts.

Note that we are not going to include Quote in this set of choices, because it is not a state that an Order can get into—it's a completely different workflow.

Adding New State Types as Requirements Change

One nice thing about using a separate type for each state is that new states can be added without breaking existing code. For example, if we have a requirement to support refunds, we can add a new RefundedOrder state with any information needed just for that state. Because the other states are defined independently, any code using them will not be affected by the change.

State Machines

In the section above, we converted a single type with flags into a set of separate types, each designed for a specific workflow stage.

This is the second time we've done this. In the EmailAddress example discussed on page 108, we converted a design with a flag into a design with two choices, one for each state: "Unverified" and "Verified."

These kinds of situations are extremely common in business modeling scenarios, so let's pause and look at using "states" as a general domain modeling tool. In a typical model, a document or record can be in one or more states, with paths from one state to another ("transitions") triggered by commands of some kind as shown in the figure on page 125. This is known as a *state machine*.

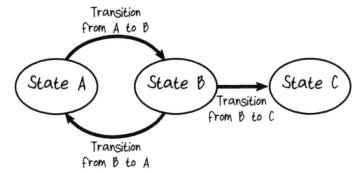

Now you might be familiar with complex state machines with tens or hundreds of states, such as those used in language parsers and regular expressions. We won't be talking about those. The kinds of state machines that we'll be discussing here are much, much simpler—just a few cases at the most, with a small number of transitions.

Some examples:

- The one we just mentioned: an email address might have states that are "Unverified" and "Verified," where you can transition from the "Unverified" state to the "Verified" state by asking the user to click a link in a confirmation email.

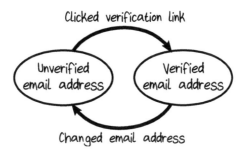

- A shopping cart might have states "Empty," "Active," and "Paid," where you can transition from the "Empty" state to the "Active" state by adding an item to the cart and to the "Paid" state by paying.

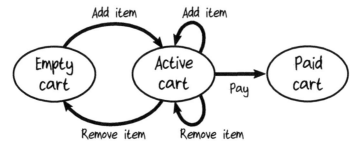

- A package delivery might have three states, "Undelivered," "Out for Delivery," and "Delivered," where you can transition from the "Undelivered" state to the "Out for Delivery" state by putting the package on the delivery truck, and so on.

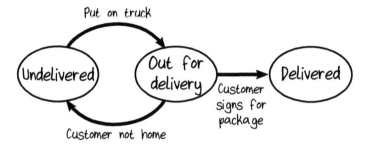

Why Use State Machines?

There are a number of benefits to using state machines in these cases:

- *Each state can have different allowable behavior.*

  For instance, in the shopping cart example, only an active cart can be paid for, and a paid cart cannot be added to. In the previous chapter, when we discussed the unverified/verified email design, we saw a business rule that said that you can only send password resets to verified email addresses. By using distinct types for each state, we could encode that requirement directly in the function signature, using the compiler to ensure that that business rule was complied with.

- *All the states are explicitly documented.*

  It's easy to have important states that are implicit but never documented. In the shopping cart example, the "empty cart" has different behavior from the "active cart," but it'd be rare to see this documented explicitly in code.

- *It is a design tool that forces you to think about every possibility that could occur.*

  A common cause of errors in a design is that certain edge cases are not handled. A state machine forces all cases to be thought about. For example:

    - What should happen if we try to verify an already verified email?

    - What should happen if we try to remove an item from an empty shopping cart?

    - What should happen if we try to deliver a package that's already in the "Delivered" state?

And so on. Thinking about a design in terms of states can force these questions to the surface and clarify the domain logic.

How to Implement Simple State Machines in F#

Complex state machines, used in language parsers and so on, are generated from rule sets or grammars and are quite complicated to implement. But the simple business-oriented state machines described above can be coded manually, without any need for special tools or libraries.

How should we implement these simple state machines, then? One thing we *don't* want to do is combine all the states into a common record, using flags, enums, or other kinds of conditional logic to distinguish them.

A much better approach is to make each state have its own type, which stores the data that is relevant to that state (if any). The entire set of states can then be represented by a choice type with a case for each state. Here's an example using the shopping cart state machine:

```
type Item = ...
type ActiveCartData = { UnpaidItems: Item list }
type PaidCartData = { PaidItems: Item list; Payment: float }

type ShoppingCart =
  | EmptyCart  // no data
  | ActiveCart of ActiveCartData
  | PaidCart of PaidCartData
```

The ActiveCartData and PaidCartData states each have their own types. The EmptyCart state has no data associated with it, so no special type is needed for it.

A command handler is then represented by a function that accepts the entire state machine (the choice type) and returns a new version of it (the updated choice type). Say we want to add an item to the cart. The state transition function addItem takes a ShoppingCart parameter and the item to add, like this:

```
let addItem cart item =
  match cart with
  | EmptyCart ->
    // create a new active cart with one item
    ActiveCart {UnpaidItems=[item]}

  | ActiveCart {UnpaidItems=existingItems} ->
    // create a new ActiveCart with the item added
    ActiveCart {UnpaidItems = item :: existingItems}

  | PaidCart _ ->
    // ignore
    cart
```

The result is a new ShoppingCart that might be in a new state, or not (in the case that it was in the "Paid" state).

Or say that we want to pay for the items in the cart. The state transition function makePayment takes a ShoppingCart parameter and the payment information, like this:

```
let makePayment cart payment =
  match cart with
  | EmptyCart ->
    // ignore
    cart

  | ActiveCart {UnpaidItems=existingItems} ->
    // create a new PaidCart with the payment
    PaidCart {PaidItems = existingItems; Payment=payment}

  | PaidCart _ ->
    // ignore
    cart
```

The result is a new ShoppingCart that might be in the "Paid" state, or not (in the case that it was already in the "Empty" or "Paid" states).

You can see that from the caller's point of view, the set of states is treated as one thing for general manipulation (the ShoppingCart type), but when processing the events internally, each state is treated separately.

Modeling Each Step in the Workflow with Types

The state machine approach is perfect for modeling our order-placing workflow, so with that in hand, let's now model the details of each step.

The Validation Step

Let's start with validation. In the earlier discussion on page 40, we documented the "ValidateOrder" substep like this:

```
substep "ValidateOrder" =
    input: UnvalidatedOrder
    output: ValidatedOrder OR ValidationError
    dependencies: CheckProductCodeExists, CheckAddressExists
```

We'll assume that we've defined the input and output types (UnvalidatedOrder and ValidatedOrder) in the same way as in the discussion earlier. In addition to the input, we can see that the substep has two dependencies, one to check that a product code exists and one to check that the address exists as shown in the figure on page 129.

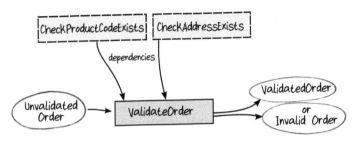

We've been talking about modeling processes as functions with inputs and outputs. But how do we model these dependencies using types? Simple, we just treat them as functions, too. The type signature of the function will become the "interface" that we need to implement later.

For example, to check that a product code exists, we need a function that takes a ProductCode and returns true if it exists in the product catalog, or false otherwise. We can define a CheckProductCodeExists type that represents this:

```
type CheckProductCodeExists =
  ProductCode -> bool
  // ^input        ^output
```

Moving on to the second dependency, we need a function that takes an UnvalidatedAddress and returns a corrected address if valid, or some kind of validation error if the address is not valid.

We also want to distinguish between a "checked address" (the output of the remote address checking service) and our Address domain object, and at some point we'll need to convert between them. For now, we might just say that a CheckedAddress is just a wrapped version of an UnvalidatedAddress:

```
type CheckedAddress = CheckedAddress of UnvalidatedAddress
```

The service then takes an UnvalidatedAddress as input and returns a Result type, with a CheckedAddress value for the success case and an AddressValidationError value for the failure case:

```
type AddressValidationError = AddressValidationError of string
```

```
type CheckAddressExists =
  UnvalidatedAddress -> Result<CheckedAddress,AddressValidationError>
  // ^input                    ^output
```

With the dependencies defined, we can now define the ValidateOrder step as a function with a primary input (the UnvalidatedOrder), two dependencies (the CheckProductCodeExists and CheckAddressExists services), and output (either a ValidatedOrder or an error). The type signature looks scary at first glance, but if you think of it as the code equivalent of the previous sentence, it should make sense.

```
type ValidateOrder =
  CheckProductCodeExists      // dependency
    -> CheckAddressExists     // dependency
    -> UnvalidatedOrder       // input
    -> Result<ValidatedOrder,ValidationError>  // output
```

The overall return value of the function must be a Result because one of the dependencies (the CheckAddressExists function) returns a Result. When Result is used anywhere, it "contaminates" all it touches, and the "result-ness" needs to be passed up until we get to a top-level function that handles it.

 We have put the dependencies *first* in the parameter order and the input type second to last, just before the output type. The reason for this is to make partial application easier (the functional equivalent of dependency injection). We'll talk about how this works in practice in the Implementation chapter on page 180.

The Pricing Step

Let's move on and design the "PriceOrder" step. Here's the original domain documentation:

```
substep "PriceOrder" =
    input: ValidatedOrder
    output: PricedOrder
    dependencies: GetProductPrice
```

Again, we see a dependency—a function returns the price given a product code.

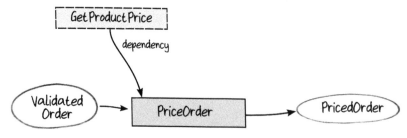

We can define a GetProductPrice type to document this dependency:

```
type GetProductPrice =
  ProductCode -> Price
```

Again, pay attention to what we've done here. The PriceOrder function needs information from the product catalog, but instead of passing some sort of heavyweight IProductCatalog interface to it, we'll just pass a *function* (GetProductPrice) that represents exactly what we need from the product catalog at this stage.

That is, GetProductPrice acts as an abstraction—it hides the existence of the product catalog and exposes to us only the functionality needed and no more.

The pricing function itself will then look like this:

```
type PriceOrder =
  GetProductPrice        // dependency
    -> ValidatedOrder    // input
    -> PricedOrder       // output
```

This function always succeeds, so there's no need to return a Result.

The Acknowledge Order Step

The next step creates an acknowledgment letter and sends it to the customer.

Let's start by modeling the acknowledgment letter. For now just say that it contains an HTML string that we are going to send in an email. We'll model the HTML string as a simple type and the OrderAcknowledgment as a record type that contains the letter and the email address to send it to:

```
type HtmlString =
  HtmlString of string

type OrderAcknowledgment = {
  EmailAddress : EmailAddress
  Letter : HtmlString
  }
```

How do we know what the content of the letter should be? Chances are that the letter will be created from some sort of template, based on the customer information and the order details. Rather than embedding that logic into the workflow, let's make it someone else's problem! That is, we'll assume that a service function will generate the content for us and that all we have to do is give it a PricedOrder.

```
type CreateOrderAcknowledgmentLetter =
  PricedOrder -> HtmlString
```

We'll then take a function of this type as a dependency for this step.

Once we have the letter, we need to send it. How should we do this? Should we call some sort of API directly, or write the acknowledgment to a message queue, or what?

Luckily, we don't need to decide these questions right now. We can punt on the exact implementation and just focus on the interface we need. As before, all we need for the design at this point is to define a function that takes an OrderAcknowledgment as input and sends it for us; we don't care how.

```
type SendOrderAcknowledgment =
  OrderAcknowledgment -> unit
```

Here we are using the unit type to indicate that there's some side effect that we don't care about, but that the function returns nothing.

But is that right, really? We want to return an OrderAcknowledgmentSent event from the overall order-placing workflow if the acknowledgment was sent, but with this design we can't tell if it was sent or not. So we need to change this. An obvious choice is to return a bool instead, which we can then use to decide whether or not to create the event:

```
type SendOrderAcknowledgment =
  OrderAcknowledgment -> bool
```

Booleans are generally a bad choice in a design, though, because they are very uninformative. It would be better to use a simple Sent/NotSent choice type instead of a bool:

```
type SendResult = Sent | NotSent
```

```
type SendOrderAcknowledgment =
  OrderAcknowledgment -> SendResult
```

Or perhaps we should have the service itself (optionally) return the OrderAcknowledgmentSent event itself?

```
type SendOrderAcknowledgment =
  OrderAcknowledgment -> OrderAcknowledgmentSent option
```

If we do that, though, we have created a coupling between our domain and the service via the event type. There's no correct answer here, so for now we'll stick with the Sent/NotSent approach. We can always change it later.

Finally, what should the output of this "Acknowledge Order" step be? Simply the "Sent" event, if created. Let's define that event type now:

```
type OrderAcknowledgmentSent = {
  OrderId : OrderId
  EmailAddress : EmailAddress
  }
```

And finally, we can put all of this together to define the function type for this step:

```
type AcknowledgeOrder =
  CreateOrderAcknowledgmentLetter    // dependency
    -> SendOrderAcknowledgment       // dependency
    -> PricedOrder                   // input
    -> OrderAcknowledgmentSent option // output
```

As you can see, the function returns an optional event, because the acknowledgment might not have been sent.

Creating the Events to Return

The previous step will have created the OrderAcknowledgmentSent event for us, but we still need to create the OrderPlaced event (for shipping) and the BillableOrderPlaced event (for billing). These are easy to define: the OrderPlaced event can just be an alias for PricedOrder, and the BillableOrderPlaced event is just a subset of the PricedOrder:

```
type OrderPlaced = PricedOrder
type BillableOrderPlaced = {
  OrderId : OrderId
  BillingAddress: Address
  AmountToBill : BillingAmount
  }
```

To actually return the events, we could create a special type to hold them, like this:

```
type PlaceOrderResult = {
  OrderPlaced : OrderPlaced
  BillableOrderPlaced : BillableOrderPlaced
  OrderAcknowledgmentSent : OrderAcknowledgmentSent option
  }
```

But it's highly likely that we'll be adding new events to this workflow over time, and defining a special record type like this makes it harder to change.

Instead, why don't we say that the workflow returns a *list* of events, where an event can be one of OrderPlaced, BillableOrderPlaced, or OrderAcknowledgmentSent.

That is, we'll define an OrderPlacedEvent that's a choice type like this:

```
type PlaceOrderEvent =
  | OrderPlaced of OrderPlaced
  | BillableOrderPlaced of BillableOrderPlaced
  | AcknowledgmentSent  of OrderAcknowledgmentSent
```

And then the final step of the workflow will emit a list of these events:

```
type CreateEvents =
  PricedOrder -> PlaceOrderEvent list
```

If we ever need to work with a new event, we can just add it to the choices, without breaking the workflow as a whole.

And if we discover that the same events appear in multiple workflows in the domain, we could even go up a level and create a more general OrderTakingDomainEvent as a choice of *all* the events in the domain.

Documenting Effects

In a previous discussion on page 87, we talked about documenting effects in the type signature: What effects could this function have? Could it return an error? Does it do I/O?

Let's quickly revisit all our dependencies and double-check if we need to be explicit about any effects like this.

Effects in the Validation Step

The validation step has two dependencies: CheckProductCodeExists and CheckAddress Exists.

Let's start with CheckProductCodeExists:

```
type CheckProductCodeExists = ProductCode -> bool
```

Could it return an error, and is it a remote call?

Let's assume it's neither of these. Instead, we will expect that a local cached copy of the product catalog is available (remember what Ollie said about autonomy in *Understanding the Domain*) and that we can access it quickly.

On the other hand, we know that the CheckAddressExists function is calling a remote service, not a local one inside the domain, and so it should also have the Async effect as well as the Result effect. In fact, the Async and Result effects are used together so often that we'll generally combine them into one type using the AsyncResult alias:

```
type AsyncResult<'success,'failure> = Async<Result<'success,'failure>>
```

With that, we can now change the return type of CheckAddressExists from Result to AsyncResult to indicate that the function has both async and error effects:

```
type CheckAddressExists =
  UnvalidatedAddress -> AsyncResult<CheckedAddress,AddressValidationError>
```

It's now clear from the type signature that the CheckAddressExists function is doing I/O and that it might fail. Earlier, when talking about bounded contexts, we said that autonomy was a key factor. So does that mean that we should try to create a local version of the address validation service? If we bring this up with Ollie, we're assured that this service has very high availability. Remember that the main reason for wanting autonomy was not for performance but to allow you to commit to a certain level of availability and service. If your implementation relies on a third party, then you really need to trust them (or otherwise work around any service issues).

Just as with Result, the Async effect is contagious for any code containing it. So changing CheckAddressExists to return an AsyncResult means we must change the whole ValidateOrder step to return an AsyncResult as well:

```
type ValidateOrder =
  CheckProductCodeExists     // dependency
    -> CheckAddressExists     // AsyncResult dependency
    -> UnvalidatedOrder       // input
    -> AsyncResult<ValidatedOrder,ValidationError list>  // output
```

Effects in the Pricing Step

The pricing step has only one dependency: GetProductPrice. We'll again assume that the product catalog is local (for example, cached in memory), and so there's no Async effect. Nor can accessing it return an error as far as we can tell. So no effects there.

However, the PriceOrder step itself might well return an error. Let's say that an item has been mispriced, and so the overall AmountToBill is very large (or negative). This is the kind of thing that we should catch when it happens. It might be a very unlikely edge case, but many real-world embarrassments have been caused by errors like this!

If we are going to return a Result now, then we also need an error type to go with it. We'll call it PricingError. The PriceOrder function now looks like this:

```
type PricingError = PricingError of string

type PriceOrder =
  GetProductPrice                       // dependency
    -> ValidatedOrder                    // input
    -> Result<PricedOrder,PricingError> // output
```

Effects in the Acknowledge Step

The AcknowledgeOrder step has two dependencies: CreateOrderAcknowledgmentLetter and SendOrderAcknowledgment.

Can the CreateOrderAcknowledgmentLetter function return an error? Probably not. And we'll assume that it's local and uses a template that's cached. So, overall, the CreateOrderAcknowledgmentLetter function does not have any effects that need to be documented in the type signature.

On the other hand, we know that SendOrderAcknowledgment will be doing I/O, so it needs an Async effect. What about errors? In this case we don't care about the error details, and even if there is an error, we want to ignore it and continue on the happy path. So that means that a revised SendOrderAcknowledgment will have an Async type but not a Result type:

```
type SendOrderAcknowledgment =
  OrderAcknowledgment -> Async<SendResult>
```

Of course, the `Async` effect ripples up to the parent function as well:

```
type AcknowledgeOrder =
  CreateOrderAcknowledgmentLetter      // dependency
    -> SendOrderAcknowledgment         // Async dependency
    -> PricedOrder                     // input
    -> Async<OrderAcknowledgmentSent option> // Async output
```

Composing the Workflow from the Steps

We've now got definitions for all the steps; so when we have implementations
for each of them, we should be able to just wire the output of one step to the
input of the next one, building up the overall workflow.

But it won't be quite that simple! Let's look at the definitions of all the steps
in one place, with the dependencies removed so that only the inputs and
outputs are listed.

```
type ValidateOrder =
  UnvalidatedOrder                                       // input
    -> AsyncResult<ValidatedOrder,ValidationError list>  // output

type PriceOrder =
  ValidatedOrder                           // input
    -> Result<PricedOrder,PricingError>    // output

type AcknowledgeOrder =
  PricedOrder                              // input
    -> Async<OrderAcknowledgmentSent option> // output

type CreateEvents =
    PricedOrder                 // input
      -> PlaceOrderEvent list // output
```

The input of the `PriceOrder` step requires a `ValidatedOrder`, but the output of ValidateOrder is an `AsyncResult<ValidatedOrder,...>`, which doesn't match at all.

Similarly, the output of the `PriceOrder` step cannot be used as the input for
AcknowledgeOrder, and so on.

In order to compose these functions then, we are going to have to juggle the
input and output types so that they are compatible and can be fitted together.
This is a common challenge when doing type-driven design, and we'll see how
to do this in the implementation chapters.

Are Dependencies Part of the Design?

In the code above, we have treated calls to other contexts (such as CheckProduct-CodeExists and ValidateAddress) as dependencies to be documented. Our design for each substep added explicit extra parameters for these dependencies:

```
type ValidateOrder =
  CheckProductCodeExists       // explicit dependency
    -> CheckAddressExists       // explicit dependency
    -> UnvalidatedOrder         // input
    -> AsyncResult<ValidatedOrder,ValidationError list>  // output

type PriceOrder =
  GetProductPrice                       // explicit dependency
    -> ValidatedOrder                   // input
    -> Result<PricedOrder,PricingError>  // output
```

You might argue that *how* any process performs its job should be hidden from us. Do we really care about what systems it needs to collaborate with in order to achieve its goal?

If you take this point of view, the process definitions would be simplified down to inputs and outputs only, looking like this:

```
type ValidateOrder =
  UnvalidatedOrder                              // input
    -> AsyncResult<ValidatedOrder,ValidationError list> // output

type PriceOrder =
  ValidatedOrder                      // input
    -> Result<PricedOrder,PricingError> // output
```

Which approach is better?

There's never a right answer when it comes to design, but let's follow this guideline:

- For functions exposed in a public API, hide dependency information from callers.

- For functions used internally, be explicit about their dependencies.

In this case, the dependencies for the top-level PlaceOrder workflow function should *not* be exposed, because the caller doesn't need to know about them. The signature should just show the inputs and outputs, like this:

```
type PlaceOrderWorkflow =
  PlaceOrder                                    // input
    -> AsyncResult<PlaceOrderEvent list,PlaceOrderError> // output
```

But for each *internal* step in the workflow, the dependencies should be made explicit, just as we did in our original designs. This helps to document what each step actually needs. If the dependencies for a step change, then we can alter the function definition for that step, which in turn will force us to change the implementation.

The Complete Pipeline

We've made a first pass at the design, so let's review what we have so far. First, we'll write down the types for the public API. We'll typically put them all in one file, such as DomainApi.fs or something similar.

Here are the inputs:

```
// ----------------------
// Input data
// ----------------------

type UnvalidatedOrder = {
  OrderId : string
  CustomerInfo : UnvalidatedCustomer
  ShippingAddress : UnvalidatedAddress
  }
and UnvalidatedCustomer = {
  Name : string
  Email : string
  }
and UnvalidatedAddress = ...

// ----------------------
// Input Command
// ----------------------

type Command<'data> = {
  Data : 'data
  Timestamp: DateTime
  UserId: string
  // etc
  }

type PlaceOrderCommand = Command<UnvalidatedOrder>
```

And here are the outputs and the workflow definition itself:

```
// ----------------------
// Public API
// ----------------------

/// Success output of PlaceOrder workflow
type OrderPlaced = ...
type BillableOrderPlaced = ...
type OrderAcknowledgmentSent = ...
```

```
type PlaceOrderEvent =
    | OrderPlaced of OrderPlaced
    | BillableOrderPlaced of BillableOrderPlaced
    | AcknowledgmentSent  of OrderAcknowledgmentSent

/// Failure output of PlaceOrder workflow
type PlaceOrderError = ...

type PlaceOrderWorkflow =
  PlaceOrderCommand                                 // input command
    -> AsyncResult<PlaceOrderEvent list,PlaceOrderError> // output events
```

The Internal Steps

We put the types used by the internal steps in a separate implementation file (such as PlaceOrderWorkflow.fs). Later on, at the bottom of this same file, we'll add the implementation.

We'll start with the internal states that represent the order life cycle:

```
// bring in the types from the domain API module
open DomainApi

// ---------------------
// Order life cycle
// ---------------------

// validated state
type ValidatedOrderLine =  ...
type ValidatedOrder = {
  OrderId : OrderId
  CustomerInfo : CustomerInfo
  ShippingAddress : Address
  BillingAddress : Address
  OrderLines : ValidatedOrderLine list
  }
and OrderId = Undefined
and CustomerInfo = ...
and Address = ...

// priced state
type PricedOrderLine = ...
type PricedOrder = ...

// all states combined
type Order =
  | Unvalidated of UnvalidatedOrder
  | Validated of ValidatedOrder
  | Priced of PricedOrder
  // etc
```

And then we can add the definitions for each internal step:

```
// ---------------------
// Definitions of Internal Steps
// ---------------------

// ----- Validate order -----

// services used by ValidateOrder
type CheckProductCodeExists =
  ProductCode -> bool

type AddressValidationError = ...
type CheckedAddress = ...
type CheckAddressExists =
  UnvalidatedAddress
    -> AsyncResult<CheckedAddress,AddressValidationError>

type ValidateOrder =
  CheckProductCodeExists     // dependency
    -> CheckAddressExists    // dependency
    -> UnvalidatedOrder      // input
    -> AsyncResult<ValidatedOrder,ValidationError list>  // output
and ValidationError = ...

// ----- Price order -----

// services used by PriceOrder
type GetProductPrice =
  ProductCode -> Price

type PricingError = ...

type PriceOrder =
  GetProductPrice        // dependency
    -> ValidatedOrder    // input
    -> Result<PricedOrder,PricingError>  // output

// etc
```

We've now got all the types in one place, ready to guide the implementation.

Long-Running Workflows

Before we move on, though, let's revisit an important assumption about the pipeline. We're expecting that even though there are calls to remote systems, the pipeline will complete within a short time, in the order of seconds.

But what if these external services took much longer to complete? For example, what if validation was done by a person rather a machine, and it took that person all day? Or what if pricing was done by a different department, and it took those folks a long time as well. If these things were true, how would it affect the design?

First, we would need to save the state into storage before calling a remote service, then we'd wait for a message telling us that the service had finished, and then we'd have to reload the state from storage and continue on with the next step in the workflow. This is much heavier than using normal asynchronous calls, because we need to persist the state between each step.

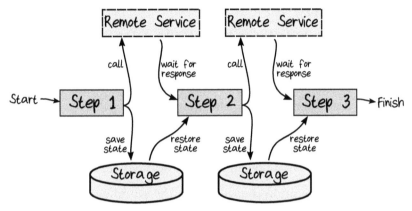

By doing this, we have broken the original workflow into smaller, independent chunks, each triggered by an event. Rather than one single workflow, you could even think of it as a series of separate mini-workflows.

This is where the state machine model is a valuable framework for thinking about the system. Before each step, the order is loaded from storage, having been persisted as one of its states. The mini-workflow transitions the order from the original state to a new state, and at the end the new state is saved back to storage again.

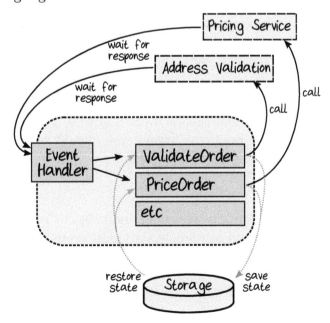

These kinds of long-running workflows are sometimes called *Sagas.*[1] They're common whenever slow humans are involved, but they can also be used whenever you want to break a workflow into decoupled, stand-alone pieces connected by events (cough...microservices).

In our example, the workflow is very simple. If the number of events and states increases and the transitions get complicated, you may need to create a special component, a *Process Manager*, that is in charge of handling incoming messages, determining what action should be taken based on the current state, and then triggering the appropriate workflow.

Wrapping Up

In this chapter, we learned how to model a workflow using only types.

We started by documenting the inputs to the workflow, and in particular, how to model commands. We then looked at how we could use state machines to model documents and other entities with life cycles. With our new understanding of states, we went back to the workflow, modeling each substep using types to represent the input and output states, and we also went to some effort to document the dependencies and effects of each step.

Along the way we created what seems like hundreds of types (actually only about thirty). Was this really necessary? Is this too many types? It might seem like a lot, but remember that we are trying to create executable documentation—code that communicates the domain. If we did not create these types, we would still have to document the difference between a validated order and a priced order, or between a widget code and a normal string. Why not let the documentation be in the code itself?

Of course, there's always a balance to be had. We've deliberately gone to an extreme here to show what it looks like if everything is documented in this way. If you find that this approach is overkill in your situation, feel free to reduce it to match your needs. As always, you should do what serves the domain and is most helpful for the task at hand.

What's Next

Having spent the last four chapters doing nothing but modeling, we have reached the end at last and can finally start getting our hands dirty with a real implementation!

---

1. http://vasters.com/archive/Sagas.html

Let's just clarify something before we move on. In this book, we've separated requirements gathering, modeling, and coding into distinct sections. This may look like we are encouraging a linear "waterfall" model of development, but this isn't the intention at all. On a real project, we should be continually mixing requirements gathering with modeling and modeling with prototyping, whatever it takes to get feedback to the customer or domain expert as soon as possible. In fact, the whole point of modeling with types is so we can go from requirements to modeling and back again in minutes rather than days because the domain expert can read the model directly.

We're ready to start the implementation chapters now. As a first step, let's make sure that we understand how functions work and how to build applications from them. We'll do that in the next chapter.

Part III

Implementing the Model

In this third part, we will take the workflow that we modeled in Part II and implement it. In the process of doing that, we'll learn how to use common functional programming techniques such as composition, partial application, and the scary-sounding "monad."

CHAPTER 8

Understanding Functions

In the preceding parts of the book, we have captured the requirements for an order-placing workflow and then modeled it using types. The next task is to implement that design using a functional programming (FP) approach.

But before we get to that, let's make sure that we understand what functional programming is and what tools and tactics we'll need in order to create the implementation. By the end of this chapter, you should have a good grasp of the key concepts in FP, which are valuable for doing any kind of programming, not just domain-driven design.

This book cannot possibly explain everything about functional programming, so we'll just focus on the basics. We'll look at what functions are and how to do function composition, which is the overarching design principle in FP.

We won't be discussing scary-sounding concepts such as monads, functors, and so on—at least not right now. We'll come across these concepts later, when the need for them arises naturally.

Finally, we won't have space to cover all of F# syntax in this book. If you see some construct you don't understand, check out some of the helpful summaries on the Internet: try searching for "F# cheat sheet" or "F# syntax."

Functions, Functions, Everywhere

First, let's look at why functional programming is so different from object-oriented programming. There are many different definitions of functional programming, but I'm going to pick a very simple one:

- Functional programming is *programming as if functions really mattered.*

In most modern languages functions are first-class objects, but using functions (or lambdas) occasionally doesn't mean that you are "doing" functional programming. The key thing about the functional programming paradigm is that functions are used *everywhere*, for *everything*.

For example, say that we have a large program that is assembled from smaller pieces.

- In an object-oriented approach, these pieces would be classes and objects.
- In a functional approach, these pieces would be functions.

Or say that we need to parameterize some aspect of the program, or we want to reduce coupling between components.

- In an object-oriented approach, we would use interfaces and dependency injection.

- In a functional approach, we would parameterize with functions.

Or let's say that we want to follow the "don't repeat yourself" principle and reuse code between many components.

- In an object-oriented approach, we might use inheritance or a technique like the Decorator pattern.

- In a functional approach, we put all the reusable code into functions and glue them together using composition.

It's important to understand that functional programming is therefore not just a stylistic difference, it's a completely different way of thinking about programming. If you are new to it, you should approach learning FP with a beginner's mind.

That is, rather than asking a question from a different paradigm (such as "How do I loop through a collection?" or "How do I implement the Strategy pattern?"), you'll be better off asking how to solve the same underlying problem ("How can I perform an action for each element of a collection?" or "How can I parameterize behavior?"). The problems we face as programmers are the same, but the solutions used in functional programming are very different from those used in object-oriented programming.

Functions Are Things

In the functional programming paradigm, functions are things in their own right. And if functions are things, then they can be passed as input to other functions:

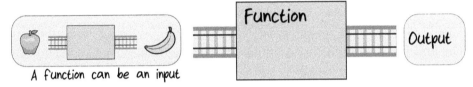

Or they can be returned as the output of a function:

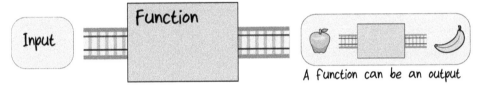

Or they can be passed as a parameter to a function to control its behavior:

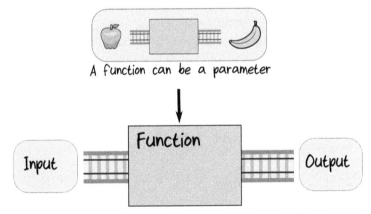

Treating functions as things opens up a world of possibilities. It's hard to get your head around at first, but you can already see that even with this basic principle you can build up complex systems quite quickly.

Jargon Alert: "Higher-Order Functions"

Functions that input or output other functions or take functions as parameters are called *higher-order functions*, often abbreviated to *HOFs*.

Treating Functions as Things in F#

Let's take a look at how "functions as things" works in F#. Here are four function definitions:

```
let plus3 x = x + 3          // plus3 : x:int -> int
let times2 x = x * 2         // times2 : x:int -> int
let square = (fun x -> x * x) // square : x:int -> int
let addThree = plus3          // addThree : (int -> int)
```

The first two definitions are just like the ones we've seen before. In the third definition, the let keyword is used to assign a name (square) to an anonymous function, also known as a *lambda* expression. In the fourth definition, the let keyword is used to assign a name (addThree) to a function defined earlier (plus3). Each of these functions is an int -> int function that takes an int as input and outputs a new int.

Now, because functions are things, we can put them in a list:

```
// listOfFunctions : (int -> int) list
let listOfFunctions =
  [addThree; times2; square]
```

 In F#, list literals use square brackets as delimiters, with semicolons (not commas!) as element separators.

We can now loop through the list and evaluate each function in turn:

```
for fn in listOfFunctions do
  let result = fn 100    // call the function
  printfn "If 100 is the input, the output is %i" result

// Result =>
// If 100 is the input, the output is 103
// If 100 is the input, the output is 200
// If 100 is the input, the output is 10000
```

The let keyword is not just for function definitions—it's used generally to assign names to values. So for example, here is let used to assign a name to the string "hello":

```
// myString : string
let myString = "hello"
```

The fact that the same keyword (let) is used to define both functions and simple values is not an accident. Let's look at an example to see why. In this first snippet, I define a function called square:

```
// square : x:int -> int
let square x = x * x
```

And in this second snippet I'm assigning the name square to an anonymous function. Is let defining a simple value here or a function?

```
// square : x:int -> int
let square = (fun x -> x * x)
```

The answer is both! A function is a thing and can be assigned a name. So the second definition of square is essentially the same as the first, and they can be used interchangeably.

Functions as Input

We said that "functions as things" means that they can be used for input and output, so let's see what that looks like in practice.

First, let's look at using a function as an input parameter. Here's a function called evalWith5ThenAdd2, which takes a function fn, calls it with 5, and then adds 2 to the result.

```
let evalWith5ThenAdd2 fn =
  fn(5) + 2

// evalWith5ThenAdd2 : fn:(int -> int) -> int
```

If we look at the type signature at the bottom, we can see that the compiler has inferred that fn must be an (int -> int) function.

Let's test it now. First, we'll define add1, which is an (int -> int) function, and then pass it in.

```
let add1 x = x + 1      // an int -> int function
evalWith5ThenAdd2 add1 // fn(5) + 2 becomes add1(5) + 2
//                      // so output is 8
```

The result is 8, as we would expect.

We can use *any* (int -> int) function as a parameter. So let's define a different one, such as square and pass it as a parameter:

```
let square x = x * x      // an int -> int function
evalWith5ThenAdd2 square // fn(5) + 2 becomes square(5) + 2
//                        // so output is 27
```

And this time the result is 27.

Functions as Output

Now let's turn to functions as output. Why would you want to do that?

Well, one very important reason to return functions is that you can "bake in" certain parameters to the function.

For example, say you have three different functions to add integers, like this:

```
let add1 x = x + 1
let add2 x = x + 2
let add3 x = x + 3
```

Obviously, we would like to get rid of the duplication. How can we do that?

The answer is to create an "adder generator"—a function that returns an "add" function with the number to add baked in:

Here's what the code would look like:

```
let adderGenerator numberToAdd =
  // return a lambda
  fun x -> numberToAdd + x

// val adderGenerator :
//    int -> (int -> int)
```

Looking at the type signature, it clearly shows us that it takes an int as input and emits an (int -> int) function as output.

We could also implement adderGenerator by returning a named function instead of an anonymous function, like this:

```
let adderGenerator numberToAdd =
  // define a nested inner function
  let innerFn x =
    numberToAdd + x

  // return the inner function
  innerFn
```

As we've seen with the square example earlier, both implementations are effectively the same. Which one do you prefer?

Finally, here's how adderGenerator might be used in practice:

```
// test
let add1 = adderGenerator 1
add1 2     // result => 3

let add100 = adderGenerator 100
add100 2   // result => 102
```

Currying

Using this trick of returning functions, *any* multiparameter function can be converted into a series of one-parameter functions. This method is called *currying*.

For example, a two-parameter function such as add:

```
// int -> int -> int
let add x y = x + y
```

can be converted into a one-parameter function by returning a new function, as we saw above:

```
// int -> (int -> int)
let adderGenerator x = fun y -> x + y
```

In F#, we don't need to do this explicitly—every function is a curried function! That is, any two-parameter function with signature 'a -> 'b -> 'c can also be interpreted as a one-parameter function that takes an 'a and returns a function ('b -> 'c), and similarly for functions with more parameters.

Partial Application

If every function is curried, that means you can take any multiparameter function and pass in just one argument, and you'll get a new function back with that parameter baked in but all the other parameters still needed.

For example, the sayGreeting function below has two parameters:

```
// sayGreeting: string -> string -> unit
let sayGreeting greeting name =
  printfn "%s %s" greeting name
```

But we can pass in just one parameter to create some new functions with the greeting baked in:

```
// sayHello: string -> unit
let sayHello = sayGreeting "Hello"

// sayGoodbye: string -> unit
let sayGoodbye = sayGreeting "Goodbye"
```

These functions now have one remaining parameter, the name. If we supply that, we get the final output:

```
sayHello "Alex"
// output: "Hello Alex"

sayGoodbye "Alex"
// output: "Goodbye Alex"
```

This approach of "baking in" parameters is called *partial application* and is a very important functional pattern. For example, we'll see it being used to do dependency injection in *Implementation: Composing a Pipeline* when we start implementing the order-taking workflow.

Total Functions

A mathematical function links each possible input to an output. In functional programming we try to design our functions the same way, so that every input has a corresponding output. These kinds of functions are called *total functions*.

Why bother? Because we want to make things *explicit* as much as possible, with all effects documented in the type signature.

Let's demonstrate the concept with a rather silly function, twelveDividedBy, which returns the result of 12 divided by the input using integer division. In pseudo-code, we could implement this with a table of cases, like this:

```
let twelveDividedBy n =
  match n with
  | 6 -> 2
  | 5 -> 2
  | 4 -> 3
  | 3 -> 4
  | 2 -> 6
  | 1 -> 12
  | 0 -> ???
```

Now what should the answer be when the input is zero? Twelve divided by zero is undefined.

If we didn't care that every possible input had a corresponding output, we could just throw an exception for the zero case, like this:

```
let twelveDividedBy n =
  match n with
  | 6 -> 2
  ...
  | 0 -> failwith "Can't divide by zero"
```

But let's look at the signature of the function defined this way:

```
twelveDividedBy : int -> int
```

This signature implies that you can pass in an int and get back an int. But that is a lie! You don't *always* get back an int; sometimes you get an exception. But that is not made explicit in the type signature.

It would be great if the type signature did *not* lie. In that case *every* input to the function would have a valid output, with no exceptions (in both senses of the word). Let's look at how we can do that.

One technique is to *restrict the input* to eliminate values that are illegal. For this example, we could create a new constrained type NonZeroInteger and pass that in. Zero wouldn't be in the set of input values at all and so would never need to be handled.

```
type NonZeroInteger =
  // Defined to be constrained to non-zero ints.
  // Add smart constructor, etc
  private NonZeroInteger of int

/// Uses restricted input
let twelveDividedBy (NonZeroInteger n) =
  match n with
  | 6 -> 2
  ...
  // 0 can't be in the input
  // so doesn't need to be handled
```

Here's the signature of this new version:

```
twelveDividedBy : NonZeroInteger -> int
```

This is much better than the previous version. You can immediately see what the requirements for the input are without having to read documentation or look at the source. This function does not lie. Everything is explicit.

Another technique is to *extend the output*. In this approach, we will be fine with accepting zero as an input, but we extend the output to be a choice between a valid int and an undefined value. We'll use the Option type to represent this choice between "something" and "nothing." Here's the implementation:

```
/// Uses extended output
let twelveDividedBy n =
  match n with
  | 6 -> Some 2 // valid
  | 5 -> Some 2 // valid
  | 4 -> Some 3 // valid
  ...
  | 0 -> None   // undefined
```

The signature of this new version would be this:

```
twelveDividedBy : int -> int option
```

This means: you give me an int and I *might* give you an int back, if the input is acceptable. Again, the signature is explicit and doesn't mislead you.

Even in a silly example like this, we can see the benefit of using a total function. In both variants, the function signatures are explicit about what all the possible inputs and outputs are. Later on in this book, especially in the chapter on error handling, we'll see some real-world uses of function signatures to document all the possible outputs.

Composition

We discussed "composition" in the context of types—creating new types by combining other types. Now let's talk about *function composition*, combining functions by connecting the output of the first to the input of the second.

For example, here are two functions. The first takes an apple as input and outputs a banana. The second takes a banana as input and outputs some cherries. The output of the first is the same type as the input of the second, and therefore we can compose them together like this:

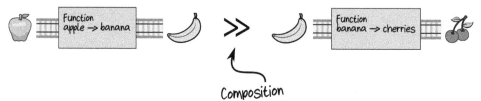

Composition

After we have composed them together, we have a new function:

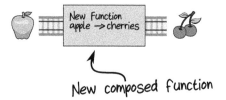

New composed function

An important aspect of this kind of composition is *information hiding*. You cannot tell that the function was composed of smaller functions, nor what the smaller functions operated on. In this case, where has the banana gone? The user of this new function is not even aware that there ever was a banana. We've successfully hidden that information from the user of the final, composed function.

Composition of Functions in F#

How does function composition work in F#?

In F#, any two functions can be glued together as long as the output type of the first one is the same as the input type of the second one. This is typically done using an approach called "piping."

Piping in F# is very similar to piping in Unix. You start with a value, feed it into the first function, take the output of the first function and feed it into the next function, and so on. The output of the last function in the series is the output of the pipeline as a whole.

The pipe operation in F# is |>. Using a pipe for the first example means the code would look like this:

```
let add1 x = x + 1      // an int -> int function
let square x = x * x    // an int -> int function

let add1ThenSquare x =
  x |> add1 |> square

// test
add1ThenSquare 5        // result is 36
```

We have defined a parameter x for add1ThenSquare. In the implementation, that parameter is fed into the first function (add) to start the data flow through the pipeline.

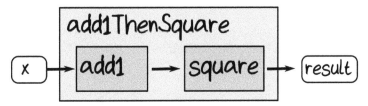

Here's another example. The first function is an int->bool function, the second function is a bool->string function, and the combined function is int->string:

```
let isEven x =
  (x % 2) = 0               // an int -> bool function

let printBool x =
  sprintf "value is %b" x  // a bool -> string function

let isEvenThenPrint x =
  x |> isEven |> printBool

// test
isEvenThenPrint 2           // result is "value is true"
```

Building an Entire Application from Functions

This principle of composition can be used to build complete applications.

For example, start with a basic function at the bottom level of the application:

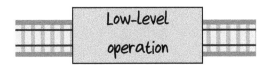

Then we compose those to create a service function, say this:

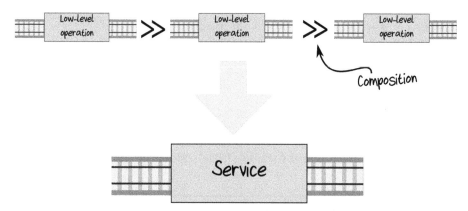

We can then use these service functions and glue them together to create a function that handles a complete workflow.

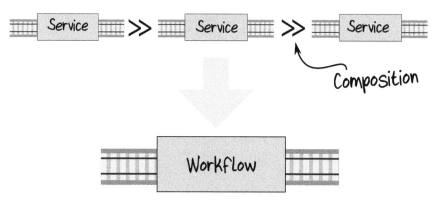

Finally we can build an application from these workflows by composing them in parallel and creating a controller/dispatcher that selects the particular workflow to call based on the input as shown in the figure on page 159.

And that is how you build a functional application. Each layer consists of a function with an input and an output. It's functions all the way up.

In Chapter 9, *Implementation: Composing a Pipeline*, on page 161, we'll see how these ideas work in practice—we'll implement the pipeline for the order-placing workflow by assembling a series of smaller functions.

Challenges in Composing Functions

Composing functions is easy when the output of one matches the input of another. But what happens if the functions don't match up so easily?

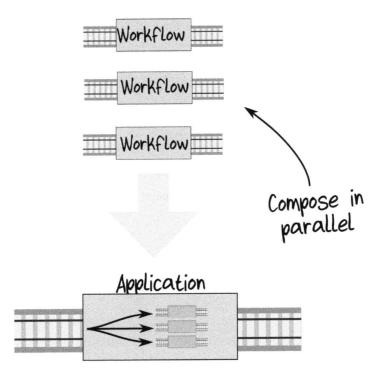

A common case is when the underlying types would fit but the "shapes" of the functions are different.

For example, one function might output an Option<int> but the second function needs a plain int. Or conversely, one function might output an int but the second function needs an Option<int>.

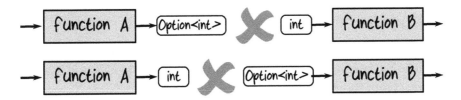

Similar mismatch issues arise with when working with lists, the success/failure Result type, async, and so on.

Many of the challenges in using composition involve trying to adjust the inputs and outputs so that they match up, allowing the functions to be connected together. A popular approach is to convert both sides to be the same type, the "lowest common multiple" of each side, as it were.

For example, if the output is an int and the input is an Option<int>, the "smallest" type that can encompass both—the lowest common multiple—is Option. If we convert the output of functionA to an Option using Some, the adjusted value can now be used as the input for functionB, and composition can occur.

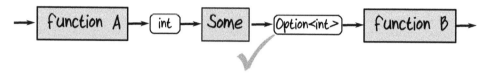

Here's a demonstration of that example using real code:

```
// a function that has an int as output
let add1 x = x + 1
```

```
// a function that has an Option<int> as input
let printOption x =
  match x with
  | Some i -> printfn "The int is %i" i
  | None -> printfn "No value"
```

To connect them, we convert the output of add1 into an Option using the Some constructor, and then that can be piped into the input of printOption:

```
5 |> add1 |> Some |> printOption
```

This is a very simple example of the type-mismatch problem. We've already seen a more complex example when we modeled the order-placing workflow and then tried to compose them on page 136. In the two implementation chapters following this one, we'll spend quite a bit of time getting functions into a uniform shape so that they can be composed.

Wrapping Up

In this chapter, we were introduced to the basic concepts of functional programming in F#—using functions everywhere as building blocks and designing them to be composable.

With these principles under our belt, we can finally start doing some real coding! In the next chapter, we'll put these concepts into practice, starting with building a pipeline for the order-placing workflow.

CHAPTER 9

Implementation: Composing a Pipeline

So far, we've spent a lot of time modeling the domain using only types. We haven't yet implemented anything! Let's remedy that now.

In the next two chapters, we'll work with the design that we did earlier (Chapter 7, *Modeling Workflows as Pipelines*, on page 119) and implement it using functional principles.

To recap the design in that chapter, the workflow can be thought of as a series of document transformations—a pipeline—with each step in the pipeline designed as a section of "pipe."

From a technical point of view, we have the following stages in our pipeline:

- Start with an UnvalidatedOrder and convert it into a ValidatedOrder, returning an error if the validation fails.

- Take the output of the validation step (a ValidatedOrder) and turn it into a PricedOrder by adding some extra information.

- Take the output of the pricing step, create an acknowledgment letter from it, and send it.

- Create a set of events representing what happened and return them.

We want to turn this into code, preserving the original requirements without getting entangled in technical details.

Here's an example of how we would like our code to look using the piping approach we discussed earlier on page 156 to connect together the functions for each step:

```
let placeOrder unvalidatedOrder =
  unvalidatedOrder
  |> validateOrder
  |> priceOrder
  |> acknowledgeOrder
  |> createEvents
```

This code—a series of steps—is easy to understand, even for a non-developer, so let's see what's needed to make this happen. There are two parts to implementing this workflow: creating the individual steps and then combining them together.

First, we'll implement each step in the pipeline as a stand-alone function, making sure that it is stateless and without side effects so it can be tested and reasoned about independently.

Next, we just compose these smaller functions into a single larger one. It sounds simple in theory. But as we mentioned before, when we actually try it, we run into a problem. The functions as designed don't fit together nicely—the output of one doesn't match the input of the next. To overcome that, we'll need to learn how to manipulate the inputs and outputs of each step so that they *can* be composed.

The functions can't be composed for two reasons:

- Some functions have extra parameters that aren't part of the data pipeline but are needed for the implementation—we called these "dependencies."

- We explicitly indicated "effects" such as error handling by using a wrapper type like Result in the function signatures. But that means that functions with effects in their output cannot be directly connected to functions that just have unwrapped plain data as their input.

In this chapter we'll deal with the first problem, working with the inputs that are dependencies, and we'll see how to do the functional equivalent of "dependency injection." We'll hold off on looking at how to work with effects until the next chapter.

For our first pass at writing some real code, then, we'll implement all the steps without worrying about effects like Result and Async. This will allow us to focus on the basics of composition.

Working with Simple Types

Before we start implementing the steps of the workflow itself, we need to first implement the "simple types," such as OrderId and ProductCode.

Since most of the types are constrained in some way, we'll follow the outline for implementing constrained types discussed earlier on page 104.

So, for each simple type we'll need at least two functions:

- A create function that constructs the type from a primitive such as string or int—for example, OrderId.create will create an OrderId from a string, or raise an error if the string is the wrong format.

- A value function that extracts the inner primitive value

We typically put these helper functions in the same file as the simple type, using a module with the same name as the type they apply to. For example, here's the definition for OrderId in the Domain module, along with its helper functions:

```
module Domain =
  type OrderId = private OrderId of string

  module OrderId =
    /// Define a "Smart constructor" for OrderId
    /// string -> OrderId
    let create str =
        if String.IsNullOrEmpty(str) then
          // use exceptions rather than Result for now
          failwith "OrderId must not be null or empty"
        elif str.Length > 50 then
          failwith "OrderId must not be more than 50 chars"
        else
          OrderId str

    /// Extract the inner value from an OrderId
    /// OrderId -> string
    let value (OrderId str) = // unwrap in the parameter!
      str                     // return the inner value
```

- The create function is similar to the guideline version, except that because we are avoiding effects for now, we'll use an exception (failwith) for errors rather than returning a Result.

- The value function demonstrates how you can pattern-match and extract the inner value in one step, directly in the parameter.

Using Function Types to Guide the Implementation

In the modeling chapters, we defined special function types to represent each step of the workflow. Now that it's time for implementation, how can we ensure that our code conforms to them?

The simplest approach is just to define a function in the normal way and trust that when we use it later, we'll get a type-checking error if we get it wrong. For example, we could define the validateOrder function as below, with no reference to the ValidateOrder type that we designed earlier:

```
let validateOrder
  checkProductCodeExists // dependency
  checkAddressExists     // dependency
  unvalidatedOrder =     // input
    ...
```

This is the standard approach for most F# code, but if we want to make it clear that we are implementing a specific function type, we can use a different style. We can write the function as a value (with no parameters) annotated with the function type, and with the body of the function written as a lambda. It looks like this:

```
// define a function signature
type MyFunctionSignature = Param1 -> Param2 -> Result

// define a function that implements that signature
let myFunc: MyFunctionSignature =
  fun param1 param2 ->
    ...
```

Applying this approach to the validateOrder function gives us this:

```
let validateOrder : ValidateOrder =
  fun checkProductCodeExists checkAddressExists unvalidatedOrder ->
    // ^dependency           ^dependency        ^input
      ...
```

What's nice about this is that all the parameters and the return value have types determined by the function type, so if you make a mistake in the implementation, you get an error locally, right inside the function definition, rather than later, when you are trying to assemble the functions.

Here's an example of type checking at work, where we accidentally pass an integer to the checkProductCodeExists function:

```
let validateOrder : ValidateOrder =
  fun checkProductCodeExists checkAddressExists unvalidatedOrder ->
    if checkProductCodeExists 42 then
      //         compiler error ^
      // This expression was expected to have type ProductCode
      // but here has type int
      ...
    ...
```

If we did not have the function type in place to determine the types of the parameters, the compiler would use type inference and might conclude that checkProductCodeExists works with integers, leading to (possibly confusing) compiler errors elsewhere.

Implementing the Validation Step

We can now start implementing the validation step. The validation step will take the unvalidated order, with all its primitive fields, and transform it into a proper, fully validated domain object.

We modeled the function types for this step like this:

```
type CheckAddressExists =
  UnvalidatedAddress -> AsyncResult<CheckedAddress,AddressValidationError>

type ValidateOrder =
  CheckProductCodeExists    // dependency
    -> CheckAddressExists    // AsyncResult dependency
    -> UnvalidatedOrder      // input
    -> AsyncResult<ValidatedOrder,ValidationError list>  // output
```

As we said, we're going to eliminate the effects for this chapter, so we can remove the AsyncResult parts, leaving us with this:

```
type CheckAddressExists =
  UnvalidatedAddress -> CheckedAddress

type ValidateOrder =
  CheckProductCodeExists    // dependency
    -> CheckAddressExists    // dependency
    -> UnvalidatedOrder      // input
    -> ValidatedOrder        // output
```

Let's convert this into an implementation. The steps to create a ValidatedOrder from an UnvalidatedOrder will be as follows:

- Create an OrderId domain type from the corresponding OrderId string in the unvalidated order.

- Create a CustomerInfo domain type from the corresponding UnvalidatedCustomerInfo field in the unvalidated order.

- Create an Address domain type from the corresponding ShippingAddress field in the unvalidated order, which is an UnvalidatedAddress.

- Do the same for BillingAddress and all the other properties.

- Once we have all the components of the ValidatedOrder available, we can then create the record in the usual way.

Here's what that looks like in code:

```
let validateOrder : ValidateOrder =
  fun checkProductCodeExists checkAddressExists unvalidatedOrder ->

    let orderId =
      unvalidatedOrder.OrderId
      |> OrderId.create

    let customerInfo =
      unvalidatedOrder.CustomerInfo
      |> toCustomerInfo   // helper function

    let shippingAddress =
      unvalidatedOrder.ShippingAddress
      |> toAddress         // helper function

    // and so on, for each property of the unvalidatedOrder

    // when all the fields are ready, use them to
    // create and return a new "ValidatedOrder" record
    {
      OrderId = orderId
      CustomerInfo = customerInfo
      ShippingAddress = shippingAddress
      BillingAddress = ...
      Lines = ...
    }
```

You can see that we are using some helper functions, such as toCustomerInfo and toAddress, that we have yet to define. These functions construct a domain type from an unvalidated type. For example, toAddress will convert an Unvalidated Address type to the corresponding domain type Address and will raise errors if the primitive values in the unvalidated address don't meet the constraints (such as being non-null and less than 50 characters long).

Once we have all these helper functions in place, the logic to convert an unvalidated order (or any non-domain type) to a domain type is straightforward: for each field of the domain type (in this case, ValidatedOrder) find the corresponding field of the non-domain type (UnvalidatedOrder) and use one of the helper functions to convert the field into a domain type.

We can use exactly the same approach when converting the subcomponents of an order as well. For example, here is the implementation of toCustomerInfo, which builds a CustomerInfo from an UnvalidatedCustomerInfo:

```
let toCustomerInfo (customer:UnvalidatedCustomerInfo) : CustomerInfo =
  // create the various CustomerInfo properties
  // and throw exceptions if invalid
  let firstName = customer.FirstName |> String50.create
  let lastName = customer.LastName |> String50.create
```

```
let emailAddress = customer.EmailAddress |> EmailAddress.create

// create a PersonalName
let name : PersonalName = {
  FirstName = firstName
  LastName = lastName
  }

// create a CustomerInfo
let customerInfo : CustomerInfo = {
  Name = name
  EmailAddress = emailAddress
  }
// ... and return it
customerInfo
```

Creating a Valid, Checked Address

The toAddress function is a bit more complex, since it not only needs to convert the raw primitive types to domain objects but also has to check that the address exists as well (using the CheckAddressExists service). Here's the complete implementation, with comments below:

```
let toAddress (checkAddressExists:CheckAddressExists) unvalidatedAddress =
  // call the remote service
  let checkedAddress = checkAddressExists unvalidatedAddress
  // extract the inner value using pattern matching
  let (CheckedAddress checkedAddress) = checkedAddress

  let addressLine1 =
    checkedAddress.AddressLine1 |> String50.create
  let addressLine2 =
    checkedAddress.AddressLine2 |> String50.createOption
  let addressLine3 =
    checkedAddress.AddressLine3 |> String50.createOption
  let addressLine4 =
    checkedAddress.AddressLine4 |> String50.createOption
  let city =
    checkedAddress.City |> String50.create
  let zipCode =
    checkedAddress.ZipCode |> ZipCode.create
  // create the address
  let address : Address = {
    AddressLine1 = addressLine1
    AddressLine2 = addressLine2
    AddressLine3 = addressLine3
    AddressLine4 = addressLine4
    City = city
    ZipCode = zipCode
    }
  // return the address
  address
```

Note that we're referring to another constructor function in the String50 module—String50.createOption—that allows the input to be null or empty, and returns None for that case.

The toAddress function needs to call checkAddressExists, so we have added it as a parameter; now pass that function along from the parent validateOrder function:

```
let validateOrder : ValidateOrder =
  fun checkProductCodeExists checkAddressExists unvalidatedOrder ->

    let orderId = ...
    let customerInfo = ...
    let shippingAddress =
      unvalidatedOrder.ShippingAddress
      |> toAddress checkAddressExists // new parameter

    ...
```

You might wonder why we are only passing in *one* parameter to toAddress when it actually has two. The second parameter (the shipping address) is being provided but via the piping process. This is an example of the partial application technique that we talked about earlier on page 153.

Creating the Order Lines

Creating the list of order lines is more complex yet again. First, we need a way to transform a single UnvalidatedOrderLine to a ValidatedOrderLine. Let's call it toValidatedOrderLine:

```
let toValidatedOrderLine checkProductCodeExists
(unvalidatedOrderLine:UnvalidatedOrderLine) =
  let orderLineId =
    unvalidatedOrderLine.OrderLineId
    |> OrderLineId.create
  let productCode =
    unvalidatedOrderLine.ProductCode
    |> toProductCode checkProductCodeExists // helper function
  let quantity =
    unvalidatedOrderLine.Quantity
    |> toOrderQuantity productCode   // helper function
  let validatedOrderLine = {
    OrderLineId = orderLineId
    ProductCode = productCode
    Quantity = quantity
    }
  validatedOrderLine
```

This is similar to the toAddress function above. There are two helper functions, toProductCode and toOrderQuantity, which we will discuss shortly.

And now, since we have a way to transform each element in the list, we can transform the whole list at once using List.map (the equivalent of Select in C# LINQ), giving us a list of ValidatedOrderLines that we can use in a ValidatedOrder:

```
let validateOrder : ValidateOrder =
  fun checkProductCodeExists checkAddressExists unvalidatedOrder ->

    let orderId = ...
    let customerInfo = ...
    let shippingAddress = ...

    let orderLines =
      unvalidatedOrder.Lines
      // convert each line using `toValidatedOrderLine`
      |> List.map (toValidatedOrderLine checkProductCodeExists)
    ...
```

Let's look at the helper function toOrderQuantity next. This is a good example of validation at the boundary of a bounded context: the input is a raw unvalidated decimal from UnvalidatedOrderLine, but the output (OrderQuantity) is a choice type with different validations for each case. Here's the code:

```
let toOrderQuantity productCode quantity =
  match productCode with
  | Widget _ ->
    quantity
    |> int                   // convert decimal to int
    |> UnitQuantity.create   // to UnitQuantity
    |> OrderQuantity.Unit    // lift to OrderQuantity type
  | Gizmo _ ->
    quantity
    |> KilogramQuantity.create  // to KilogramQuantity
    |> OrderQuantity.Kilogram   // lift to OrderQuantity type
```

We're using the case of the ProductCode choice type to guide the constructor. For example, if the ProductCode is a Widget, then we cast the raw decimal into an int and create a UnitQuantity from that. And similarly for the GizmoCode case.

But we can't stop there. If we did, one branch would return a UnitQuantity and the other would return a KilogramQuantity. These are different types, so we would get a compiler error. By converting both branches into the choice type OrderQuantity, we ensure that both branches return the same type and keep the compiler happy!

The other helper function, toProductCode, should at first glance be straightforward to implement. We want to write our functions using pipelines as much as possible, so the code should look something like this:

```
let toProductCode (checkProductCodeExists:CheckProductCodeExists) productCode =
  productCode
  |> ProductCode.create
  |> checkProductCodeExists
  // returns a bool :(
```

But now we have a problem. We want the toProductCode function to return a ProductCode, but the checkProductCodeExists function returns a bool, which means the whole pipeline returns a bool. Somehow, then, we need to make checkProductCodeExists return a ProductCode instead. Oh dear, does that mean we have to change our spec? Luckily, no. Let's see how.

Creating Function Adapters

We have a function that returns a bool, but we really want a function that returns the original ProductCode input (if everything goes well). Rather than changing the spec, let's create an "adapter" function that takes the original function as input and emits a new function with the right "shape" to be used in the pipeline.

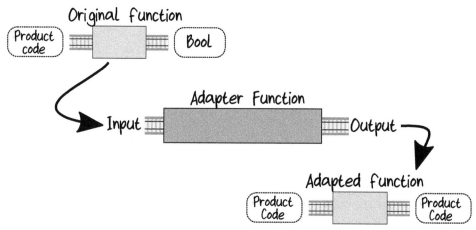

Here's the obvious implementation, with parameters for the bool-returning predicate (checkProductCodeExists) and the value to check (productCode):

```
let convertToPassthru checkProductCodeExists productCode =
  if checkProductCodeExists productCode then
    productCode
  else
    failwith "Invalid Product Code"
```

What's interesting about this implementation is that the compiler has determined that it is completely generic—it's not specific to our particular case at all! If you look at the function signature, you'll see there's no mention of the ProductCode type anywhere:

```
val convertToPassthru :
  checkProductCodeExists:('a -> bool) -> productCode:'a -> 'a
```

In fact, we've accidentally created a generic adapter that will convert *any* predicate function into a "passthrough" function suitable for a pipeline. Calling the parameters "checkProductCodeExists" or "productCode" doesn't make sense now—they could be anything at all. This is the reason so many standard library functions have such short parameter names, such as f and g for function parameters, and x and y for other values.

Let's rewrite the function to use more abstract names, then, like this:

```
let predicateToPassthru f x =
  if f x then
    x
  else
    failwith "Invalid Product Code"
```

And now the hard-coded error message sticks out, so let's parameterize that too. Here's the final version:

```
let predicateToPassthru errorMsg f x =
  if f x then
    x
  else
    failwith errorMsg
```

Note that we have put the error message *first* in the parameter order so that we can bake it in with partial application.

The signature of this function is this:

```
val predicateToPassthru : errorMsg:string -> f:('a -> bool) -> x:'a -> 'a
```

We can interpret this as, "You give me an error message and a function of type 'a -> bool, and I'll give you back a function of type 'a -> 'a." This predicate-ToPassthru function is thus a "function transformer"—you feed it one function and it'll transform it into another function.

This technique is extremely common in functional programming, so it's important to understand what's going on and to recognize the pattern when you see it. Even the humble List.map function can be thought of as a function transformer—it transforms a "normal" function 'a -> 'b into a function that works on lists ('a list -> 'b list).

OK, now let's use this generic function to create a new version of toProductCode that we can use in our implementation:

```
let toProductCode (checkProductCodeExists:CheckProductCodeExists) productCode =

  // create a local ProductCode -> ProductCode function
  // suitable for using in a pipeline
  let checkProduct productCode =
    let errorMsg = sprintf "Invalid: %A" productCode
    predicateToPassthru errorMsg checkProductCodeExists productCode

  // assemble the pipeline
  productCode
  |> ProductCode.create
  |> checkProduct
```

And that's it—now we have a basic sketch of a validateOrder implementation
that we can build on. Notice that the low-level validation logic, such as "a
product must start with a *W* or a *G*," is not explicitly implemented in our
validation functions but is built into the constructors of the constrained
simple types, such as OrderId and ProductCode. Using types can boost our confidence that the code is correct—the very fact that we can successfully create
a ValidatedOrder from an UnvalidatedOrder means we can trust that it is validated!

Implementing the Rest of the Steps

Now that we've seen how to implement validateOrder, we can use the same
techniques to build the rest of the pipeline functions.

Here's the original design of the pricing step function, with effects:

```
type PriceOrder =
  GetProductPrice        // dependency
    -> ValidatedOrder   // input
    -> Result<PricedOrder, PlaceOrderError>  // output
```

But again, we'll eliminate the effects for now, leaving this design:

```
type GetProductPrice = ProductCode -> Price
type PriceOrder =
  GetProductPrice        // dependency
    -> ValidatedOrder   // input
    -> PricedOrder       // output
```

And here's the outline of the implementation. It simply transforms each order
line to a PricedOrderLine and builds a new PricedOrder with them:

```
let priceOrder : PriceOrder =
  fun getProductPrice validatedOrder ->
    let lines =
      validatedOrder.Lines
      |> List.map (toPricedOrderLine getProductPrice)
    let amountToBill =
      lines
```

```
      // get each line price
      |> List.map (fun line -> line.LinePrice)
      // add them together as a BillingAmount
      |> BillingAmount.sumPrices
  let pricedOrder : PricedOrder = {
    OrderId   = validatedOrder.OrderId
    CustomerInfo = validatedOrder.CustomerInfo
    ShippingAddress = validatedOrder.ShippingAddress
    BillingAddress = validatedOrder.BillingAddress
    Lines = lines
    AmountToBill = amountToBill
    }
  pricedOrder
```

By the way, if you have many steps in the pipeline and you don't want to implement them yet (or don't know how to), you can just fail with a "not implemented" message, like this:

```
let priceOrder : PriceOrder =
  fun getProductPrice validatedOrder ->
    failwith "not implemented"
```

Using a "not implemented" exception can be convenient when sketching out an implementation. It allows us to ensure that our project is fully compilable at all times. For example, we could use this approach to build a dummy version of a particular pipeline stage that conforms to the function type and then use it with the other stages before a proper implementation is available.

Going back to the implementation of priceOrder, we've introduced two new helper functions: toPricedOrderLine and BillingAmount.sumPrices.

We've added the BillingAmount.sumPrices function to the shared BillingAmount module (along with create and value). It simply adds up a list of Prices and wraps it as a BillingAmount. Why have we defined a BillingAmount type in the first place? Because it's distinct from a Price and the validation rules might be different.

```
/// Sum a list of prices to make a billing amount
/// Raise exception if total is out of bounds
let sumPrices prices =
  let total = prices |> List.map Price.value |> List.sum
  create total
```

The toPricedOrderLine function is similar to what we've seen before. It's a helper function that converts a single line only:

```
/// Transform a ValidatedOrderLine to a PricedOrderLine
let toPricedOrderLine getProductPrice (line:ValidatedOrderLine) : PricedOrderLine =
  let qty = line.Quantity |> OrderQuantity.value
  let price = line.ProductCode |> getProductPrice
  let linePrice = price |> Price.multiply qty
```

```
{
  OrderLineId = line.OrderLineId
  ProductCode = line.ProductCode
  Quantity = line.Quantity
  LinePrice = linePrice
}
```

And within this function, we've introduced another helper function, Price.multiply, to multiply a Price by a quantity.

```
/// Multiply a Price by a decimal qty.
/// Raise exception if new price is out of bounds.
let multiply qty (Price p) =
  create (qty * p)
```

The pricing step is now complete!

Implementing the Acknowledgment Step

Here's the design for the acknowledgment step, with effects removed:

```
type HtmlString = HtmlString of string
type CreateOrderAcknowledgmentLetter =
  PricedOrder -> HtmlString

type OrderAcknowledgment = {
  EmailAddress : EmailAddress
  Letter : HtmlString
}
type SendResult = Sent | NotSent
type SendOrderAcknowledgment =
  OrderAcknowledgment -> SendResult

type AcknowledgeOrder =
  CreateOrderAcknowledgmentLetter     // dependency
    -> SendOrderAcknowledgment        // dependency
    -> PricedOrder                    // input
    -> OrderAcknowledgmentSent option // output
```

And here's the implementation:

```
let acknowledgeOrder : AcknowledgeOrder =
  fun createAcknowledgmentLetter sendAcknowledgment pricedOrder ->
    let letter = createAcknowledgmentLetter pricedOrder
    let acknowledgment = {
      EmailAddress = pricedOrder.CustomerInfo.EmailAddress
      Letter = letter
    }

    // if the acknowledgment was successfully sent,
    // return the corresponding event, else return None
    match sendAcknowledgment acknowledgment with
    | Sent ->
```

```
    let event = {
      OrderId = pricedOrder.OrderId
      EmailAddress = pricedOrder.CustomerInfo.EmailAddress
      }
    Some event
  | NotSent ->
    None
```

The implementation is straightforward. No helper functions were needed, so that was easy!

What about the sendAcknowledgment dependency, though? At some point, we'll have to decide on an implementation for it. However, for now we can just leave it alone. That's one of the great benefits of using functions to parameterize dependencies—you can avoid making decisions until the last responsible moment, yet you can still build and assemble most of the code.

Creating the Events

Finally, we just need to create the events to be returned from the workflow. Let's add a wrinkle to the requirements and say that the billing event should only be sent when the billable amount is greater than zero. Here's the design:

```
/// Event to send to shipping context
type OrderPlaced = PricedOrder

/// Event to send to billing context
/// Will only be created if the AmountToBill is not zero
type BillableOrderPlaced = {
    OrderId : OrderId
    BillingAddress: Address
    AmountToBill : BillingAmount
    }

type PlaceOrderEvent =
    | OrderPlaced of OrderPlaced
    | BillableOrderPlaced of BillableOrderPlaced
    | AcknowledgmentSent  of OrderAcknowledgmentSent

type CreateEvents =
  PricedOrder                        // input
    -> OrderAcknowledgmentSent option  // input (event from previous step)
    -> PlaceOrderEvent list            // output
```

We don't need to create the OrderPlaced event because it's just the same as the PricedOrder event; and the OrderAcknowledgmentSent event will have been created in the previous step, so we don't need to create it either.

The BillableOrderPlaced event is needed, though, so let's make a createBillingEvent function. And because we need to test for a non-zero billing amount, the function must return an *optional* event.

```
// PricedOrder -> BillableOrderPlaced option
let createBillingEvent (placedOrder:PricedOrder) : BillableOrderPlaced option =
  let billingAmount = placedOrder.AmountToBill |> BillingAmount.value
  if billingAmount > 0M then
    let order = {
      OrderId = placedOrder.OrderId
      BillingAddress = placedOrder.BillingAddress
      AmountToBill = placedOrder.AmountToBill
    }
    Some order
  else
    None
```

So now we have an OrderPlaced event, an optional OrderAcknowledgmentSent event, and an optional BillableOrderPlaced. How should we return them? We'll use the "lowest common multiple" approach on page 158 to convert everything to a common type.

We decided earlier that we would create a choice type (PlaceOrderEvent) for each one and then return a list of those. So first we need to convert each event to the choice type. For the OrderPlaced event, we can just use the PlaceOrderEvent.Order-Placed constructor directly, but for OrderAcknowledgmentSent and BillableOrderPlaced, we need to use Option.map, since they are optional.

```
let createEvents : CreateEvents =
  fun pricedOrder acknowledgmentEventOpt ->
    let event1 =
      pricedOrder
      // convert to common choice type
      |> PlaceOrderEvent.OrderPlaced
    let event2Opt =
      acknowledgmentEventOpt
      // convert to common choice type
      |> Option.map PlaceOrderEvent.AcknowledgmentSent
    let event3Opt =
      pricedOrder
      |> createBillingEvent
      // convert to common choice type
      |> Option.map PlaceOrderEvent.BillableOrderPlaced

    // return all the events how?
    ...
```

Now they're all the same type, but some are optional. How should we deal with that? Well, we'll do the same trick again and convert them all to a more general type—in this case, a list.

For OrderPlaced we can convert it to a list using List.singleton, and for the options we can create a helper called listOfOption:

```
/// convert an Option into a List
let listOfOption opt =
  match opt with
  | Some x -> [x]
  | None -> []
```

With that, all three event types are the same and we can return them inside another list:

```
let createEvents : CreateEvents =
  fun pricedOrder acknowledgmentEventOpt ->
    let events1 =
      pricedOrder
      // convert to common choice type
      |> PlaceOrderEvent.OrderPlaced
      // convert to list
      |> List.singleton
    let events2 =
      acknowledgmentEventOpt
      // convert to common choice type
      |> Option.map PlaceOrderEvent.AcknowledgmentSent
      // convert to list
      |> listOfOption
    let events3 =
      pricedOrder
      |> createBillingEvent
      // convert to common choice type
      |> Option.map PlaceOrderEvent.BillableOrderPlaced
      // convert to list
      |> listOfOption

    // return all the events
    [
    yield! events1
    yield! events2
    yield! events3
    ]
```

This approach of converting or "lifting" non-compatible things to a shared type is a key technique for handling composition problems. For example, in the next chapter we'll use it to deal with the mismatch between different kinds of Result types.

Composing the Pipeline Steps Together

Now we're ready to complete the workflow by composing the implementations of the steps into a pipeline. We want the code to look something like this:

```
let placeOrder : PlaceOrderWorkflow =
  fun unvalidatedOrder ->
    unvalidatedOrder
    |> validateOrder
    |> priceOrder
    |> acknowledgeOrder
    |> createEvents
```

But we have a problem, which is that validateOrder has two extra inputs in addition to UnvalidatedOrder. As it stands, there's no easy way to connect the input of the PlaceOrder workflow to the validateOrder function, because the inputs and outputs don't match.

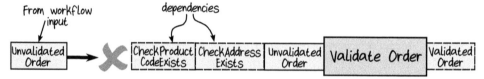

priceOrder has two inputs, so it can't be connected to the output of validateOrder:

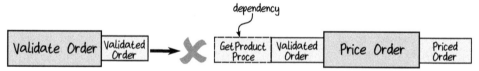

As we noted on page 136, composing functions with different "shapes" like this is one of the main challenges in functional programming, and many techniques have been developed to solve the problem. Most solutions involve the dreaded "monad," so for now we'll use a very simple approach, which is to use *partial application*, as presented on page 153. What we'll do is apply just two of the three parameters to validateOrder (the two dependencies), giving us a new function with only one input.

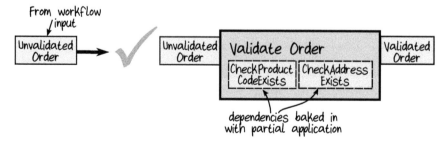

In code, it would look like this:

```
let validateOrderWithDependenciesBakedIn =
  validateOrder checkProductCodeExists checkAddressExists

// new function signature after partial application:
// UnvalidatedOrder -> ValidatedOrder
```

Of course, that's a horrible name! Luckily in F#, you can use the same name (validateOrder) locally for the new function as well—this is called "shadowing":

```
let validateOrder =
  validateOrder checkProductCodeExists checkAddressExists
```

Alternatively, you can use a tick mark in the name (validateOrder') to show that it's a variant of the original function, like this:

```
let validateOrder' =
  validateOrder checkProductCodeExists checkAddressExists
```

We can bake in the dependencies to priceOrder and acknowledgeOrder in the same way, so that they also become functions with a single input parameter.

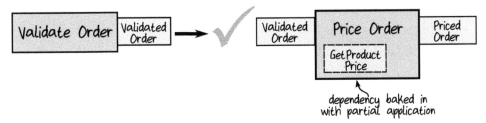

The main workflow function, placeOrder, would now look something like this:

```
let placeOrder : PlaceOrderWorkflow =

  // set up local versions of the pipeline stages
  // using partial application to bake in the dependencies
  let validateOrder =
    validateOrder checkProductCodeExists checkAddressExists
  let priceOrder =
    priceOrder getProductPrice
  let acknowledgeOrder =
    acknowledgeOrder createAcknowledgmentLetter sendAcknowledgment

  // return the workflow function
  fun unvalidatedOrder ->

    // compose the pipeline from the new one-parameter functions
    unvalidatedOrder
    |> validateOrder
    |> priceOrder
    |> acknowledgeOrder
    |> createEvents
```

Sometimes, even by doing this, the functions don't fit together. In our case, the output of acknowledgeOrder is just the event, not the priced order, so it doesn't match the input of createEvents.

We could write a little adapter for this, or we could simply switch to a more imperative style of code, where the output of each step is explicitly assigned to a value, like this:

```
let placeOrder : PlaceOrderWorkflow =
  // return the workflow function
  fun unvalidatedOrder ->
    let validatedOrder =
      unvalidatedOrder
      |> validateOrder checkProductCodeExists checkAddressExists
    let pricedOrder =
      validatedOrder
      |> priceOrder getProductPrice
    let acknowledgmentOption =
      pricedOrder
      |> acknowledgeOrder createAcknowledgmentLetter sendAcknowledgment
    let events =
      createEvents pricedOrder acknowledgmentOption
    events
```

It's not quite as elegant as the pipeline, but it's still easy to understand and maintain.

Next issue: Where do checkProductCodeExists and checkAddressExists and priceOrder and the other dependencies come from? We don't want to have to define them globally, so let's look at how to "inject" these dependencies.

Injecting Dependencies

We have a number of low-level helper functions, such as toValidProductCode, that take a function parameter representing a service. These are quite deep in the design, so how do we get dependencies from the top level down to the functions that need them?

If we were doing object-oriented programming, we would use dependency injection, and possibly an IoC container. In functional programming, we don't want to do that because the dependencies become implicit. Instead we always want to pass dependencies around as explicit parameters, which ensures that the dependencies are obvious.

There are a number of techniques for doing this kind of thing in functional programming, such as the "Reader Monad" and the "Free Monad," but since this is an introductory book, we'll stick with the simplest approach, which is to pass all the dependencies into the top-level function, which then passes them into the inner functions, which in turn passes them down to *their* inner functions, and so on.

Let's say that we implemented the helper functions as we defined them earlier:

```
// low-level helper functions
let toAddress checkAddressExists unvalidatedAddress =
  ...

let toProductCode checkProductCodeExists productCode =
  ...
```

They both have an explicit parameter for their dependency.

Now as part of creating an order line, we need to create a product code, so that means that toValidatedOrderLine needs to use toProductCode, which implies that toValidatedOrderLine also needs to have the checkProductCodeExists parameter:

```
// helper function
let toValidatedOrderLine checkProductExists unvalidatedOrderLine =
//                        ^ needed for toProductCode, below

  // create the components of the line
  let orderLineId = ...
  let productCode =
    unvalidatedOrderLine.ProductCode
    |> toProductCode checkProductExists //use service

  ...
```

And moving one level up, the validateOrder function needs to use both toAddress and toValidatedOrderLine, so it in turn needs *both* services to be passed in as extra parameters:

```
let validateOrder : ValidateOrder =
  fun checkProductExists // dependency for toValidatedOrderLine
    checkAddressExists   // dependency for toAddress
    unvalidatedOrder ->

      // build the validated address using the dependency
      let shippingAddress =
        unvalidatedOrder.ShippingAddress
        |> toAddress checkAddressExists

      ...

      // build the validated order lines using the dependency
      let lines =
        unvalidatedOrder.Lines
        |> List.map (toValidatedOrderLine checkProductExists)

      ...
```

And so on up the chain until you get to a top-level function that sets up all the services and other dependencies. In object-oriented design this top-level function is generally called the *composition root*, so let's use that term here.

Should the placeOrder workflow function act as the composition root? No, because setting up the services will typically involve accessing configuration, and so on. Better that the placeOrder workflow itself be provided with the services it needs as parameters, like this:

```
let placeOrder
  checkProductExists                  // dependency
  checkAddressExists                  // dependency
  getProductPrice                     // dependency
  createOrderAcknowledgmentLetter     // dependency
  sendOrderAcknowledgment             // dependency
  : PlaceOrderWorkflow =              // function definition

    fun unvalidatedOrder ->
      ...
```

This has the added benefit that the entire workflow is easily testable because all the dependencies are fake-able.

In practice, the composition root function should be as close as possible to the application's entry point—the main function for console apps or the OnStartup/Application_Start handler for long-running apps such as web services.

Here's an example of a composition root for a web service using the Suave framework.[1] First the services are set up, then the workflows are passed all their dependencies, and finally the routings are set up in order to direct the input to the appropriate workflow:

```
let app : WebPart =

  // set up the services used by the workflow
  let checkProductExists = ...
  let checkAddressExists = ...
  let getProductPrice = ...
  let createOrderAcknowledgmentLetter = ...
  let sendOrderAcknowledgment = ...
  let toHttpResponse = ...

  // set up the "placeOrder" workflow
  // by partially applying the services to it
  let placeOrder =
    placeOrder
      checkProductExists
      checkAddressExists
```

---

1. https://suave.io/

```
        getProductPrice
        createOrderAcknowledgmentLetter
        sendOrderAcknowledgment

// set up the other workflows
let changeOrder = ...
let cancelOrder = ...

// set up the routing
choose
  [ POST >=> choose
    [ path "/placeOrder"
        >=> deserializeOrder  // convert JSON to UnvalidatedOrder
        >=> placeOrder        // do the workflow
        >=> postEvents        // post the events onto queues
        >=> toHttpResponse    // return 200/400/etc based on the output
      path "/changeOrder"
        >=> ...
      path "/cancelOrder"
        >=> ...
    ]
  ]
```

You can see that if the path is /placeOrder, we start the "place order" process, starting with deserializing the input, then calling the main placeOrder pipeline, then posting the events, and then converting the output to an HTTP response. We don't have space to discuss the functions other than placeOrder, but deserialization techniques are discussed in the Serialization chapter on page 221.

Too Many Dependencies?

validateOrder has two dependencies. What happens if it needs four or five, or more? And if other steps need lots of other dependencies, you might have an explosion of them. If this happens, what should you do?

First, it may be that your function is doing too many things. Can you split it into smaller pieces? If that's not possible, you could group the dependencies into a single record structure, say, and pass that around as one parameter.

A common situation is when the dependencies for the child functions are particularly complicated in turn. For example, let's say that the checkAddressExists function is talking to a web service that requires a URI endpoint and credentials:

```
let checkAddressExists endPoint credentials =
  ...
```

Are we going to have to pass these extra two parameters into the caller of toAddress as well, like this?

```
let toAddress checkAddressExists endPoint credentials unvalidatedAddress =
//                              only ^ needed ^ for checkAddressExists

  // call the remote service
  let checkedAddress = checkAddressExists endPoint credentials unvalidatedAddress
  //                      2 extra parameters ^ passed in ^
  ...
```

Then we'd also have to pass these extra parameters into the caller of toAddress, and so on, all the way to the top:

```
let validateOrder
  checkProductExists
  checkAddressExists
  endPoint     // only needed for checkAddressExists
  credentials // only needed for checkAddressExists
  unvalidatedOrder =
    ...
```

No, of course we shouldn't do this. These intermediate functions shouldn't need to know anything about the dependencies of the checkAddressExists function. A much better approach is to set up the low-level functions *outside* the top-level function and then just pass in a prebuilt child function with all of its dependencies already baked in.

For example, in the code below, we bake the URI and credentials into the checkAddressExists function during setup so that it can be used as a one-parameter function thereafter. This simplified function can be passed in everywhere just as before:

```
let placeOrder : PlaceOrderWorkflow =

  // initialize information (e.g from configuration)
  let endPoint = ...
  let credentials = ...

  // make a new version of checkAddressExists
  // with the credentials baked in
  let checkAddressExists = checkAddressExists endPoint credentials
  // etc

  // set up the steps in the workflow
  let validateOrder =
    validateOrder checkProductCodeExists checkAddressExists
    //                the new checkAddressExists ^
    //                is a one parameter function
  // etc

  // return the workflow function
  fun unvalidatedOrder ->
    // compose the pipeline from the steps
    ...
```

This approach of reducing parameters by passing in "prebuilt" helper functions is a common technique that helps to hide complexity. When one function is passed into another function, the "interface"—the function type—should be as minimal as possible, with all dependencies hidden.

Testing Dependencies

One great thing about passing in dependencies like this is that it makes the core functions very easy to test because it's easy to provide fake, but working, dependencies without any need for a special mocking library.

For example, say that we want to test whether the product code aspect of the validation is working. One test should check that if the checkProductCodeExists succeeds, the whole validation succeeds. And another test should check that if the checkProductCodeExists fails, the whole validation fails. Let's look at how to write these tests now.

Here's a tip before we start: F# allows you to create identifiers with spaces and punctuation in them, as long as they are enclosed in double-backticks. It's not a good idea to do this for normal code, but for test functions it's acceptable because it makes the test output far more readable.

Here's some sample code for the "success" case, using the Arrange/Act/Assert model of testing:

```
open NUnit.Framework

[<Test>]
let ``If product exists, validation succeeds``() =
  // arrange: set up stub versions of service dependencies
  let checkAddressExists address =
    CheckedAddress address // succeed
  let checkProductCodeExists productCode =
    true                   // succeed

  // arrange: set up input
  let unvalidatedOrder = ...

  // act: call validateOrder
  let result = validateOrder checkProductCodeExists checkAddressExists ...

  // assert: check that result is a ValidatedOrder, not an error
  ...
```

You can see that the stub versions of the checkAddressExists and checkProductCode-Exists functions (that represent the services) are trivial to write and can be defined right there in the test.

We are using the NUnit framework to demonstrate testing here, but you can use any .NET test framework, or even better, one of the F#-friendly libraries, like FsUnit, Unquote, Expecto, or FsCheck.

To write the code for the failure case, all we need to do is change the checkProductCodeExists function to fail for any product code:

```
let checkProductCodeExists productCode =
  false  // fail
```

Here's the complete test:

```
[<Test>]
let ``If product doesn't exist, validation fails``() =
  // arrange: set up stub versions of service dependencies
  let checkAddressExists address = ...
  let checkProductCodeExists productCode =
    false // fail

  // arrange: set up input
  let unvalidatedOrder = ...

  // act: call validateOrder
  let result = validateOrder checkProductCodeExists checkAddressExists ...

  // assert: check that result is a failure
  ...
```

Of course, for this chapter, we've said that a service failure will be indicated by throwing an exception, which is something we want to avoid. We'll fix this in the next chapter.

This is a tiny example, but already we can see the practical benefit of using functional programming principles for testing:

- The validateOrder function is stateless. It's not mutating anything, and if you call it with the same input you get the same output. This makes the function simple to test.

- All dependencies are explicitly passed in, making it easy to understand how it works.

- All side effects are encapsulated in parameters, not directly in the function itself. Again, this makes the function simple to test and simple to control what the side effects are.

Testing is a large topic that we don't have space to go into here. Here are some popular F#-friendly testing tools that are worth investigating:

- FsUnit wraps standard test frameworks like NUnit and XUnit with F#-friendly syntax.

- Unquote shows all the values leading up to a test failure ("unrolling the stack," as it were).

- If you're only familiar with "example-based" testing approaches such as NUnit, you should definitely look into the "property-based" approach to testing. FsCheck is the main property-based testing library for F#.

- Expecto is a lightweight F# testing framework that uses standard functions as test fixtures instead of requiring special attributes like [<Test>].

The Assembled Pipeline

We've seen the code in scattered fragments throughout this chapter. Let's gather it all together and show how the complete pipeline would be assembled.

1. We put all the code that implements a particular workflow in the same module, named after the workflow (PlaceOrderWorkflow.fs, for example).

2. At the top of the file, we put the type definitions.

3. After that, we put the implementations for each step.

4. At the very bottom, we assemble the steps into the main workflow function.

In order to save space, we'll just show an outline of the file content. If you would like to see the complete file, all the code for this chapter is available in the code repository associated with this book.

First, then, the types:

Now the types of the workflow that are "public" (part of the contract with the caller of the workflow) will be defined elsewhere, perhaps in an API module, so we only need to include in this file the types (designed in *Modeling Workflows as Pipelines*) that represent the internal stages of the workflow.

```
module PlaceOrderWorkflow =

  // make the shared simple types (such as
  // String50 and ProductCode) available.
  open SimpleTypes

  // make the public types exposed to the
  // callers available
  open API

  // ==============================
  // Part 1: Design
  // ==============================
```

```
// NOTE: the public parts of the workflow -- the API --
// such as the `PlaceOrderWorkflow` function and its
// input `UnvalidatedOrder`, are defined elsewhere.
// The types below are private to the workflow implementation.

// ----- Validate Order -----

type CheckProductCodeExists =
  ProductCode -> bool
type CheckedAddress =
  CheckedAddress of UnvalidatedAddress
type CheckAddressExists =
  UnvalidatedAddress -> CheckedAddress
type ValidateOrder =
  CheckProductCodeExists    // dependency
    -> CheckAddressExists   // dependency
    -> UnvalidatedOrder     // input
    -> ValidatedOrder       // output


// ----- Price order -----

type GetProductPrice = ...
type PriceOrder = ...
// etc
```

After the types, in the same file, we can put the implementations that are
based on those types. Here's the first step, validateOrder, summarized from
implementation earlier in this chapter, on page 165.

```
// ===============================
// Part 2: Implementation
// ===============================

// -----------------------------
// ValidateOrder implementation
// -----------------------------

let toCustomerInfo (unvalidatedCustomerInfo: UnvalidatedCustomerInfo) =
  ...

let toAddress (checkAddressExists:CheckAddressExists) unvalidatedAddress =
  ...

let predicateToPassthru = ...

let toProductCode (checkProductCodeExists:CheckProductCodeExists) productCode =
  ...

let toOrderQuantity productCode quantity =
  ...

let toValidatedOrderLine checkProductExists (unvalidatedOrderLine:UnvalidatedOrderLine) =
  ...

/// Implementation of ValidateOrder step
```

```
let validateOrder : ValidateOrder =
  fun checkProductCodeExists checkAddressExists unvalidatedOrder ->
    let orderId =
      unvalidatedOrder.OrderId
      |> OrderId.create
    let customerInfo = ...
    let shippingAddress = ...
    let billingAddress = ...
    let lines =
      unvalidatedOrder.Lines
      |> List.map (toValidatedOrderLine checkProductCodeExists)
    let validatedOrder : ValidatedOrder = {
      OrderId  = orderId
      CustomerInfo = customerInfo
      ShippingAddress = shippingAddress
      BillingAddress = billingAddress
      Lines = lines
    }
    validatedOrder
```

We'll skip over the implementations of the rest of the steps (again, you can see all the code in the repository associated with this book) and jump to the very bottom of the file, where the top-level PlaceOrder function is implemented:

```
// ------------------------------
// The complete workflow
// ------------------------------
let placeOrder
  checkProductExists            // dependency
  checkAddressExists            // dependency
  getProductPrice               // dependency
  createOrderAcknowledgmentLetter // dependency
  sendOrderAcknowledgment       // dependency
  : PlaceOrderWorkflow =        // definition of function

  fun unvalidatedOrder ->
    let validatedOrder =
      unvalidatedOrder
      |> validateOrder checkProductExists checkAddressExists
    let pricedOrder =
      validatedOrder
      |> priceOrder getProductPrice
    let acknowledgmentOption =
      pricedOrder
      |> acknowledgeOrder createOrderAcknowledgmentLetter sendOrderAcknowledgment
    let events =
      createEvents pricedOrder acknowledgmentOption
    events
```

Wrapping Up

In this chapter, we concentrated entirely on implementing the steps in the pipeline and working with dependencies. The implementation for each step was narrowly focused on doing just one incremental transformation and was easy to reason about and test in isolation.

When it came time to compose the steps, the types didn't always match up, so we introduced three important functional programming techniques:

- Using an "adapter function" to transform a function from one "shape" to a different shape—in this case, to change the output of checkProductCodeExists from a bool to a ProductCode

- "Lifting" disparate types into a common type, as we did with the events, converting them all to the common PlaceOrderEvent type

- Using partial application to bake dependencies into a function, allowing the function to be composed more easily and also hiding unneeded implementation details from callers

We'll be using these same techniques again later in this book.

There's one area we haven't addressed yet. In this chapter we avoided working with effects and instead used exceptions for error handling. That was convenient for composition but horrible for documentation, leading to deceptive function signatures rather than the more explicit ones that we'd prefer. In the next chapter, we'll rectify that. We'll add all the Result types back into the function types and learn how to work with them.

CHAPTER 10

Implementation: Working with Errors

What happens if a product code is malformed, or a customer name is too long, or the address validation service times out? Any system will have errors, and how we handle them is important. Consistent and transparent error handling is critical to any kind of production-ready system.

In the previous chapter, we deliberately removed the error "effect" (the Result type) from the steps in the pipeline so that we could focus on composition and dependencies.

But this effect is important! In this chapter, we'll restore the Result to the type signatures and learn how to work with them.

More generally, we'll explore the functional approach to error handling, developing a technique that allows you to capture errors elegantly, without contaminating your code with ugly conditionals and try/catch statements. We'll also see why we should treat certain kinds of errors as *domain* errors, deserving of the same attention as the rest of the domain-driven design.

Using the Result Type to Make Errors Explicit

Functional programming techniques focus on making things *explicit* as much as possible, and this applies to error handling, too. We want to create functions that are explicit about whether they succeeded or not, and if they failed, what the error cases are.

All too often, errors are treated as second-class citizens in our code. But in order to have a robust, production-worthy system, we should treat errors as first-class citizens. And that goes double for errors that are part of the domain.

In the previous chapter, we used exceptions to raise errors. That was convenient, but it meant that all the function signatures were misleading. For example, the function to check an address had this signature:

```
type CheckAddressExists =
  UnvalidatedAddress -> CheckedAddress
```

This is extremely unhelpful because it doesn't indicate what could go wrong. Instead, what we want is a *total function* (see *Total Functions*, on page 154) where all possible outcomes are documented explicitly by the type signature. As we have already learned in *Modeling Errors*, on page 70, we can use the Result type to make it clear that the function could succeed or fail, and then the signature would look something like this:

```
type CheckAddressExists =
    UnvalidatedAddress -> Result<CheckedAddress,AddressValidationError>

and AddressValidationError =
  | InvalidFormat of string
  | AddressNotFound of string
```

This tells us several important things:

- The input is an UnvalidatedAddress.

- If the validation was successful, the output is a (possibly different) CheckedAddress.

- If the validation was not successful, the reason is because the format was invalid or because the address was not found.

This shows how a function signature can act as documentation. If another developer comes along and needs to use these functions, they can tell a lot about them just by looking at the signature.

Working with Domain Errors

Software systems are complex, and we can't handle every conceivable error using types like this, nor would we want to. So before we do anything else, let's come up with a consistent approach to classifying and handling errors.

We can classify errors into three groups:

- *Domain Errors*. These are errors that are to be expected as part of the business process and therefore must be included in the design of the domain, such as an order that is rejected by billing or an order that contains an invalid product code. The business will already have procedures in place to deal with this kind of thing, and the code will need to reflect these processes.

- *Panics*. These are errors that leave the system in an unknown state, such as unhandleable system errors (such as "out of memory") or errors caused by programmer oversight (for example, "divide by zero" or "null reference").

- *Infrastructure Errors.* These are errors that are to be expected as part of the architecture but are not part of any business process and are not included in the domain, such as a network timeout or an authentication failure.

Sometimes it's not clear whether something is a domain error or not. If you're unsure, just ask a domain expert!

> You: Hi, Ollie. Quick question: If we get a connection abort accessing the load balancer, is that something you care about?
>
> Ollie: ????
>
> You: OK, let's just call that an infrastructure error and tell the user to try again later.

These different kinds of errors require different implementations.

Domain errors are part of the domain, like anything else, and so should be incorporated into our domain modeling, discussed with domain experts, and documented in the type system, if possible.

Panics are best handled by abandoning the workflow and raising an exception that is then caught at the highest appropriate level (such as the main function of the application or equivalent). Here's an example:

```
/// A workflow that panics if it gets bad input
let workflowPart2 input =
  if input = 0 then
    raise (DivideByZeroException())
  ...

/// Top level function for the application
/// which traps all exceptions from workflows.
let main() =

  // wrap all workflows in a try/with block
  try
    let result1 = workflowPart1()
    let result2 = workflowPart2 result1
    printfn "the result is %A" result2

  // top level exception handling
  with
  | :? OutOfMemoryException ->
    printfn "exited with OutOfMemoryException"
  | :? DivideByZeroException ->
    printfn "exited with DivideByZeroException"
  | ex ->
    printfn "exited with %s" ex.Message
```

Infrastructure errors can be handled using either of the above approaches. The exact choice depends on the architecture you're using. If the code consists of many small services, then exceptions might be cleaner, but if you have a more monolithic app, you might want to make the error handling more explicit. In fact, it's often useful to treat many infrastructure errors in the same way as domain errors, because it will force us as developers to think about what can go wrong. Indeed, in some cases, these kinds of errors *will* need to be escalated to a domain expert. For example, if the remote address validation service is unavailable, how should the business process change? What should we tell the customers? Those kinds of questions cannot be addressed by the development team alone but must be considered by the domain experts and product owners as well.

In the rest of this chapter, we're only going to focus on errors that we want to explicitly model as part of the domain. Panics and errors that we don't want to model should just throw exceptions and be caught by a top-level function, as shown above.

Modeling Domain Errors in Types

When we were modeling the domain, we avoided using primitives such as strings and instead created types that were domain-specific, using domain vocabulary (the Ubiquitous Language).

Well, errors deserve to get the same treatment. If certain kinds of errors come up in a discussion about the domain, they should be modeled just like everything else in the domain. Generally we'll model errors as a choice type, with a separate case for each kind of error that needs special attention.

For example, we might model the errors in our order-placing workflow like this:

```
type PlaceOrderError =
  | ValidationError of string
  | ProductOutOfStock of ProductCode
  | RemoteServiceError of RemoteServiceError
  ...
```

- The ValidationError case would be used for the validation of properties, such as any length or format errors.

- The ProductOutOfStock case would be used when the customer attempts to buy an out-of-stock product. There might be a special business process to handle this.

- The RemoteServiceError case is an example of how to handle an infrastructure error. Rather than just throwing an exception, we could handle this case by, say, retrying a certain number of times before giving up.

What's nice about using a choice type like this is that it acts as explicit documentation *in the code* of all the things that might go wrong. And any extra information associated with the error is shown explicitly as well. Furthermore, it's not only easy to expand (or contract) the choice type as requirements change, but it's *safe* as well, because the compiler will ensure that any code that pattern-matches against this list will have warnings if it misses a case.

When we were designing the workflow earlier (Chapter 7, *Modeling Workflows as Pipelines*, on page 119), we knew that errors could happen, but we didn't dig deeply into exactly what they could be. That was deliberate. There's no need to try to define all possible errors up front during the design stage. Typically, error cases will arise as the application is developed, and then you can make a decision whether to treat them as domain errors or not. If a case is a domain error, you can then add it to the choice type.

Of course, adding a new case to the choice type will probably cause warnings in some of your code, saying you haven't handled all the cases. That's great, because now you are forced to have a discussion with the domain expert or product owner on what exactly to do for that case. When choice types are used like this, it's hard to accidentally overlook an edge case.

Error Handling Makes Your Code Ugly

One nice thing about exceptions is that they keep your "happy path" code clean. For example, our validateOrder function in the previous chapter looked like this (in pseudocode):

```
let validateOrder unvalidatedOrder =
  let orderId = ... create order id (or throw exception)
  let customerInfo = ... create info (or throw exception)
  let shippingAddress = ... create and validate shippingAddress...
  // etc
```

If we return errors from each step, then the code gets much uglier. We would typically have conditionals after each potential error, as well as try/catch blocks to trap potential exceptions. Here's some more pseudocode that demonstrates this:

```
let validateOrder unvalidatedOrder =
  let orderIdResult = ... create order id (or return Error)
  if orderIdResult is Error then
    return
```

```
let customerInfoResult = ... create name (or return Error)
if customerInfoResult is Error then
    return

try
    let shippingAddressResult = ... create valid address (or return Error)
    if shippingAddress is Error then
      return

    // ...

with
  | ?: TimeoutException -> Error "service timed out"
  | ?: AuthenticationException -> Error "bad credentials"

// etc
```

The problem with this approach is that two-thirds of the code is now devoted to error handling—our original simple and clean code has now been ruined. We have a challenge: how can we introduce proper error handling while preserving the elegance of the pipeline model?

Chaining Result-Generating Functions

Before we deal with our specific situation, we should step back and look at the big picture. In general, if we have some Result-generating functions, how can we compose them together in a clean way?

Here's a visual representation of the problem. A normal function can be visualized as piece of railroad track:

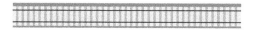

But a function with a Result output can be visualized as a railroad track that splits into two, like this:

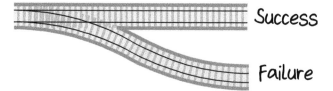

I'm going to call these kinds of functions *switch functions*, after the railroad analogy. They're often called "monadic" functions as well.

So how should we connect two of these "switch" functions? Well, if the output is successful, we want to go on to the next function in the series, but if the output is an error, we want to bypass it as shown in the figure on page 197.

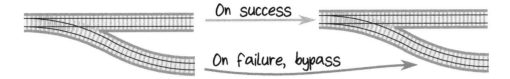

How do we combine these two switches so that both failure tracks are connected? It's obvious—like this:

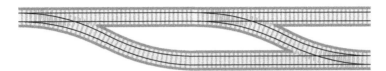

And if you connect all the steps in the pipeline in this way, you get what I call the "two-track" model of error handling, or "railroad-oriented programming," which looks like this:

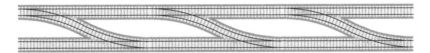

In this approach, the top track is the happy path, and the bottom track is the failure path. You start off on the success track, and if you're lucky you stay on it to the end. But if there is an error, you get shunted onto the failure track and bypass the rest of the steps in the pipeline.

This looks great but there's a big problem: we can't compose these kinds of result-generating functions together, because the type of the two-track output is not the same as the type of the one-track input:

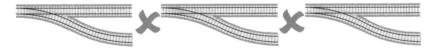

How can we solve this issue? How can we connect a two-track output to a one-track input? Well, let's observe that if the second function had a *two*-track input, then there would be no problem connecting them:

So we need to convert a "switch" function, with one input and two outputs, into a two-track function. To do this, let's create a special "adapter block" that has a slot for a switch function and which converts it into a two-track function:

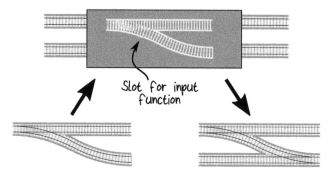

If we then convert all our steps into two-track functions, we can compose them together nicely after they have been converted:

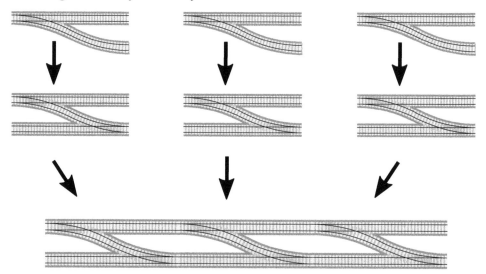

The final result is a two-track pipeline, with a "success" track and a "failure" track, just as we want.

Implementing the Adapter Blocks

We discussed the concept of "function adapters" earlier on page 170. The adapter that converts switch functions to two-track functions is a very important one in the functional programming toolkit—it's commonly called bind or flatMap in FP terminology. It's surprisingly easy to implement. Here's the logic:

- The input is a "switch" function. The output is a new two-track-only function, represented as a lambda that has a two-track input and a two-track output.

- If the two-track input is a success, then pass that input to the switch function. The output of the switch function is a two-track value, so we don't need to do anything further with it.

- If the two-track input is a failure, then bypass the switch function and return the failure.

The implementation in code looks like this:

```
let bind switchFn =
  fun twoTrackInput ->
    match twoTrackInput with
    | Ok success -> switchFn success
    | Error failure -> Error failure
```

An equivalent but more common implementation is to have *two* input parameters to bind—the "switch" function and a two-track value (a Result)—and to eliminate the lambda, like this:

```
let bind switchFn twoTrackInput =
  match twoTrackInput with
  | Ok success -> switchFn success
  | Error failure -> Error failure
```

Both implementations of bind are equivalent: the second implementation, when curried, is the same as the first (see *Currying*, on page 152).

Another useful adapter block is one that converts single-track functions into two-track functions.

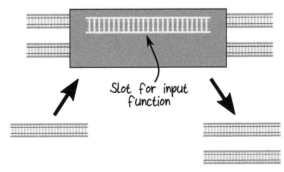

Slot for input function

It's commonly called map in FP terminology. Here's the logic:

- The input is a one-track function and a two-track value (a Result).

- If the input Result is a success, then pass that input to the one-track function and wrap the output in Ok to make it into a Result again (because the output needs to be two-track).

- If the input Result is a failure, then bypass the function, as before.

The implementation in code looks like this:

```
let map f aResult =
  match aResult with
  | Ok success -> Ok (f success)
  | Error failure -> Error failure
```

With bind, map, and a few other similar functions, we'll have a powerful toolkit that we can use to compose all sorts of mismatched functions.

Organizing the Result Functions

Where should we put these new functions in our code organization? The standard approach is to put them in a module with the same name as the type, in this case Result. The module would then look like this:

```
/// Define the Result type
type Result<'Success,'Failure> =
    | Ok of 'Success
    | Error of 'Failure

/// Functions that work with Result
module Result =

  let bind f aResult = ...

  let map f aResult = ...
```

Since Result and its associated functions are used everywhere in the domain, we would typically create a new utility module (such as Result.fs) and place it before the domain types in our project structure.

Composition and Type Checking

We've focused on getting the "shapes" of the functions to match up by converting a "switch" function into a "two-track" function. But of course, type checking is also going on, so we need to make sure that the types are matched up as well for composition to work.

On the success branch, the types can change along the track, as long as the output type of one step matches the input type of the next step. For example, the three functions below can be composed in a pipeline using bind because the output (Bananas) of FunctionA matches the input of FunctionB and the output (Cherries) of FunctionB matches the input of FunctionC.

```
type FunctionA = Apple -> Result<Bananas,...>
type FunctionB = Bananas -> Result<Cherries,...>
type FunctionC = Cherries -> Result<Lemon,...>
```

The bind function would be used like this:

```
let functionA : FunctionA = ...
let functionB : FunctionB = ...
let functionC : FunctionC = ...

let functionABC input =
  input
  |> functionA
  |> Result.bind functionB
  |> Result.bind functionC
```

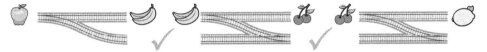

On the other hand, FunctionA and FunctionC can't be composed directly, even with bind, because the types are different:

Converting to a Common Error Type

Unlike the success track, where the type can change at each step, the error track has the same uniform type all the way along the track. That is, every function in the pipeline must have the *same* error type.

In many cases, that means we'll need to tweak the error types to make them compatible with each other. To do that, let's create a function that is similar to map but which acts on the value in the *failure* track. That function is called mapError and would be implemented like this:

```
let mapError f aResult =
  match aResult with
  | Ok success -> Ok success
  | Error failure -> Error (f failure)
```

For example, let's say that we have an AppleError and a BananaError and we have two functions that use them as their error types.

```
type FunctionA = Apple -> Result<Bananas,AppleError>
type FunctionB = Bananas -> Result<Cherries,BananaError>
```

The mismatch in the error types means that FunctionA and FunctionB cannot be composed. What we need to do is create a new type that both AppleError and BananaError can be converted to—a choice between the two. Let's call this FruitError:

```
type FruitError =
  | AppleErrorCase of AppleError
  | BananaErrorCase of BananaError
```

We can then convert functionA to have a result type of FruitError like this:

```
let functionA : FunctionA = ...

let functionAWithFruitError input =
  input
  |> functionA
  |> Result.mapError (fun appleError -> AppleErrorCase appleError)
```

This can be simplified as follows:

```
let functionAWithFruitError input =
  input
  |> functionA
  |> Result.mapError AppleErrorCase
```

Here's a diagram of the transformation:

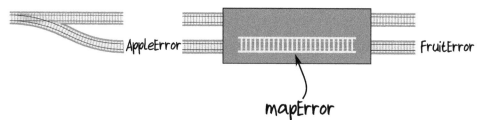

If we look at the signatures of functionA and functionAWithFruitError, we can see that they now have different types in the error case, just as we want:

```
// type of functionA
Apple -> Result<Bananas,AppleError>

// type of functionAWithFruitError
Apple -> Result<Bananas,FruitError>
```

Similarly we can convert the error case of functionB from a BananaError to a FruitError as well. When we put it all together, the code would look something like this:

```
let functionA : FunctionA = ...
let functionB : FunctionB = ...

// convert functionA to use "FruitError"
let functionAWithFruitError input =
  input |> functionA |> Result.mapError AppleErrorCase
```

```
// convert functionB to use "FruitError"
let functionBWithFruitError input =
  input |> functionB |> Result.mapError BananaErrorCase

// and now we can compose the new versions with "bind"
let functionAB input =
  input
  |> functionAWithFruitError
  |> Result.bind functionBWithFruitError
```

The signature of the combined functionAB is this:

```
val functionAB : Apple -> Result<Cherries,FruitError>
```

Using bind and map in Our Pipeline

We understand the concepts now, so let's put them into practice. We'll compose the workflow pipeline using our error-generating functions, tweaking
them as necessary so that they fit together.

Let's quickly revisit the components of our pipeline, focusing on Result and
ignoring the Async effect and the service dependencies for now.

First, ValidateOrder will return an error if the input data is not in the right format,
so it's a "switch" function and its signature will be like this:

```
type ValidateOrder =
  // ignoring additional dependencies for now
  UnvalidatedOrder                          // input
    -> Result<ValidatedOrder, ValidationError> // output
```

The PriceOrder step may also fail for a variety of reasons, so its signature will
be this:

```
type PriceOrder =
  ValidatedOrder                          // input
    -> Result<PricedOrder, PricingError>  // output
```

The AcknowledgeOrder and CreateEvents steps will always succeed, so their signatures will be:

```
type AcknowledgeOrder =
  PricedOrder                          // input
    -> OrderAcknowledgmentSent option // output

type CreateEvents =
  PricedOrder                          // input
    -> OrderAcknowledgmentSent option  // input (event from previous step)
    -> PlaceOrderEvent list            // output
```

Let's start by combining ValidateOrder and PriceOrder. The failure type for Validate-Order is ValidationError, while the failure type for PriceOrder is PricingError. As we saw above, the functions are incompatible because the error types are different. We need to convert both functions to return the *same* error type—a common error type to be used throughout the pipeline, which we'll call PlaceOrderError. PlaceOrderError will be defined like this:

```
type PlaceOrderError =
  | Validation of ValidationError
  | Pricing of PricingError
```

And now, by using mapError, we can define new versions of validateOrder and priceOrder that can be composed, just as we did for the FruitError example above:

```
// Adapted to return a PlaceOrderError
let validateOrderAdapted input =
  input
  |> validateOrder // the original function
  |> Result.mapError PlaceOrderError.Validation

// Adapted to return a PlaceOrderError
let priceOrderAdapted input =
  input
  |> priceOrder // the original function
  |> Result.mapError PlaceOrderError.Pricing
```

When this is done, we can finally chain them together using bind:

```
let placeOrder unvalidatedOrder =
  unvalidatedOrder
  |> validateOrderAdapted          // adapted version
  |> Result.bind priceOrderAdapted // adapted version
```

Note that the validateOrderAdapted function doesn't need to have bind in front of it because it's first in the pipeline.

Next, acknowledgeOrder and createEvents have no errors—they are "one-track" functions—so we can use Result.map to convert them into two-track functions that can be slotted into the pipeline:

```
let placeOrder unvalidatedOrder =
  unvalidatedOrder
  |> validateOrderAdapted
  |> Result.bind priceOrderAdapted
  |> Result.map acknowledgeOrder   // use map to convert to two-track
  |> Result.map createEvents       // convert to two-track
```

This placeOrder function has this signature:

```
UnvalidatedOrder -> Result<PlaceOrderEvent list,PlaceOrderError>
```

Which is very close to what we need it to be.

Let's analyze this new version of the workflow pipeline:

- Each function in the pipeline can generate errors, and the errors it can produce are indicated in its signature. We can test the functions in isolation, confident that when they are assembled we won't get any unexpected behavior.

- The functions are still chained together, but now using a two-track model. An error in one step causes the remainder of the functions in the pipeline to be skipped.

- The overall flow in the top-level placeOrder is still clean. There are no special conditionals or try/catch blocks.

Unfortunately, this placeOrder implementation won't actually compile! Even when we use bind and map, the functions don't always fit together. In particular, the output of acknowledgeOrder doesn't match the input of createEvents, because the output is just the event, not the priced order. We'll see how to deal with this issue shortly.

Adapting Other Kinds of Functions to the Two-Track Model

So far, we have seen two function "shapes" in our pipeline: one-track functions and "switch" functions. But of course we may need to work with many other kinds of functions. Let's look at two of them now:

- Functions that throw exceptions
- "Dead-end" functions that don't return anything

Handling Exceptions

We've avoided throwing exceptions in *our* code, but what about exceptions that are raised in code not controlled by us, such as in a library or service. Earlier, we suggested that many exceptions are not part of the domain design and need not be caught except at the top level. But if we *do* want to treat an exception as part of the domain, how should we do that?

The solution is straightforward—we can just create another "adapter block" function that converts an exception-throwing function into a Result-returning function as shown in the figure on page 206.

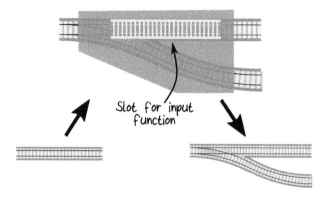

Slot for input function

For example, say that we want to trap timeouts from remote services and turn them into a RemoteServiceError. We'll be working with many services, so let's first define a ServiceInfo to keep track of the service that caused the error:

```
type ServiceInfo = {
  Name : string
  Endpoint: Uri
  }
```

And then we can define an error type that builds on this:

```
type RemoteServiceError = {
  Service : ServiceInfo
  Exception : System.Exception
  }
```

We pass in the service info and the original service function to an adapter block that catches some of the exceptions and returns a Result in those cases. Here's an example for when the service function takes a single parameter (x in the code below):

```
/// "Adapter block" that converts exception-throwing services
/// into Result-returning services.
let serviceExceptionAdapter serviceInfo serviceFn x =
  try
    // call the service and return success
    Ok (serviceFn x)
  with
  | :? TimeoutException as ex ->
    Error {Service=serviceInfo; Exception=ex}
  | :? AuthorizationException as ex ->
    Error {Service=serviceInfo; Exception=ex}
```

Note that we are not catching *all* possible exceptions, only the ones that are relevant to the domain.

If the service function has two parameters, we need to define another adapter to support that case, and so on.

```
let serviceExceptionAdapter2 serviceInfo serviceFn x y =
  try
    Ok (serviceFn x y)
  with
  | :? TimeoutException as ex -> ...
  | :? AuthorizationException as ex -> ...
```

These are generic adapter blocks that will adapt *any* function. In some cases you might prefer a custom adapter block for a particular service, such as one that converts database exceptions to a DatabaseError choice type with domain-friendly cases like "record not found" and "duplicate key."

Now to use this adapter, we create a ServiceInfo and then pass in the service function. For example, if the service function is the address-checking function, the code would look something like this:

```
let serviceInfo = {
  Name = "AddressCheckingService"
  Endpoint = ...
  }
// exception-throwing service
let checkAddressExists address =
    ...

// Result-returning service
let checkAddressExistsR address =
    // adapt the service
    let adaptedService =
      serviceExceptionAdapter serviceInfo checkAddressExists
    // call the service
    adaptedService address
```

To make it clear that the new function is a variant that returns a Result, we'll name it checkAddressExistsR, with an *R* at the end. (In real-world code, you would probably just give it the same name as the original function—"shadowing" it).

Again, let's check the signatures to make sure that we have what we want. The original function indicated that it always returned a CheckedAddress:

```
checkAddressExists :
  UnvalidatedAddress -> CheckedAddress
```

But we know that the signature was misleading. If we look at the signature of the new "adapted" function, we can see that it's much more descriptive. It indicates that it might fail and return an error.

```
checkAddressExistsR :
  UnvalidatedAddress -> Result<CheckedAddress,RemoteServiceError>
```

The error type is RemoteServiceError, so if we want to use this function in our pipeline, we would have to add a case for remote errors in our PlaceOrderError type:

```
type PlaceOrderError =
  | Validation of ValidationError
  | Pricing of PricingError
  | RemoteService of RemoteServiceError // new!
```

Then we must convert the RemoteServiceError into the shared PlaceOrderError when creating the *R* version of the function, just as we did earlier:

```
let checkAddressExistsR address =
  // adapt the service
  let adaptedService =
    serviceExceptionAdapter serviceInfo checkAddressExists
  // call the service
  address
  |> adaptedService
  |> Result.mapError RemoteService // lift to PlaceOrderError
```

Handling Dead-End Functions

Another common type of function is what you might call a "dead-end" or "fire-and-forget" function: a function that takes input but doesn't return any output.

Most of these kinds of functions are writing to I/O somehow. For example, the logging function below has no output:

```
// string -> unit
let logError msg =
  printfn "ERROR %s" msg
```

Other examples include writing to a database, posting to a queue, and so on.

To make a dead-end function work with the two-track pipeline, we'll need yet another adapter block. To construct this, we'll first need a way to call the dead-end function with the input and then return the original input—a "pass-through" function. Let's call this function tee:

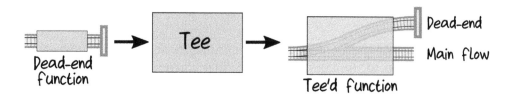

Here's the code:

```
// ('a -> unit) -> ('a -> 'a)
let tee f x =
  f x
  x
```

The signature shows that it takes any unit-returning function and emits a one-track function.

We can then use Result.map to convert the output of tee to a two-track function:

```
// ('a -> unit) -> (Result<'a,'error> -> Result<'a,'error>)
let adaptDeadEnd f =
  Result.map (tee f)
```

So now we have a way to take a dead-end function like logError and convert it into a two-track function that can be slotted into our pipeline.

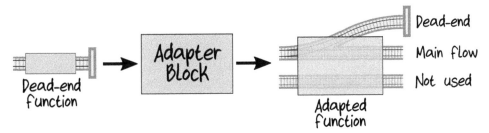

Making Life Easier with Computation Expressions

So far we've been dealing with straightforward error-handling logic. We've been able to chain together Result-generating functions using bind; and for those functions that were not two-track, we've been able to make them fit the two-track model using various "adapter" functions.

Sometimes, though, the workflow logic is more complicated. You may need to work within conditional branches, or loops, or work with deeply nested Result-generating functions. In cases like these, F# offers some relief in the form of "computation expressions." A computation expression is a special kind of expression block that hides the messiness of bind behind the scenes.

It's easy to create your own computation expressions. For example, we can make one for Result called result (lowercase). All you need to get started is two functions:

- bind, which we've already seen used with Result
- return, which just constructs a value—in the case of Result, that would be the Ok constructor.

We won't show the implementation details for the result computation expression here—you can browse the code in the Result.fs file in the code repository for this book. Instead, let's look at how a computation expression can be used in practice to simplify code with lots of Results.

In the earlier version of placeOrder, we used bind to connect the output of the Result-returning validateOrder to the input of priceOrder, like this:

```
let placeOrder unvalidatedOrder =
  unvalidatedOrder
  |> validateOrderAdapted
  |> Result.bind priceOrderAdapted
  |> Result.map acknowledgeOrder
  |> Result.map createEvents
```

With a computation expression, however, we can work with the outputs of validateOrder and priceOrder directly, just as if they were *not* wrapped in Result.

Here's how that same code looks using a computation expression:

```
let placeOrder unvalidatedOrder =
  result {
    let! validatedOrder =
      validateOrder unvalidatedOrder
      |> Result.mapError PlaceOrderError.Validation
    let! pricedOrder =
      priceOrder validatedOrder
      |> Result.mapError PlaceOrderError.Pricing
    let acknowledgmentOption =
      acknowledgeOrder pricedOrder
    let events =
      createEvents pricedOrder acknowledgmentOption
    return events
  }
```

Let's see how this code works:

- The result computation expression starts with the word *result* and then encompasses the block delimited by curly braces.

- The special let! keyword looks like a let but in fact "unwraps" the result to get at the inner value. The validatedOrder in let! validatedOrder = ... is a normal value that can be passed directly into the priceOrder function.

- The error type must be the same throughout the block, so Result.mapError is used to lift the error types to the common type, just as before. The errors are not explicit in the result expression, but their types still need to match up.

- The last line in the block uses the return keyword, which indicates what the overall value of the block is.

In practice, you just use let! everywhere you would have used a bind. For other functions that don't need bind, such as acknowledgeOrder, you can just use normal syntax—you don't need to use Result.map.

As you can see, computation expressions make the code look as if we were not using Result at all. It hides the complexity nicely.

We won't go deeply into how to define a computation expression, but it's quite straightforward. For example, here is a basic definition of the result computation expression used above:

```
type ResultBuilder() =
  member this.Return(x) = Ok x
  member this.Bind(x,f) = Result.bind f x

let result = ResultBuilder()
```

We'll see some more computation expressions later in this book, notably the async computation expression, which is used to manage asynchronous callbacks in the same elegant way.

Composing Computation Expressions

One attractive thing about computation expressions is that they are *composable*, which is a quality we always aim for.

For example, let's say that validateOrder and priceOrder were defined using result computation expressions:

```
let validateOrder input = result {
  let! validatedOrder = ...
  return validatedOrder
  }
let priceOrder input = result {
  let! pricedOrder = ...
  return pricedOrder
  }
```

Then these can be used within a bigger result expression, just like a normal function:

```
let placeOrder unvalidatedOrder = result {
  let! validatedOrder = validateOrder unvalidatedOrder
  let! pricedOrder = priceOrder validatedOrder
  ...
  return ...
  }
```

And placeOrder, in turn, could be used in an even bigger result expression, and so on.

Validating an Order with Results

We can now revisit the implementation of the validateOrder function, this time using a result computation expression to hide the error-handling logic.

As a reminder, here is the implementation without any Results:

```
let validateOrder : ValidateOrder =
  fun checkProductCodeExists checkAddressExists unvalidatedOrder ->
    let orderId =
      unvalidatedOrder.OrderId
      |> OrderId.create
    let customerInfo =
      unvalidatedOrder.CustomerInfo
      |> toCustomerInfo
    let shippingAddress =
      unvalidatedOrder.ShippingAddress
      |> toAddress checkAddressExists
    let billingAddress = ...
    let lines = ...

    let validatedOrder : ValidatedOrder = {
      OrderId  = orderId
      CustomerInfo = customerInfo
      ShippingAddress = shippingAddress
      BillingAddress = billingAddress
      Lines = lines
    }
    validatedOrder
```

But when we change all the helper functions to return Result, that code will no longer work. For example, the OrderId.create function will return a Result<OrderId,string>, not a plain OrderId (and similarly for toCustomerInfo, toAddress, and so on). However, if we use a result computation expression and use let! rather than let, we can access the OrderId, CustomerInfo, and so forth as plain values. Here's what the implementation looks like now:

```
let validateOrder : ValidateOrder =
  fun checkProductCodeExists checkAddressExists unvalidatedOrder ->
    result {
      let! orderId =
        unvalidatedOrder.OrderId
        |> OrderId.create
        |> Result.mapError ValidationError
      let! customerInfo =
        unvalidatedOrder.CustomerInfo
        |> toCustomerInfo
```

```
    let! shippingAddress = ...
    let! billingAddress  = ...
    let! lines = ...

    let validatedOrder : ValidatedOrder = {
      OrderId  = orderId
      CustomerInfo = customerInfo
      ShippingAddress = shippingAddress
      BillingAddress = billingAddress
      Lines = lines
    }
    return validatedOrder
  }
```

As before, though, we'll need to use Result.mapError to make sure that all the error types match. OrderId.create returns a string in the error case, so we must use mapError to lift it to a ValidationError. The other helper functions will need to do the same thing when they are dealing with simple types. We'll assume that the output toCustomerInfo and toAddress functions are already a ValidationError, so we don't need to use mapError for them.

Working with Lists of Results

When we originally validated the order lines without using a Result type, we could just use List.map to convert each line:

```
let validateOrder unvalidatedOrder =
  ...

  // convert each line into an OrderLine domain type
  let lines =
      unvalidatedOrder.Lines
      |> List.map (toValidatedOrderLine checkProductCodeExists)

  // create and return a ValidatedOrder
  let validatedOrder : ValidatedOrder = {
    ...
    Lines = lines
    // etc
    }
  validatedOrder
```

But this approach no longer works when toValidatedOrderLine returns a Result. After using map, we end up with a list of Result<ValidatedOrderLine,...>, rather than a list of ValidatedOrderLine.

That's not at all helpful to us: when we set the value of ValidatedOrder.Lines, we need a Result of list rather than a list of Result.

```
let validateOrder unvalidatedOrder =
  ...

  let lines = // lines is a "list of Result"
      unvalidatedOrder.Lines
      |> List.map (toValidatedOrderLine checkProductCodeExists)

  let validatedOrder : ValidatedOrder = {
    ...
    Lines = lines  // compiler error
    //         ^ expecting a "Result of list" here
    }
  ...
```

Using a result expression won't help us here—the problem is that we have a type mismatch. So now the question is this: how can we convert a list of Result into a Result of list?

Let's create a helper function that will do that: it'll loop through the list of Results, and if any of them are bad, the overall result will be the error. Otherwise, if they're all good, the overall result will be a list of all the successes.

The trick to implementing it is to remember that in F#, the standard list type is a linked list, built by prepending each element onto a smaller list. To solve our problem, we first need a new version of the prepend action (also known in the FP world as the "cons" operator) that prepends a Result containing one item onto a Result containing a list of items. The implementation is straightforward:

- If both parameters are Ok, prepend the contents and wrap the resulting list back up into a Result.

- Otherwise, if either parameter is an Error, return the error.

Here's the code:

```
/// Prepend a Result<item> to a Result<list>
let prepend firstR restR =
  match firstR, restR with
  | Ok first, Ok rest -> Ok (first::rest)
  | Error err1, Ok _ -> Error err1
  | Ok _, Error err2 -> Error err2
  | Error err1, Error _ -> Error err1
```

If you look at the type signature of this prepend function, you can see that it's completely generic: it takes a Result<'a> and a Result<'a list> and combines them into a new Result<'a list>.

With that in hand, we can build a Result<'a list> from a Result<'a> list by iterating over the list starting with the last one (using foldBack) and then prepending each Result element to the list that we've built so far. We'll call this function sequence and add it as another useful function in the Result module. Here's its implementation:

```
let sequence aListOfResults =
  let initialValue = Ok [] // empty list inside Result

  // loop through the list in reverse order,
  // prepending each element to the initial value
  List.foldBack prepend aListOfResults initialValue
```

Don't worry too much about how this code works. Once written and included in your library, you only need to know how and when to use it!

Let's define a Result type to play with (we'll call it IntOrError) and then test sequence with a list of successes:

```
type IntOrError = Result<int,string>

let listOfSuccesses : IntOrError list = [Ok 1; Ok 2]
let successResult =
  Result.sequence listOfSuccesses    // Ok [1; 2]
```

You can see that the list of Results ([Ok 1; Ok 2]) has been transformed into a Result containing a list (Ok [1; 2]).

Let's try with a list of failures:

```
let listOfErrors : IntOrError list = [ Error "bad"; Error "terrible" ]

let errorResult =
  Result.sequence listOfErrors  // Error "bad"
```

We get another Result, but this time it contains an error (Error "bad").

> In the failure example, only the first error is returned. In many cases, though, we want to preserve *all* the errors, especially when doing validation. The functional programming technique for doing this is called *applicatives*. We'll mention it briefly in the next section, but we won't discuss a detailed implementation in this book.

With Result.sequence in our toolkit, we can finally write the code to construct the ValidatedOrder:

```
let validateOrder : ValidateOrder =
  fun checkProductCodeExists checkAddressExists unvalidatedOrder ->
    result {
      let! orderId = ...
      let! customerInfo = ...
      let! shippingAddress = ...
      let! billingAddress  = ...
```

```
let! lines =
  unvalidatedOrder.Lines
  |> List.map (toValidatedOrderLine checkProductCodeExists)
  |> Result.sequence // convert list of Results to a single Result

let validatedOrder : ValidatedOrder = {
  OrderId      = orderId
  CustomerInfo = customerInfo
  ShippingAddress = shippingAddress
  BillingAddress = billingAddress
  Lines = lines
  }
  return validatedOrder
}
```

If you care about performance, the List.map followed by Result.sequence can be made more efficient by combining them into a single function generally called traverse,[1] but we won't get sidetracked with that here.

We're almost done, but there's one final hiccup. The output of validateOrder has as its error case the ValidationError type.

In the main pipeline, however, we need the error case to be a PlaceOrderError. So now, in the placeOrder function, we need to convert the type Result<Validated-Order,ValidationError> to the type Result<ValidatedOrder,PlaceOrderError>. Just as we did before, we can transform the type of error value using mapError. Similarly, we need to convert the output of priceOrder from a PricingError to a PlaceOrderError as well.

Here's what the implementation of the overall workflow looks like now, with mapError in use:

```
let placeOrder : PlaceOrder =          // definition of function
  fun unvalidatedOrder ->
    result {
      let! validatedOrder =
        validateOrder checkProductExists checkAddressExists unvalidatedOrder
        |> Result.mapError PlaceOrderError.Validation
      let! pricedOrder =
        priceOrder getProductPrice validatedOrder
        |> Result.mapError PlaceOrderError.Pricing
      let acknowledgmentOption = ...
      let events = ...
      return events
    }
```

The output is now Result<ValidatedOrder,PlaceOrderError>, just as we want.

---

1.   https://fsharpforfunandprofit.com/posts/elevated-world-4/

Monads and More

This book tries to avoid too much jargon, but one word that comes up all the time in functional programming is *monad*. So let's pause and talk a little about monads now. The *m*-word has a reputation for being scary, but in fact we've already created and used one in this very chapter!

A monad is just a programming pattern that allows you to chain "monadic" functions together in series. OK, then what's a "monadic" function? It's a function that takes a "normal" value and returns some kind of "enhanced" value. In the error-handling approach developed in this chapter, the "enhanced" value is something wrapped in the Result type, so a monadic function is exactly the kind of Result-generating "switch" functions that we've been working with.

Technically, a "monad" is simply a term for something with three components:

* A data structure
* Some related functions
* Some rules about how the functions must work

The data structure in our case is the Result type.

To be a monad, the data type must have two related functions as well, return and bind:

* return (also known as pure) is a function that turns a normal value into a monadic type. Since the type we're using is Result, the return function is just the Ok constructor.

* bind (also known as flatMap) is a function that lets you chain together monadic functions (in our case, Result-generating functions). We saw how to implement bind for Result earlier in this chapter.

The rules about how these functions should work are called the "monad laws," which sound intimidating but are actually commonsense guidelines to make sure the implementations are correct and not doing anything weird. I won't go into the monad laws here—you can easily find them on the Internet.

So, that's all a monad is. I hope you can see that it's not as mysterious as you might have thought.

Composing in Parallel with Applicatives

While we're at it, let's also talk about a related pattern called *applicatives*.

Applicatives are similar to monads; but rather than chaining monadic functions *in series*, an applicative allows you to combine monadic values *in parallel*.

For example, if we need to do validation, we would probably use an applicative approach to combine all the errors, rather than only keeping the first one. Unfortunately, we haven't got space to go into more details in this book, but there's a detailed discussion on fsharpforfunandprofit.com.[2]

I won't use the terms *monad* or *applicative* much in this book, but now if you do run into them, you'll have an idea what they mean.

Jargon Alert

For reference, here are the terms that we have introduced in this chapter:

- In the error-handling context, the bind function converts a Result-generating function into a two-track function. It's used to chain Result-generating functions "in series." More generally, the bind function is a key component of a monad.

- In the error-handling context, the map function converts a one-track function into a two-track function.

- The *monadic* approach to composition refers to combining functions in series using bind.

- The *applicative* approach to composition refers to combining results in parallel.

Adding the Async Effect

In our original design, we didn't only use an error effect (Result). In most of the pipeline, we also used an async effect as well. Combining effects can be tricky in general, but since these two effects often appear together, we'll define an asyncResult computation expression to go along with the AsyncResult type we defined earlier. We won't show the implementation now, but you can find it in the code repository for this book.

Using asyncResult is just like using result. For example, the validateOrder implementation looks like this:

```
let validateOrder : ValidateOrder =
  fun checkProductCodeExists checkAddressExists unvalidatedOrder ->
    asyncResult {
      let! orderId =
        unvalidatedOrder.OrderId
        |> OrderId.create
        |> Result.mapError ValidationError
        |> AsyncResult.ofResult    // lift a Result to AsyncResult
      let! customerInfo =
```

```
    unvalidatedOrder.CustomerInfo
    |> toCustomerInfo
    |> AsyncResult.ofResult
  let! checkedShippingAddress = // extract the checked address
    unvalidatedOrder.ShippingAddress
    |> toCheckedAddress checkAddressExists
  let! shippingAddress =        // process checked address
    checkedShippingAddress
    |> toAddress
    |> AsyncResult.ofResult
  let! billingAddress = ...
  let! lines =
    unvalidatedOrder.Lines
    |> List.map (toValidatedOrderLine checkProductCodeExists)
    |> Result.sequence // convert list of Results to a single Result
    |> AsyncResult.ofResult
  let validatedOrder : ValidatedOrder = {
    OrderId  = orderId
    CustomerInfo = customerInfo
    ShippingAddress = shippingAddress
    BillingAddress = billingAddress
    Lines = lines
  }
  return validatedOrder
}
```

In addition to replacing result with asyncResult, we have to ensure that everything is an AsyncResult now. For example, the output of OrderId.create is just a Result, so we have to "lift" it to an AsyncResult using the helper function AsyncResult.ofResult.

We've also broken up the address validation into two parts. The reason is that when we add all the effects back in, the CheckAddressExists function returns an AsyncResult.

```
type CheckAddressExists =
  UnvalidatedAddress -> AsyncResult<CheckedAddress,AddressValidationError>
```

That has the wrong error type to fit into our workflow, so let's create a helper function (toCheckedAddress) that handles that result and maps the service-specific error (AddressValidationError) to our own ValidationError:

```
/// Call the checkAddressExists and convert the error to a ValidationError
let toCheckedAddress (checkAddress:CheckAddressExists) address =
  address
  |> checkAddress
  |> AsyncResult.mapError (fun addrError ->
    match addrError with
    | AddressNotFound -> ValidationError "Address not found"
    | InvalidFormat -> ValidationError "Address has bad format"
    )
```

The output of the toCheckedAddress function still returns an AsyncResult around a CheckedAddress, so we unwrap it into a checkedAddress value using let!, which we can then pass in to the validation stage (toAddress) in the usual way.

It's also straightforward to convert the main placeOrder function to use asyncResult:

```
let placeOrder : PlaceOrder =
  fun unvalidatedOrder ->
    asyncResult {
      let! validatedOrder =
        validateOrder checkProductExists checkAddressExists unvalidatedOrder
        |> AsyncResult.mapError PlaceOrderError.Validation
      let! pricedOrder =
        priceOrder getProductPrice validatedOrder
        |> AsyncResult.ofResult
        |> AsyncResult.mapError PlaceOrderError.Pricing
      let acknowledgmentOption = ...
      let events = ...
      return events
    }
```

And the rest of the pipeline code can be converted to using asyncResult in the same way, but we won't show it here. You can see the full implementation in the code repository.

Wrapping Up

We're now done with the revised implementation of the pipeline, incorporating our type-safe approach to error-handling and async effects. The main placeOrder implementation above is still quite clear, and there's no ugly error-handling code to disrupt the flow. Yes, we did have to do some awkward transformations to get all the types aligned correctly, but that extra effort pays for itself in the confidence that all the pipeline components will work together without any problems.

In the next few chapters, we'll work on implementing the interactions between the domain and the outside world: how to serialize and deserialize data and how to persist state to a database.

CHAPTER 11

Serialization

In the examples in this book, we have designed our workflows as functions with inputs and outputs, where the inputs come from Commands and the outputs are Events. But where do these commands come from? And where do the events go? They come from, or go to, some infrastructure that lives outside our bounded context—a message queue, a web request, and so on.

This infrastructure has no understanding of our particular domain, and therefore we must convert types in our domain model into something that the infrastructure *does* understand, such as JSON, XML, or a binary format like protobuf.[1]

We'll also need some way of keeping track of the internal state needed by a workflow, such as the current state of an Order. Again, we'll probably use an external service such as a database.

It's clear that an important aspect of working with external infrastructure is the ability to convert the types in our domain model into things that can be serialized and deserialized easily.

Therefore, in this chapter, we'll learn how to do just this; we'll see how to design types that can be serialized, and then we'll see how to convert our domain objects to and from these intermediate types.

Persistence vs. Serialization

Let's start with some definitions. We'll say that *persistence* simply means state that outlives the process that created it. And we'll say that *serialization* is the process of converting from a domain-specific representation to a representation that can be persisted easily, such as binary, JSON, or XML.

---

1. https://developers.google.com/protocol-buffers/

For example, our order-placing workflow implementation is instantiated and run every time an "order form arrived" event occurs. But when the code stops running, we want its output to stay around somehow ("be persisted") so that other parts of the business can use that data. "Staying around" does not necessarily mean being stored in a proper database—it could be stored as a file or in a queue. And we shouldn't make assumptions about the lifetime of the persisted data—it could be kept around for just a few seconds (such as in a queue) or it could be kept around for decades (such as in a data warehouse).

In this chapter, we'll focus on serialization, and in the next chapter we'll look at persistence.

Designing for Serialization

As we discussed in *Transferring Data Between Bounded Contexts*, on page 46, our complex domain types, with special types for choices and constraints nested together deeply, are not well suited for a serializer to work with. So the trick to pain-free serialization is to convert your domain objects to a type specifically designed for serialization—a Data Transfer Object—and then serialize that DTO instead of the domain type.

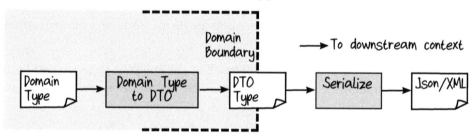

For deserialization, we do the same thing in the other direction:

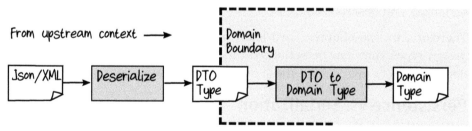

In general, we want the deserialization to be as clean as possible. That means that the deserialization into a DTO should *always* succeed unless the underlying data is corrupt somehow. Any kind of domain-specific validation (such as validating integer bounds for an OrderQty or checking that a ProductCode is valid) should be done in the DTO-to-domain-type conversion process, inside the bounded context, where we have better control of error handling.

Connecting the Serialization Code to the Workflow

The serialization process is just another component that can be added to the workflow pipeline: the deserialization step is added at the front of the workflow, and the serialization step at the end of the workflow.

For example, say that we have a workflow that looks like this (we'll ignore error handling and Results for now):

```
type MyInputType = ...
type MyOutputType = ...

type Workflow = MyInputType -> MyOutputType
```

Then the function signatures for the deserialization step might look like this:

```
type JsonString = string
type MyInputDto = ...

type DeserializeInputDto = JsonString -> MyInputDto
type InputDtoToDomain = MyInputDto -> MyInputType
```

And the serialization step might look like this:

```
type MyOutputDto = ...

type OutputDtoFromDomain = MyOutputType -> MyOutputDto
type SerializeOutputDto = MyOutputDto -> JsonString
```

It's clear all these functions can be chained together in a pipeline, like this:

```
let workflowWithSerialization jsonString =
  jsonString
  |> deserializeInputDto    // JSON to DTO
  |> inputDtoToDomain       // DTO to domain object
  |> workflow               // the core workflow in the domain
  |> outputDtoFromDomain    // Domain object to DTO
  |> serializeOutputDto     // DTO to JSON
  // final output is another JsonString
```

And then this workflowWithSerialization function would be the one that is exposed to the infrastructure. The inputs and outputs are just JsonStrings or similar, so that the infrastructure is isolated from the domain.

Of course, it's not quite that simple in practice! We need to handle errors, async, and so on. But this demonstrates the basic concepts.

DTOs as a Contract Between Bounded Contexts

The commands we consume are triggered by the outputs of other bounded contexts, and the events that our workflow emits become the inputs for other bounded contexts. These events and commands form a kind of contract that our bounded context must support. It's a loose contract, to be sure, because we want to avoid tight coupling between the bounded contexts. Nevertheless, the serialized format of these events and commands, which are DTOs, should only be changed carefully, if at all. This means that you should always have complete control of the serialization format, and you shouldn't just allow a library to do things auto-magically!

A Complete Serialization Example

To demonstrate the practice of serializing and deserializing a domain object to and from JSON, let's build a small example. Say that we want to persist a domain type Person that's defined like this:

```
module Domain = // our domain-driven types

  /// constrained to be not null and at most 50 chars
  type String50 = String50 of string

  /// constrained to be bigger than 1/1/1900 and less than today's date
  type Birthdate = Birthdate of DateTime

  /// Domain type
  type Person = {
    First: String50
    Last: String50
    Birthdate : Birthdate
    }
```

The String50 and Birthdate types cannot be serialized directly, so we first create a corresponding DTO type Dto.Person (a Person in a Dto module) where all the fields are primitives, like this:

```
/// A module to group all the DTO-related
/// types and functions.
module Dto =

  type Person = {
    First: string
    Last: string
    Birthdate : DateTime
    }
```

Next, we need "toDomain" and "fromDomain" functions. These are associated with the DTO type, not the domain type, because the domain shouldn't know about DTOs, so let's also put them in the Dto module in a submodule called Person.

```
module Dto =

  module Person =
    let fromDomain (person:Domain.Person) :Dto.Person =
      ...
```

```
let toDomain (dto:Dto.Person) :Result<Domain.Person,string> =
  ...
```

 As mentioned earlier, we need to use the CompilationRepresentation attribute in versions of F# before 4.1 when a module has the same name as a type.

This pattern of having a pair of fromDomain and toDomain functions is something we'll use consistently.

Let's start with the fromDomain function that converts a domain type into a DTO. This function always succeeds (Result is not needed) because a complex domain type can always be converted to a DTO without errors.

```
let fromDomain (person:Domain.Person) :Dto.Person =
  // get the primitive values from the domain object
  let first = person.First |> String50.value
  let last = person.Last |> String50.value
  let birthdate = person.Birthdate |> Birthdate.value

  // combine the components to create the DTO
  {First = first; Last = last; Birthdate = birthdate}
```

Going in the other direction, the toDomain function converts a DTO into a domain type; and because the various validations and constraints might fail, toDomain returns a Result<Person,string> rather than a plain Person.

```
let toDomain (dto:Dto.Person) :Result<Domain.Person,string> =
  result {
    // get each (validated) simple type from the DTO as a success or failure
    let! first = dto.First |> String50.create "First"
    let! last = dto.Last |> String50.create "Last"
    let! birthdate = dto.Birthdate |> Birthdate.create

    // combine the components to create the domain object
    return {
      First = first
      Last = last
      Birthdate = birthdate
    }
  }
```

We're using a result computation expression to handle the error flow, because the simple types, such as String50 and Birthdate, return Result from their create methods.

For example, we might implement String50.create using the approach discussed in *The Integrity of Simple Values*, on page 104. The code is shown below. Notice that we include the field name as a parameter so that we get helpful error messages:

```
let create fieldName str : Result<String50,string> =
  if String.IsNullOrEmpty(str) then
    Error (fieldName + " must be non-empty")
  elif str.Length > 50 then
    Error (fieldName + " must be less that 50 chars")
  else
    Ok (String50 str)
```

Wrapping the JSON Serializer

Serializing JSON or XML is not something we want to code ourselves—we'll probably prefer to use a third-party library. However, the API of the library might not be functional-friendly, so we may want to wrap the serialization and deserialization routines to make them suitable for use in a pipeline and to convert any exceptions into Results. Here's how to wrap part of the standard .NET JSON serialization library (Newtonsoft.Json), for example:

```
module Json =

  open Newtonsoft.Json

  let serialize obj =
    JsonConvert.SerializeObject obj

  let deserialize<'a> str =
    try
      JsonConvert.DeserializeObject<'a> str
      |> Result.Ok
    with
    // catch all exceptions and convert to Result
    | ex -> Result.Error ex
```

We're creating our own Json module to put the adapted versions in so we can call the serialization functions Json.serialize and Json.deserialize.

A Complete Serialization Pipeline

With the DTO-to-domain converter and the serialization functions in place, we can take a domain type—the Person record—all the way to a JSON string:

```
/// Serialize a Person into a JSON string
let jsonFromDomain (person:Domain.Person) =
  person
  |> Dto.Person.fromDomain
  |> Json.serialize
```

If we test it, we get the JSON string that we expect:

```
// input to test with
let person : Domain.Person = {
  First = String50 "Alex"
  Last = String50 "Adams"
  Birthdate = Birthdate (DateTime(1980,1,1))
  }

// use the serialization pipeline
jsonFromDomain person

// The output is
// "{"First":"Alex","Last":"Adams","Birthdate":"1980-01-01T00:00:00"}"
```

Composing the serialization pipeline is straightforward because all stages are
Result-free, but composing the deserialization pipeline is trickier because both
the Json.deserialize and the PersonDto.fromDomain can return Results. The solution is
to use Result.mapError to convert the potential failures to a common choice type
and then use a result expression to hide the errors, just as we learned in
Converting to a Common Error Type, on page 201:

```
type DtoError =
  | ValidationError of string
  | DeserializationException of exn

/// Deserialize a JSON string into a Person
let jsonToDomain jsonString :Result<Domain.Person,DtoError> =
  result {
    let! deserializedValue =
      jsonString
      |> Json.deserialize
      |> Result.mapError DeserializationException

    let! domainValue =
      deserializedValue
      |> Dto.Person.toDomain
      |> Result.mapError ValidationError

    return domainValue
    }
```

Let's test it with an input that has no errors:

```
// JSON string to test with
let jsonPerson = """{
  "First": "Alex",
  "Last": "Adams",
  "Birthdate": "1980-01-01T00:00:00"
  }"""

// call the deserialization pipeline
jsonToDomain jsonPerson |> printfn "%A"
```

```
// The output is:
//   Ok {First = String50 "Alex";
//       Last = String50 "Adams";
//       Birthdate = Birthdate 01/01/1980 00:00:00;}
```

We can see that the overall result is Ok and the Person domain object has been successfully created.

Let's now tweak the JSON string to have errors—a blank name and a bad date—and run the code again:

```
let jsonPersonWithErrors = """{
  "First": "",
  "Last": "Adams",
  "Birthdate": "1776-01-01T00:00:00"
  }"""

// call the deserialization pipeline
jsonToDomain jsonPersonWithErrors |> printfn "%A"

// The output is:
//   Error (ValidationError [
//        "First must be non-empty"
//        ])
```

You can see that we do indeed get the Error case of Result and one of the validation error messages. In a real application, you could log this and perhaps return the error to the caller. (In this implementation we only return the first error. To return all the errors, see *Composing in Parallel with Applicatives*, on page 217.)

Another approach to error handling during deserialization is not to do it at all and instead just let the deserialization code throw exceptions. Which approach you choose depends on whether you want to handle deserialization errors as an expected situation or as a "panic" that crashes the entire pipeline. And that in turn depends on how public your API is, how much you trust the callers, and how much information you want to provide the callers about these kinds of errors.

Working with Other Serializers

The code above uses the Newtonsoft.Json serializer. You can use other serializers, but you may need to add attributes to the PersonDto type. For example, to serialize a record type using the DataContractSerializer (for XML) or DataContractJson-Serializer (for JSON), you must decorate your DTO type with DataContractAttribute and DataMemberAttribute:

```
module Dto =
  [<DataContract>]
  type Person = {
    [<field: DataMember>]
    First: string
    [<field: DataMember>]
    Last: string
    [<field: DataMember>]
    Birthdate : DateTime
    }
```

This shows one of the other advantages of keeping the serialization type separate from the domain type—the domain type is not contaminated with complex attributes like this. As always, it's good to separate the domain concerns from the infrastructure concerns.

Another useful attribute to know about with serializers is the CLIMutableAttribute, which emits a (hidden) parameterless constructor, often needed by serializers that use reflection.

Finally, if you know that you're only going to be working with other F# components, you can use a F#-specific serializer such as FsPickler[2] or Chiron.[3] Note that by doing this, you're now introducing a coupling between the bounded contexts in that they all must use the same programming language.

Working with Multiple Versions of a Serialized Type

Over time, as the design evolves, the domain types may need to change, with fields added or removed or renamed. This in turn may affect the DTO types, too. The DTO types act as a contract between the bounded contexts, and it's important not to break this contract. This means that you may have to support multiple versions of a DTO type over time. There are many ways to do this, but we haven't got space to go into that here. Greg Young's book, *Versioning in an Event Sourced System,*[4] has a good discussion of the various approaches available.

How to Translate Domain Types to DTOs

The domain types that we define can be quite complex, yet the corresponding DTO types must be simple structures containing only primitive types. How then do we design a DTO given a particular domain type? Let's look at some guidelines.

---

2. https://github.com/mbraceproject/FsPickler
3. https://github.com/xyncro/chiron
4. https://leanpub.com/esversioning

Single-Case Unions

Single-case unions—what we are calling "simple types" in this book—can be represented by the underlying primitive in the DTO.

For example, if ProductCode is this domain type:

```
type ProductCode = ProductCode of string
```

Then the corresponding DTO type is just string.

Options

For options, we can replace the None case with null. If the option wraps a reference type, we don't need to do anything because null is a valid value. For value types like int, we'll need to use the nullable equivalent, such as Nullable<int>.

Records

Domain types defined as records can stay as records in the DTO, as long as the type of each field is converted to the DTO equivalent.

Here's an example demonstrating single-case unions, optional values, and a record type:

```
/// Domain types
type OrderLineId = OrderLineId of int
type OrderLineQty = OrderLineQty of int
type OrderLine = {
  OrderLineId : OrderLineId
  ProductCode : ProductCode
  Quantity : OrderLineQty option
  Description : string option
  }

/// Corresponding DTO type
type OrderLineDto = {
  OrderLineId : int
  ProductCode : string
  Quantity : Nullable<int>
  Description : string
  }
```

Collections

Lists, sequences, and sets should be converted to arrays, which are supported in every serialization format.

```
/// Domain type
type Order = {
  ...
```

```
  Lines : OrderLine list
  }
/// Corresponding DTO type
type OrderDto = {
  ...
  Lines : OrderLineDto[]
  }
```

For maps and other complex collections, the approach you take depends on the serialization format. When using JSON format, you should be able to serialize directly from a map to a JSON object, since JSON objects are just key-value collections.

For other formats you may need to create a special representation. For example, a map might be represented in a DTO as an array of records, where each record is a key-value pair:

```
/// Domain type
type Price = Price of decimal
type PriceLookup = Map<ProductCode,Price>

/// DTO type to represent a map
type PriceLookupPair = {
  Key : string
  Value : decimal
  }
type PriceLookupDto = {
  KVPairs : PriceLookupPair []
  }
```

Alternatively a map can be represented as two parallel arrays that can be zipped together on deserialization.

```
/// Alternative DTO type to represent a map
type PriceLookupDto = {
  Keys : string []
  Values : decimal []
  }
```

Discriminated Unions Used as Enumerations

In many cases, you have unions where every case is just a name with no extra data. These can be represented by .NET enums, which in turn are generally represented by integers when serialized.

```
/// Domain type
type Color =
  | Red
  | Green
  | Blue
```

```
/// Corresponding DTO type
type ColorDto =
    | Red = 1
    | Green = 2
    | Blue = 3
```

Note that when deserializing, you *must* handle the case where the .NET enum value is not one of the enumerated ones.

```
let toDomain dto : Result<Color,_> =
  match dto with
  | ColorDto.Red -> Ok Color.Red
  | ColorDto.Green -> Ok Color.Green
  | ColorDto.Blue -> Ok Color.Blue
  | _ -> Error (sprintf "Color %O is not one of Red,Green,Blue" dto)
```

Alternatively, you can serialize an enum-style union as a string, using the name of the case as the value. This is more sensitive to renaming issues, though.

Tuples

Tuples should not occur often in the domain, but if they do they'll probably need to be represented by a specially defined record, since tuples are not supported in most serialization formats. In the example below, the domain type Card is a tuple, but the corresponding CardDto type is a record.

```
/// Components of tuple
type Suit = Heart | Spade | Diamond | Club
type Rank = Ace | Two | Queen | King // incomplete for clarity

// Tuple
type Card = Suit * Rank

/// Corresponding DTO types
type SuitDto = Heart = 1 | Spade = 2 | Diamond = 3 | Club = 4
type RankDto = Ace = 1 | Two = 2 | Queen = 12 | King = 13
type CardDto = {
  Suit : SuitDto
  Rank : RankDto
  }
```

Choice Types

Choice types can be represented as a record with a "tag" that represents which choice is used and then a field for each possible case that contains the data associated with that case. When a specific case is converted in the DTO, the field for that case will have data and all the other fields, for the other cases, will be null (or for lists, empty).

Some serializers can handle F# discriminated union types directly, but you won't have control over the format they use. This could be a problem if another bounded context, using a different serializer, doesn't know how to interpret them. Since the DTOs are part of a contract, it's better to have explicit control over the format.

Here's an example of a domain type (Example) with four choices:

- An empty case, tagged as A
- An integer, tagged as B
- A list of strings, tagged as C
- A name (using the Name type from above), tagged as D

```fsharp
/// Domain types
type Name = {
  First : String50
  Last : String50
  }
type Example =
  | A
  | B of int
  | C of string list
  | D of Name
```

And here's how the corresponding DTO types would look, with the type of each case being replaced with a serializable version: int to Nullable<int>, string list to string[] and Name to NameDto.

```fsharp
/// Corresponding DTO types
type NameDto = {
  First : string
  Last : string
  }
type ExampleDto = {
  Tag : string // one of "A","B", "C", "D"
  // no data for A case
  BData : Nullable<int>  // data for B case
  CData : string[]       // data for C case
  DData : NameDto        // data for D case
  }
```

Serialization is straightforward—you just need to convert the appropriate data for the selected case and set the data for all the other cases to null:

```fsharp
let nameDtoFromDomain (name:Name) :NameDto =
    let first = name.First |> String50.value
    let last = name.Last |> String50.value
    {First=first; Last=last}
```

```
let fromDomain (domainObj:Example) :ExampleDto =
  let nullBData = Nullable()
  let nullCData = null
  let nullDData = Unchecked.defaultof<NameDto>
  match domainObj with
  | A ->
      {Tag="A"; BData=nullBData; CData=nullCData; DData=nullDData}
  | B i ->
      let bdata = Nullable i
      {Tag="B"; BData=bdata; CData=nullCData; DData=nullDData}
  | C strList ->
      let cdata = strList |> List.toArray
      {Tag="C"; BData=nullBData; CData=cdata; DData=nullDData}
  | D name ->
      let ddata = name |> nameDtoFromDomain
      {Tag="D"; BData=nullBData; CData=nullCData; DData=ddata}
```

Here's what's going on in this code:

- We set up the null values for each field at the top of the function and then assign them to the fields that aren't relevant to the case being matched.

- In the "B" case, Nullable<_> types cannot be assigned null directly. We must use the Nullable() function instead.

- In the "C" case, an Array can be assigned null because it's a .NET class.

- In the "D" case, an F# record such as NameDto cannot be assigned null either, so we are using the "backdoor" function Unchecked.defaultOf<_> to create a null value for it. This should never be used in normal code, only when you need to create nulls for interop or serialization.

When deserializing a choice type with a tag like this, we match on the "tag" field and then handle each case separately. And before we attempt the deserialization, we must always check the data associated with the tag is not null:

```
let nameDtoToDomain (nameDto:NameDto) :Result<Name,string> =
    result {
      let! first = nameDto.First |> String50.create
      let! last = nameDto.Last |> String50.create
      return {First=first; Last=last}
    }

let toDomain dto : Result<Example,string> =
  match dto.Tag with
    | "A" ->
      Ok A
    | "B" ->
      if dto.BData.HasValue then
        dto.BData.Value |> B |> Ok
      else
```

```
      Error "B data not expected to be null"
  | "C" ->
    match dto.CData with
    | null ->
      Error "C data not expected to be null"
    | _ ->
      dto.CData |> Array.toList |> C |> Ok
  | "D" ->
    match box dto.DData with
    | null ->
      Error "D data not expected to be null"
    | _ ->
      dto.DData
      |> nameDtoToDomain  // returns Result...
      |> Result.map D     // ...so must use "map"
  | _ ->
    // all other cases
    let msg = sprintf "Tag '%s' not recognized" dto.Tag
    Error msg
```

In the "B" and "C" cases, the conversion from the primitive value to the domain values is error-free (after ensuring that the data is not null). In the "D" case, the conversion from NameDto to Name might fail, so it returns a Result that we must map over (using Result.map) with the D case constructor.

Serializing Records and Choice Types Using Maps

An alternative serialization approach for compound types (records and discriminated unions) is to serialize *everything* as a key-value map. In other words, all DTOs will be implemented in the same way: as the .NET type IDictionary<string,obj>. This approach is particularly applicable for working with the JSON format, where it aligns well with the JSON object model.

The advantage of this approach is that there's no "contract" implicit in the DTO structure&emdash;a key-value map can contain anything&emdash;so it promotes highly decoupled interactions. The downside is that there's no contract at all! That means that it's hard to know when there is a mismatch in expectations between producer and consumer. Sometimes a little bit of coupling can be useful. Let's look at some code. Using this approach, we would serialize a Name record like this:

```
let nameDtoFromDomain (name:Name) :IDictionary<string,obj> =
  let first = name.First |> String50.value :> obj
  let last = name.Last |> String50.value :> obj
  [
    ("First",first)
    ("Last",last)
  ] |> dict
```

Here we're creating a list of key/value pairs and then using the built-in function dict to build an IDictionary from them. If this dictionary is then serialized to JSON, the output looks just as if we created a separate NameDto type and serialized it.

One thing to note is that the IDictionary uses obj as the type of the value. That means that all the values in the record must be explicitly cast to obj using the upcast operator :>.

For choice types, the dictionary that is returned will have exactly one entry, but the value of the key will depend on the choice. For example, if we are serializing the Example type, the key would be one of "A," "B," "C," or "D."

```
let fromDomain (domainObj:Example) :IDictionary<string,obj> =
  match domainObj with
  | A ->
    [ ("A",null) ] |> dict
  | B i ->
    let bdata = Nullable i :> obj
    [ ("B",bdata) ] |> dict
  | C strList ->
    let cdata = strList |> List.toArray :> obj
    [ ("C",cdata) ] |> dict
  | D name ->
    let ddata = name |> nameDtoFromDomain :> obj
    [ ("D",ddata) ] |> dict
```

The code above shows a similar approach to nameDtoFromDomain. For each case, we convert the data into a serializable format and then cast that to obj. In the "D" case, where the data is a Name, the serializable format is just another IDictionary.

Deserialization is a bit trickier. For each field we need to (a) look in the dictionary to see if it's there, and (b) if present, retrieve it and attempt to cast it into the correct type.

This calls out for a helper function, which we'll call getValue:

```
let getValue key (dict:IDictionary<string,obj>) :Result<'a,string> =
  match dict.TryGetValue key with
  | (true,value) ->  // key found!
    try
      // downcast to the type 'a and return Ok
      (value :?> 'a) |> Ok
    with
    | :? InvalidCastException ->
      // the cast failed
      let typeName = typeof<'a>.Name
```

```
    let msg = sprintf "Value could not be cast to %s" typeName
    Error msg
| (false,_) ->      // key not found
  let msg = sprintf "Key '%s' not found" key
  Error msg
```

Let's look at how to deserialize a Name, then. We first have to get the value at the "First" key (which might result in an error). If that works, we call String50.create on it to get the First field (which also might result in an error). Similarly for the "Last" key and the Last field. As always, we'll use a result expression to make our lives easier.

```
let nameDtoToDomain (nameDto:IDictionary<string,obj>) :Result<Name,string> =
  result {
    let! firstStr = nameDto |> getValue "First"
    let! first = firstStr |> String50.create
    let! lastStr = nameDto |> getValue "Last"
    let! last = lastStr |> String50.create
    return {First=first; Last=last}
  }
```

To deserialize a choice type such as Example, we need to test whether a key is present for each case. If one is, we can attempt to retrieve it and convert it into a domain object. Again, there's lots of potential for errors, so for each case we'll use a result expression.

```
let toDomain (dto:IDictionary<string,obj>) : Result<Example,string> =
  if dto.ContainsKey "A" then
    Ok A    // no extra data needed
  elif dto.ContainsKey "B" then
    result {
      let! bData = dto |> getValue "B" // might fail
      return B bData
      }
  elif dto.ContainsKey "C" then
    result {
      let! cData = dto |> getValue "C" // might fail
      return cData |> Array.toList |> C
      }
  elif dto.ContainsKey "D" then
    result {
      let! dData = dto |> getValue "D" // might fail
      let! name = dData |> nameDtoToDomain  // might also fail
      return name |> D
      }
  else
    // all other cases
    let msg = sprintf "No union case recognized"
    Error msg
```

Generics

In many cases, the domain type is generic. If the serialization library supports generics, then you can create DTOs using generics as well.

For example, the Result type is generic and can be converted into a generic ResultDto like this:

```
type ResultDto<'OkData,'ErrorData when 'OkData : null and 'ErrorData: null> = {
  IsError : bool  // replaces "Tag" field
  OkData : 'OkData
  ErrorData : 'ErrorData
  }
```

Note that the generic types 'OkData and 'ErrorData must be constrained to be nullable because they might be missing or null in the associated JSON object.

If the serialization library does not support generics, then you'll have to create a special type for each concrete case. That might sound tedious, but you'll probably find that, in practice, very few generic types need to be serialized.

For example, here's the Result type from the order-placing workflow converted to a DTO using concrete types rather than generic types:

```
type PlaceOrderResultDto = {
  IsError : bool
  OkData : PlaceOrderEventDto[]
  ErrorData : PlaceOrderErrorDto
  }
```

Wrapping Up

In this chapter, we left our bounded context and clean domain and stepped into the messy world of infrastructure. We learned how to design serializable Data Transfer Objects to act as the intermediaries between the bounded contexts and the outside world, and we looked at a number of guidelines that can help you with your own implementations.

Serialization is one kind of interaction with the outside world, but it's not the only one. In most applications we'll need to talk to a database of some sort. In the next chapter, we'll turn our attention to the techniques and challenges of persistence—how to make our domain model work with relational and NoSQL databases.

CHAPTER 12

Persistence

Throughout this book, we've designed our domain models to be "persistence-ignorant"—not letting the design be distorted by implementation issues associated with storing data or interacting with other services.

But there comes a point in most applications where we have state that needs to last longer than the lifetime of a process or workflow. At this point, we need to turn to some sort of persistence mechanism such as a file system or database. Sadly, there's almost always a mismatch when moving from our perfect domain to the messy world of infrastructure.

This chapter aims to help you deal with the issues associated with persisting a domain-driven data model. We'll start by discussing some high-level principles, such as command-query separation, and then we'll switch to low-level implementations. In particular, we'll see how to persist our domain model in two different ways: in a NoSQL document database and then in a traditional SQL database.

By the end of the chapter, you should have all the tools you need to integrate a database or other persistence mechanism into your application.

Before we dive into the mechanics of persistence, though, let's look at some general guidelines that help us work with persistence in the context of domain-driven design:

- Push persistence to the edges.
- Separate commands (updates) from queries (reads).
- Bounded contexts must own their own data store.

Pushing Persistence to the Edges

As we discussed earlier on page 54, we would ideally like all our functions to be "pure," which makes them easier to reason about and test. Functions that read from or write to the outside world cannot be pure, so when designing our workflows, we want to avoid any kind of I/O or persistence-related logic inside the workflow. This generally means separating workflows into two parts:

- A domain-centric part that contains the business logic
- An "edge" part that contains the I/O-related code

For example, let's say we have a workflow that implements the logic for paying an invoice. In a model that mixes up domain logic and I/O, the implementation might be designed like this:

- Load the invoice from the database.

- Apply the payment.

- If the invoice is fully paid, mark it as fully paid in the database and post an InvoicePaid event.

- If the invoice is not fully paid, mark it as partially paid in the database and don't post any event.

Here's what that code might look like in F#:

```
// workflow mixes domain logic and I/O
let payInvoice invoiceId payment =
  // load from DB
  let invoice = loadInvoiceFromDatabase(invoiceId)

  // apply payment
  invoice.ApplyPayment(payment)

  // handle different outcomes
  if invoice.IsFullyPaid then
    markAsFullyPaidInDb(invoiceId)
    postInvoicePaidEvent(invoiceId)
  else
    markAsPartiallyPaidInDb(invoiceId)
```

The problem is that the function is not pure and would be hard to test.

Let's extract the pure business logic into an applyPayment function that does not touch the database but instead returns a decision about what to do next, which we'll call InvoicePaymentResult:

```
type InvoicePaymentResult =
  | FullyPaid
  | PartiallyPaid of ...

// domain workflow: pure function
let applyPayment unpaidInvoice payment :InvoicePaymentResult =
  // apply payment
  let updatedInvoice = unpaidInvoice |> applyPayment payment
```

```
// handle different outcomes
if isFullyPaid updatedInvoice then
  FullyPaid
else
  PartiallyPaid updatedInvoice
// return PartiallyPaid or FullyPaid
```

This function is completely pure. It does not load any data—all the data it needs is passed to it as parameters. And it doesn't save any data. It makes a decision but returns that decision as a choice type, rather than acting on it immediately. As a result, it's easy to test that the logic in this function is working.

Once this function is written, we'll use it as part of a command handler at the boundaries of our bounded context, where I/O is allowed, like this:

```
type PayInvoiceCommand = {
  InvoiceId : ...
  Payment : ...
  }
// command handler at the edge of the bounded context
let payInvoice payInvoiceCommand =
  // load from DB
  let invoiceId = payInvoiceCommand.InvoiceId
  let unpaidInvoice =
    loadInvoiceFromDatabase invoiceId   // I/O

  // call into pure domain
  let payment =
    payInvoiceCommand.Payment           // pure
  let paymentResult =
    applyPayment unpaidInvoice payment  // pure

  // handle result
  match paymentResult with
  | FullyPaid ->
    markAsFullyPaidInDb invoiceId       // I/O
    postInvoicePaidEvent invoiceId      // I/O
  | PartiallyPaid updatedInvoice ->
    updateInvoiceInDb updatedInvoice    // I/O
```

Note that this function does not make any decisions itself, it just handles the decision made by the inner domain-centric function. As a result, this function doesn't really need to be tested with a unit test, because the persistence logic is generally trivial. That doesn't mean it shouldn't be tested, of course, but you might be better off testing it as part of an end-to-end integration test.

You can think of this composite function as a sandwich—I/O at the edges with a pure center as shown in the figure on page 242.

However, if we *do* want to test this function in isolation, all we need to do is add additional function parameters to it to represent all the I/O actions that we call, like this:

```
// command handler at the edge of the bounded context
let payInvoice
  loadUnpaidInvoiceFromDatabase // dependency
  markAsFullyPaidInDb           // dependency
  updateInvoiceInDb             // dependency
  payInvoiceCommand =

  // load from DB
  let invoiceId = payInvoiceCommand.InvoiceId
  let unpaidInvoice =
    loadUnpaidInvoiceFromDatabase invoiceId

  // call into pure domain
  let payment =
    payInvoiceCommand.Payment
  let paymentResult =
    applyPayment unpaidInvoice payment

  // handle result
  match paymentResult with
  | FullyPaid ->
    markAsFullyPaidInDb(invoiceId)
    postInvoicePaidEvent(invoiceId)
  | PartiallyPaid updatedInvoice ->
    updateInvoiceInDb updatedInvoice
```

And now you can easily test this function by providing stubs for the parameters in the usual way.

Composite functions that use I/O like this should of course be located at the top level of the application—either in the "composition root" or in a controller.

Making Decisions Based on Queries

The example above assumed that all of the data could be loaded outside the domain function and then passed in to it. But what happens if you need to make a decision based on reading from a database, right in the middle of the "pure" code?

The solution is to keep the pure functions intact but sandwich them between impure I/O functions, like this.

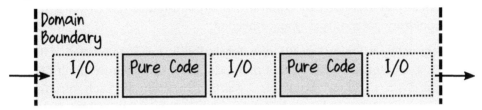

The pure functions contain the business logic and make the decisions, and the I/O functions read and write data.

For example, let's say that we need to extend the workflow: after payment, we'll calculate the total amount owed and send a warning message to the customer if it's too large. With the additional requirements, the steps in the pipeline would look something like this:

```
--- I/O---
Load invoice from DB

--- Pure ---
Do payment logic

--- I/O ---
Pattern match on output choice type:
  if "FullyPaid" -> Mark invoice as paid in DB
  if "PartiallyPaid" -> Save updated invoice to DB

--- I/O ---
Load all amounts from unpaid invoices in DB

--- Pure ---
Add the amounts up and decide if amount is too large

--- I/O ---
Pattern match on output choice type:
  If "OverdueWarningNeeded" -> Send message to customer
  If "NoActionNeeded" -> do nothing
```

If there's too much mixing of I/O and logic, the simple "sandwich" may become more of a "layer cake." In that case, you might want to break the workflow into shorter mini-workflows, as discussed in *Long-Running Workflows*, on page 140. This way each workflow can stay as a small, simple sandwich.

Where's the Repository Pattern?

In the original *Domain-Driven Design* book, there's a pattern for accessing databases called the Repository pattern. If you are familiar with the book, you might be wondering how that pattern fits in with a functional approach.

The answer is that it doesn't. The Repository pattern is a nice way of hiding persistence in an object-oriented design that relies on mutability. But when we model everything as functions and push persistence to the edges, then the Repository pattern is no longer needed.

This approach also has a benefit in maintainability, because instead of having a single I/O interface with tens of methods, most of which we don't need to use in a given workflow, we define a distinct function for each specific I/O access and use them only as needed.

Command-Query Separation

The next principle we'll look at is *command-query separation*, or CQS.

In the functional approach to domain modeling, all our objects are designed to be immutable. Let's think of the storage system as some kind of immutable object too. That is, every time we change the data in the storage system, it transforms into a new version of itself.

For example, if we want to model inserting a record in a functional way, we can think of the insert function as having two parameters: the data to insert and the original state of the data store. The output of the function, after the insert is completed, is a new version of the data store with the data added to it.

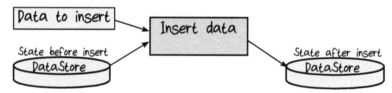

In code, we could model it using this type signature:

```
type InsertData = DataStoreState -> Data -> NewDataStoreState
```

There are four basic ways of interacting with a data store: "Create" (or "insert"), "Read" (or "query"), "Update," and "Delete." We just looked at "Insert"—let's diagram the other ones too:

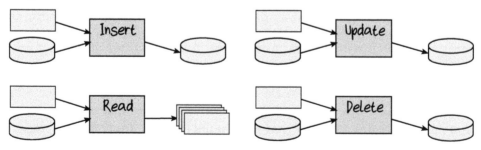

Or in code:

```
type InsertData = DataStoreState -> Data -> NewDataStoreState
type ReadData = DataStoreState -> Query -> Data
type UpdateData = DataStoreState -> Data -> NewDataStoreState
type DeleteData = DataStoreState -> Key -> NewDataStoreState
```

One of these is not like the others. It's clear that we have two different kinds of operations:

- The insert, update, and delete operations change the state of the database and (in general) do not return any useful data.

- The read or query operation, on the other hand, does *not* change the state of the database, and it's the only one of the four that returns a useful result.

Command-query separation is a design principle based on these distinctions. It states that code that returns data ("queries") should not be mixed up with code that updates data ("commands"). Or to put it more simply: asking a question should not change the answer.

Applied to functional programming, the CQS principle proposes this:

- Functions that return data should not have side effects.
- Functions that have side effects (updating state) should not return data—that is, they should be unit-returning functions.

That's nothing new—we've been doing this anyway throughout our design—but let's now apply this specifically to databases.

Let's work on those function signatures a bit.

- On the input side, we can replace the DataStoreState with some kind of handle to the data store, such as a DbConnection.

- The output (NewDataStoreState) is not relevant for a real-world data store because the data store is mutable and doesn't return a new state. Therefore we can replace that type with the Unit type.

Our signatures would now look like this:

```
type InsertData = DbConnection -> Data -> Unit
type ReadData = DbConnection -> Query -> Data
type UpdateData = DbConnection -> Data -> Unit
type DeleteData = DbConnection -> Key -> Unit
```

The DbConnection type is specific to a particular data store, so we'll want to hide this dependency from the callers using partial application or a similar technique (see *Partial Application*, on page 153), which means our persistence-related functions, as seen from the domain code, will be database-agnostic and will have signatures like this:

```
type InsertData = Data -> Unit
type ReadData = Query -> Data
type UpdateData = Data -> Unit
type DeleteData = Key -> Unit
```

This is just what we saw in the previous chapters.

Of course, since we're dealing with I/O and possible errors, the actual signatures need to include some effects. It's common to create an alias such as DataStoreResult or DbResult that includes the Result type and possibly Async as well, and then our signatures will look like this:

```
type DbError = ...
type DbResult<'a> = AsyncResult<'a,DbError>

type InsertData = Data -> DbResult<Unit>
type ReadData = Query -> DbResult<Data>
type UpdateData = Data -> DbResult<Unit>
type DeleteData = Key -> DbResult<Unit>
```

Command-Query Responsibility Segregation

It's often tempting to try to reuse the same objects for reading and writing. For example, if we have a Customer record, we might save it to a database and load it from a database with side-effecting functions like these:

```
type SaveCustomer = Customer -> DbResult<Unit>
type LoadCustomer = CustomerId -> DbResult<Customer>
```

However, it's not really a good idea to reuse the same type for both reading and writing for a number of reasons.

First, the data returned by the query is often different than what is needed when writing. For example, a query might return denormalized data or calculated values, but these wouldn't be used when writing data. Also, when creating a new record, fields such as generated IDs or versions wouldn't be used, yet would be returned in a query. Rather than trying to make one data type serve multiple purposes, it's better to design each data type for one specific use. In F#, it's easy to create as many data types as needed, as we've seen before.

A second reason to avoid reuse is that the queries and commands tend to evolve independently and therefore shouldn't be coupled. For example, you may find that over time you need three or four different queries on the same data, with only one update command. It gets awkward if the query type and the command type are forced to be the same.

Finally, some queries may need to return multiple entities at once for performance reasons. For example, when you load an order, you may also want to load the customer data associated with that order, rather than making a second trip to the database to get the customer. Of course, when you are saving the order to the DB, you would use only the reference to the customer (the CustomerId) rather than the entire customer.

Based on these observations, it's clear that queries and commands are almost always different from a domain-modeling point of view, and therefore they should be modeled with different types. This separation of query types and command types leads naturally to a design where they are *segregated* into different modules so that they are truly decoupled and can evolve independently. One module would be responsible for queries (known as the *read model*) and the other for commands (the *write model*), hence *command-query responsibility segregation* or *CQRS*.

For example, if we wanted to have separate read and write models for a customer, we might define a WriteModel.Customer type and a ReadModel.Customer type, and the data access functions would look like this:

```
type SaveCustomer = WriteModel.Customer -> DbResult<Unit>
type LoadCustomer = CustomerId -> DbResult<ReadModel.Customer>
```

CQRS and Database Segregation

The CQRS principle can be applied to databases too. In that case, you would have two different data stores, one optimized for writing (no indexes, transactional, and so on), and one optimized for queries (denormalized, heavily indexed, and so on).

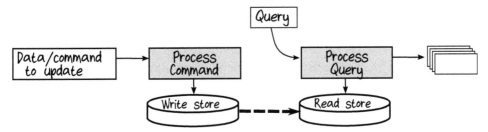

This is the "logical" view, of course—you don't need to have two separate physical databases. In a relational database, for example, the "write" model could simply be tables and the "read" model could be predefined views on those tables.

If you *do* have physically separate data stores, you must implement a special process that copies data from the "write store" to the "read store." This is extra work, so you must decide whether the design benefits of separate data stores are worth it. More importantly, the data on the read-side may be out of date compared to the data on the write-side, which means that the read store is "eventually consistent" rather than immediately consistent. This may or may not be a problem, depending on your domain (see also the discussion on consistency on page 114).

However, once you have committed to segregating the reads and writes, you then have the flexibility to use many distinct read stores, each of which is optimized for a certain domain. In particular, you can have a read store that contains aggregated data from many bounded contexts, which is very useful for doing reports or analytics.

Event Sourcing

CQRS is often associated with event sourcing.[1] In an event-sourcing approach, the current state is not persisted as a single object. Instead, every time there is a change to the state, an event representing the change (such as InvoicePaid) is persisted. In this way, each difference between the old state and the new state is captured, somewhat like a version control system. To restore the current state at the beginning of a workflow, all the previous events are replayed. There are many advantages to this approach, not least that it matches the model of many domains where everything is audited. As they say, "Accountants don't use erasers." Event sourcing is a large topic and we don't have space to do it justice here.

Bounded Contexts Must Own Their Data Storage

Another key guideline for persistence is that each bounded context must be isolated from others in terms of their data storage. That means the following:

- A bounded context must own its own data storage and associated schemas, and it can change them at any time without having to coordinate with other bounded contexts.

- No other system can directly access the data owned by the bounded context. Instead, the client should either use the public API of the bounded context or use some kind of copy of the data store.

The goal here, as always, is to ensure that the bounded contexts stay decoupled and can evolve independently. If system *A* accesses the data store of

---

1. http://microservices.io/patterns/data/event-sourcing.html

system *B*, then even if the codebases are completely independent, the two systems are still coupled in practice because of the shared data.

Now the implementation of "isolation" can vary depending on the needs of the design and the requirements of the operations team. At one extreme, each bounded context might have a physically distinct database or data store that is deployed completely separately from all the others. At the other extreme, all the data from all contexts could be stored in one physical database (making deployment easier) but use some kind of namespace mechanism to keep the data for each context logically separate.

Working with Data from Multiple Domains

What about reporting and business analytics systems? They'll need to access data from multiple contexts, but we've just said that this is a bad idea.

The solution is to treat "Reporting" or "Business Intelligence" as a separate domain and to copy the data owned by the other bounded contexts to a separate system designed for reporting. This approach, although more work, does allow the source systems and the reporting system to evolve independently and allows each to be optimized for its own concerns. Of course, this approach is not new—the distinction between OLTP[2] and OLAP[3] systems has been around for decades.

There are various ways to get data from the other bounded contexts to the Business Intelligence context. The "pure" way would be to have it subscribe to events emitted by other systems. For example, every time an order is created, an event will be triggered and the Business Intelligence (or "BI") context can listen to that event and insert a corresponding record in its own data store. This approach has the advantage that the Business Intelligence context is just another domain and does not require any special treatment in the design.

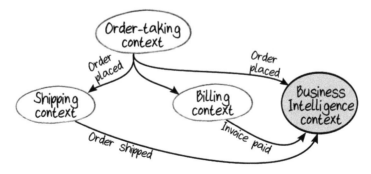

---

2.   https://en.wikipedia.org/wiki/Online_transaction_processing
3.   https://en.wikipedia.org/wiki/Online_analytical_processing

Another way is to use a traditional ETL process[4] to copy the data from the source systems to the BI system. This has the advantage of being easier to implement initially, but it may impose extra maintenance since it'll probably need to be altered when the source systems change their database schemas.

Note that within the Business Intelligence domain, there's very little need for a formal domain model. It's probably more important to develop a multidimensional database (colloquially known as a "cube") that efficiently supports ad hoc queries and many different access paths.

We can handle the data required for operations using a similar approach. We treat "Operational Intelligence" as a separate domain and then send logging, metrics, and other kinds of data to it for analysis and reporting.

Working with Document Databases

We've talked about some of the general principles of persistence. We'll now shift gears completely and dive into some implementation examples, starting with a so-called "document database," designed to store semistructured data in JSON or XML format.

Persisting to a document database is easy. We use the techniques discussed in the previous chapter (Chapter 11, *Serialization*, on page 221) to convert a domain object into a DTO and then into a JSON string (or XML string or whatever) and then store and load it through the API of the storage system.

For example, if we are using Azure blob storage to save PersonDto objects, we can set up the storage like this:

```
open Microsoft.WindowsAzure
open Microsoft.WindowsAzure.Storage
open Microsoft.WindowsAzure.Storage.Blob

let connString = "... Azure connection string ..."
let storageAccount = CloudStorageAccount.Parse(connString)
let blobClient = storageAccount.CreateCloudBlobClient()

let container = blobClient.GetContainerReference("Person");
container.CreateIfNotExists()
```

And then we can save a DTO to a blob with a few lines of code:

```
type PersonDto = {
  PersonId : int
  ...
  }
```

---

4. https://en.wikipedia.org/wiki/Extract,_transform,_load

```
let savePersonDtoToBlob personDto =
  let blobId = sprintf "Person%i" personDto.PersonId
  let blob = container.GetBlockBlobReference(blobId)
  let json = Json.serialize personDto
  blob.UploadText(json)
```

And that's all there is to it. In the same way, we can create code that loads from the storage using the deserialization techniques from the previous chapter.

Working with Relational Databases

Relational databases have a very different model from most code, and traditionally this has been the cause of a lot of pain—the so-called "impedance mismatch" between objects and databases.

Data models developed using functional programming principles tend to be more compatible with relational databases, primarily because functional models do not mix data and behavior, so the saving and retrieving of records is more straightforward. Nevertheless, we still need to address some issues. Let's look at how a relational database model compares to a functional model.

First, the good news is that tables in relational databases correspond nicely to collections of records in the functional model. And the set-oriented operations (SELECT, WHERE) in a database are similar to the list-oriented operations (map, filter) in functional languages.

So our strategy will be to use the serialization techniques from the previous chapter to design record types that can be mapped directly to tables. For example, say we have a domain type like this:

```
type CustomerId = CustomerId of int
type String50 = String50 of string
type Birthdate = Birthdate of DateTime

type Customer = {
  CustomerId : CustomerId
  Name : String50
  Birthdate : Birthdate option
  }
```

Then the corresponding table design is straightforward:

```
CREATE TABLE Customer (
  CustomerId int NOT NULL,
  Name NVARCHAR(50) NOT NULL,
  Birthdate DATETIME NULL,
  CONSTRAINT PK_Customer PRIMARY KEY (CustomerId)
)
```

The bad news is that relational databases only store primitives such as strings or ints, which means that we will have to unwrap our nice domain types, such as ProductCode or OrderId.

Even worse, relational tables do not map nicely to choice types. That's something we need to look at in more detail.

Mapping Choice Types to Tables

How should we model choice types in a relational database? If we think of choice types as a one-level inheritance hierarchy, then we can borrow some of the approaches used to map object hierarchies to the relational model.[5]

The two most useful approaches for mapping choice types are these:

- All cases live in the same table.
- Each case has its own table.

For example, say that we have a type like Contact (below), which contains a choice type, and we want to store it in a database:

```
type Contact = {
  ContactId : ContactId
  Info : ContactInfo
  }

and ContactInfo =
  | Email of EmailAddress
  | Phone of PhoneNumber

and EmailAddress = EmailAddress of string
and PhoneNumber = PhoneNumber of string
and ContactId = ContactId of int
```

The first approach ("all cases in one table") is similar to the approach discussed on page 232. We'll use just one table to store all the data from all the cases, which in turn means that (a) we'll need a flag or flags to indicate which case is being used and (b) there will have to be NULLable columns that are used for only some of the cases.

```
CREATE TABLE ContactInfo (
  -- shared data
  ContactId int NOT NULL,
  -- case flags
  IsEmail bit NOT NULL,
  IsPhone bit NOT NULL,
  -- data for the "Email" case
  EmailAddress NVARCHAR(100), -- Nullable
```

---

5.   http://www.agiledata.org/essays/mappingObjects.html

```
-- data for the "Phone" case
PhoneNumber NVARCHAR(25), -- Nullable
-- primary key constraint
CONSTRAINT PK_ContactInfo PRIMARY KEY (ContactId)
)
```

We have used a bit field flag for each case rather than a single Tag VARCHAR field because it's slightly more compact and easier to index.

The second approach (where each case has its own table) means that we create two child tables in addition to the main table, one child table for each case. All tables share the same primary key. The main table stores the ID and some flags to indicate which case is active, while the child tables store the data for each case. In exchange for more complexity, we have better constraints in the database (such as NOT NULL columns in the child tables).

```
-- Main table
CREATE TABLE ContactInfo (
  -- shared data
  ContactId int NOT NULL,
  -- case flags
  IsEmail bit NOT NULL,
  IsPhone bit NOT NULL,
  CONSTRAINT PK_ContactInfo PRIMARY KEY (ContactId)
)

-- Child table for "Email" case
CREATE TABLE ContactEmail (
  ContactId int NOT NULL,
  -- case-specific data
  EmailAddress NVARCHAR(100) NOT NULL,
  CONSTRAINT PK_ContactEmail PRIMARY KEY (ContactId)
)

-- Child table for "Phone" case
CREATE TABLE ContactPhone (
  ContactId int NOT NULL,
  -- case-specific data
  PhoneNumber NVARCHAR(25) NOT NULL,
  CONSTRAINT PK_ContactPhone PRIMARY KEY (ContactId)
)
```

This "multitable" approach might be better when the data associated with cases are very large and have little in common, but otherwise we'll use the first, "one-table" approach by default.

Mapping Nested Types to Tables

What if a type contains other types? How should these be handled? The general advice is this:

- If the inner type is an DDD Entity, with its own identity, it should be stored in a separate table.

- If the inner type is a DDD Value Object, without its own identity, it should be stored "inline" with the parent data.

For example, our Order type contains a list of OrderLine values. The OrderLine type is an Entity, and therefore it should be stored in its own table, with a pointer (foreign key) to its parent object.

```
CREATE TABLE Order (
  OrderId int NOT NULL,
  -- and other columns
)

CREATE TABLE OrderLine (
  OrderLineId int NOT NULL,
  OrderId int NOT NULL,
  -- and other columns
)
```

On the other hand, the Order type contains two Address values, which are Value Objects. The corresponding Order table should therefore directly include all the Address columns.

```
CREATE TABLE Order (
  OrderId int NOT NULL,

  -- inline the shipping address Value Object
  ShippingAddress1 varchar(50)
  ShippingAddress2 varchar(50)
  ShippingAddressCity varchar(50)
  -- and so on

  -- inline the billing address Value Object
  BillingAddress1 varchar(50)
  BillingAddress2 varchar(50)
  BillingAddressCity varchar(50)
  -- and so on

  -- other columns
)
```

Reading from a Relational Database

In F#, we tend not to use an object-relational mapper (ORM), but instead work directly with raw SQL commands. The most convenient way to do this is to use an F# SQL type provider. A few of these are available—for this example, we'll use the FSharp.Data.SqlClient type provider.[6]

---

6.   http://fsprojects.github.io/FSharp.Data.SqlClient/

What's special about using a type provider rather than a typical runtime library is that the SQL type provider will create types that match the SQL queries or SQL commands *at compile time*. If the SQL query is incorrect, you will get a compile time error, not a runtime error. And if the SQL is correct, it will generate an F# record type that matches the output of the SQL code exactly.

Let's say that we want to read a single Customer using a CustomerId. Here's how this could be done using the type provider.

First we define a connection string to be used at compile time, which typically references a local database.

```
open FSharp.Data

[< Literal>]
let CompileTimeConnectionString =
  @"Data Source=(localdb)\MsSqlLocalDb; Initial Catalog=DomainModelingExample;"
```

Then we define our query as a type called ReadOneCustomer, like this:

```
type ReadOneCustomer = SqlCommandProvider<"""
  SELECT CustomerId, Name, Birthdate
  FROM Customer
  WHERE CustomerId = @customerId
  """, CompileTimeConnectionString>
```

At compile time, the type provider will run this query on the local database and generate a type to represent it. This is similar to SqlMetal[7] or EdmGenerator[8] utilities, except no separate files are generated—the types are created in place. Later, when we use this type, we'll provide a different "production" connection from the compile-time one.

Next, just as we did with the serialization examples in the previous chapter, we should create a toDomain function. This one validates the fields in the database and then assembles them using a result expression.

That is, we will treat the database as an untrusted source of data that needs to be validated just like any other source of data, so the toDomain function will need to return a Result<Customer,_> rather than a plain Customer. Here's the code:

```
let toDomain (dbRecord:ReadOneCustomer.Record) : Result<Customer,_> =
  result {
    let! customerId =
      dbRecord.CustomerId
      |> CustomerId.create
```

---

7. https://msdn.microsoft.com/en-us/library/bb386987.aspx
8. https://msdn.microsoft.com/en-us/library/bb387165.aspx

```
  let! name =
    dbRecord.Name
    |> String50.create "Name"
  let! birthdate =
    dbRecord.Birthdate
    |> Result.bindOption Birthdate.create
  let customer = {
    CustomerId = customerId
    Name = name
    Birthdate = birthdate
    }
  return customer
  }
```

We've seen this kind of code before, in the *Serialization* chapter. There is one new addition, however. The Birthdate column in the database is nullable, so the type provider makes the dbRecord.Birthdate field an Option type. But the Birthdate.create function doesn't accept options. To fix this, we'll create a little helper function called bindOption that allows a "switch" function to work on options.

```
let bindOption f xOpt =
  match xOpt with
  | Some x -> f x |> Result.map Some
  | None -> Ok None
```

Writing a custom toDomain function like this and working with all the Results is a bit complicated, but once written, we can be sure that we'll never have unhandled errors.

On the other hand, if we're very confident that the database will never contain bad data and we're willing to panic if it does, then we can throw exceptions for invalid data instead. In that case, we can change the code to use a panicOn-Error helper function (that converts error Results into exceptions), which in turn means that the output of the toDomain function is a plain Customer without being wrapped in a Result. The code looks like this:

```
let toDomain (dbRecord:ReadOneCustomer.Record) : Customer =

  let customerId =
    dbRecord.CustomerId
    |> CustomerId.create
    |> panicOnError "CustomerId"

  let name =
    dbRecord.Name
    |> String50.create "Name"
    |> panicOnError "Name"

  let birthdate =
    dbRecord.Birthdate
```

```
|> Result.bindOption Birthdate.create
|> panicOnError "Birthdate"

// return the customer
{CustomerId = customerId; Name = name; Birthdate = birthdate}
```

where the panicOnError helper function looks something like this:

```
exception DatabaseError of string

let panicOnError columnName result =
  match result with
  | Ok x -> x
  | Error err ->
    let msg = sprintf "%s: %A" columnName err
    raise (DatabaseError msg)
```

Either way, once we have a toDomain function, we can now write the code that reads the database and returns the results as a domain type. For example, here's a readOneCustomer function that performs the ReadOneCustomer query and then converts it into a domain type.

```
type DbReadError =
  | InvalidRecord of string
  | MissingRecord of string

let readOneCustomer (productionConnection:SqlConnection) (CustomerId customerId) =
  // create the command by instantiating the type we defined earlier
  use cmd = new ReadOneCustomer(productionConnection)

  // execute the command
  let records = cmd.Execute(customerId = customerId) |> Seq.toList

  // handle the possible cases
  match records with
  // none found
  | [] ->
    let msg = sprintf "Not found. CustomerId=%A" customerId
    Error (MissingRecord msg)  // return a Result

  // exactly one found
  | [dbCustomer] ->
    dbCustomer
    |> toDomain
    |> Result.mapError InvalidRecord

  // more than one found?
  | _ ->
    let msg = sprintf "Multiple records found for CustomerId=%A" customerId
    raise (DatabaseError msg)
```

First, note that we are now explicitly passing in a SqlConnection to use as the "production" connection.

Next, we have three possible cases to handle: no record found, exactly one record found, and more than one record found. We need to decide which cases should be handled as part of the domain and which should never happen (and can be handled as a panic). In this case, we'll say that a missing record is possible and will be treated as a Result.Error, while more than one record will be treated as a panic.

Handling these various cases seems like a lot of work, but the benefit is that you are explicitly making decisions about the possible errors (and this is documented in the code) rather than assuming that everything works and then getting a NullReferenceException somewhere down the line.

And of course, we can make this code cleaner by following the "parameterize all the things" principle to make a general function, convertSingleDbRecord say, where the table name, ID, records, and toDomain converter are all passed in as parameters:

```
let convertSingleDbRecord tableName idValue records toDomain =
  match records with
  // none found
  | [] ->
    let msg = sprintf "Not found. Table=%s Id=%A" tableName idValue
    Error msg  // return a Result

  // exactly one found
  | [dbRecord] ->
    dbRecord
    |> toDomain
    |> Ok   // return a Result

  // more than one found?
  | _ ->
    let msg = sprintf "Multiple records found. Table=%s Id=%A" tableName idValue
    raise (DatabaseError msg)
```

With this generic helper function, the code can be reduced to a few lines:

```
let readOneCustomer (productionConnection:SqlConnection) (CustomerId customerId) =
  use cmd = new ReadOneCustomer(productionConnection)
  let tableName = "Customer"

  let records = cmd.Execute(customerId = customerId) |> Seq.toList
  convertSingleDbRecord tableName customerId records toDomain
```

Reading Choice Types from a Relational Database

We can read choice types the same way, although it's a bit more complicated. Let's say that we're using the one-table approach to store ContactInfo records and we want to read a single ContactInfo using a ContactId. Just as before, we define our query as a type, like this:

```
type ReadOneContact = SqlCommandProvider<"""
  SELECT ContactId,IsEmail,IsPhone,EmailAddress,PhoneNumber
  FROM ContactInfo
  WHERE ContactId = @contactId
  """, CompileTimeConnectionString>
```

Next, we create a toDomain function. This one checks the flag in the database (IsEmail) to see which case of ContactInfo to create and then assembles the data for each case using child result expressions (yay for composability!).

```
let toDomain (dbRecord:ReadOneContact.Record) : Result<Contact,_> =
  result {
    let! contactId =
      dbRecord.ContactId
      |> ContactId.create

    let! contactInfo =
      if dbRecord.IsEmail then
        result {
          // get the primitive string which should not be NULL
          let! emailAddressString =
            dbRecord.EmailAddress
            |> Result.ofOption "Email expected to be non null"
          // create the EmailAddress simple type
          let! emailAddress =
            emailAddressString |> EmailAddress.create
          // lift to the Email case of Contact Info
          return (Email emailAddress)
          }
      else
        result {
          // get the primitive string which should not be NULL
          let! phoneNumberString =
            dbRecord.PhoneNumber
            |> Result.ofOption "PhoneNumber expected to be non null"
          // create the PhoneNumber simple type
          let! phoneNumber =
            phoneNumberString |> PhoneNumber.create
          // lift to the PhoneNumber case of Contact Info
          return (Phone phoneNumber)
          }

    let contact = {
      ContactId = contactId
      Info = contactInfo
      }
    return contact
    }
```

You can see that in the Email case, for example, the EmailAddress column in the database is nullable, so the dbRecord.EmailAddress created by the type provider is an Option type. So first we must use Result.ofOption to convert the Option into a Result (in case it's missing), then create the EmailAddress type, and then lift that to the Email case of ContactInfo.

It's even more complicated than the earlier Customer example, but again, we have a lot of confidence that we'll never have an unexpected error.

By the way, if you're wondering what the code for the Result.ofOption function looks like, here it is:

```
module Result =
  /// Convert an Option into a Result
  let ofOption errorValue opt =
    match opt with
    | Some v -> Ok v
    | None -> Error errorValue
```

As before, once we have a toDomain function, we can use it in conjunction with the convertSingleDbRecord helper function we created earlier.

```
let readOneContact (productionConnection:SqlConnection) (ContactId contactId) =
  use cmd = new ReadOneContact(productionConnection)
  let tableName = "ContactInfo"

  let records = cmd.Execute(contactId = contactId) |> Seq.toList
  convertSingleDbRecord tableName contactId records toDomain
```

You can see that creating the toDomain function is the hard part. Once that's done, the actual database access code is relatively simple.

You might be thinking: Isn't this all a lot of work? Can't we just use something like Entity Framework or NHibernate that will do all this mapping automatically? The answer is no, not if you want to ensure the integrity of your domain. ORMs like those mentioned cannot validate email addresses and order quantities, deal with nested choice types, and so on. Yes, it's tedious to write this kind of database code, but the process is mechanical and straightforward and isn't the hardest part of writing an application!

Writing to a Relational Database

Writing to a relational database follows the same pattern as reading: we convert our domain object to a DTO and then execute an insert or update command.

The simplest way to do database inserts is to let the SQL type provider generate a mutable type that represents the structure of a table, and then we just set the fields of that type.

Here's a demonstration. First, we use the type provider to set up types for all the tables:

```
type Db = SqlProgrammabilityProvider<CompileTimeConnectionString>
```

And now we can define a writeContact function that takes a Contact and sets all the fields in the corresponding Contact from the database:

```
let writeContact (productionConnection:SqlConnection) (contact:Contact) =

  // extract the primitive data from the domain object
  let contactId = contact.ContactId |> ContactId.value
  let isEmail,isPhone,emailAddressOpt,phoneNumberOpt =
    match contact.Info with
    | Email emailAddress->
      let emailAddressString = emailAddress |> EmailAddress.value
      true,false,Some emailAddressString,None
    | Phone phoneNumber ->
      let phoneNumberString = phoneNumber |> PhoneNumber.value
      false,true,None,Some phoneNumberString

  // create a new row
  let contactInfoTable = new Db.dbo.Tables.ContactInfo()
  let newRow = contactInfoTable.NewRow()
  newRow.ContactId <- contactId
  newRow.IsEmail <- isEmail
  newRow.IsPhone <- isPhone
  // use optional types to map to NULL in the database
  newRow.EmailAddress <- emailAddressOpt
  newRow.PhoneNumber <- phoneNumberOpt

  // add to table
  contactInfoTable.Rows.Add newRow

  // push changes to the database
  let recordsAffected = contactInfoTable.Update(productionConnection)
  recordsAffected
```

An alternative approach with more control is to use handwritten SQL statements. For example, to insert a new Contact, we first define a type representing a SQL INSERT statement:

```
type InsertContact = SqlCommandProvider<"""
  INSERT INTO ContactInfo
  VALUES (@ContactId,@IsEmail,@IsPhone,@EmailAddress,@PhoneNumber)
  """, CompileTimeConnectionString>
```

And now we can define a writeContact function that takes a Contact, extracts the primitives from the choice type, and then executes the command.

```
let writeContact (productionConnection:SqlConnection) (contact:Contact) =
  // extract the primitive data from the domain object
  let contactId = contact.ContactId |> ContactId.value
  let isEmail,isPhone,emailAddress,phoneNumber =
    match contact.Info with
    | Email emailAddress->
      let emailAddressString = emailAddress |> EmailAddress.value
      true,false,emailAddressString,null
    | Phone phoneNumber ->
      let phoneNumberString = phoneNumber |> PhoneNumber.value
      false,true,null,phoneNumberString

  // write to the DB
  use cmd = new InsertContact(productionConnection)
  cmd.Execute(contactId,isEmail,isPhone,emailAddress,phoneNumber)
```

Transactions

All the code so far has been of the form "one aggregate = one transaction." But in many situations, we have a number of things that need to be saved together atomically—all or nothing.

Some data stores support transactions as part of their API. Multiple calls to the service can be enlisted in the same transaction, like this:

```
let connection = new SqlConnection()
let transaction = connection.BeginTransaction()

// do two separate calls to the database
// in the same transaction
markAsFullyPaid connection invoiceId
markPaymentCompleted connection paymentId

// completed
transaction.Commit()
```

Some data stores only support transactions as long as everything is done in a single connection. In practice, that means that you'll have to combine multiple operations in a single call, like this:

```
let connection = new SqlConnection()
// do one call to service
markAsFullyPaidAndPaymentCompleted connection paymentId invoiceId
```

Sometimes, though, you are communicating with different services, and there's no way to have a cross-service transaction.

Gregor Hohpe's article "Starbucks Does Not Use Two-Phase Commit," mentioned on page 114 points out that businesses generally do not require transactions across different systems because the overhead and coordination cost is too heavy and slow. Instead, we assume that most of the time things go well, and then we use reconciliation processes to detect inconsistency and compensating transactions to correct errors.

For example, here's a simple demonstration of a compensating transaction to roll back a database update:

```
// do first call
markAsFullyPaid connection invoiceId
// do second call
let result = markPaymentCompleted connection paymentId

// if second call fails, do compensating transaction
match result with
| Error err ->
  // compensate for error
  unmarkAsFullyPaid connection invoiceId
| Ok _ -> ...
```

Wrapping Up

In this chapter, we started by looking at some high-level principles of persistence: separating queries from commands, keeping the I/O at the edges, and ensuring that bounded contexts own their own data store. We then dived down into the low-level mechanics of interacting with a relational database.

And that brings us to the end of the third part of this book. We've now got all the tools we need to design and create a full implementation of a bounded context: the pure types and functions inside the domain (*Implementation: Composing a Pipeline*), the error handling (*Implementation: Working with Errors*), the serialization at the edges (*Serialization*), and, in this chapter, the database for storing state.

But we're not quite done yet. As the military saying goes, "No plan survives contact with the enemy." So what happens when we learn new things and need to change the design? That will be the topic of the next and final chapter.

CHAPTER 13

Evolving a Design and Keeping It Clean

We have completed our domain model and implementation, but we all know that that's not the end of the story. It's all too common for a domain model to start off clean and elegant; but as the requirements change, the model gets messy and the various subsystems become entangled and hard to test. So here's our final challenge: can we evolve the model without it becoming a big ball of mud?

Domain-driven design is not meant to be a static, once-only process. It is meant to be a continuous collaboration between developers, domain experts, and other stakeholders. So if the requirements change, we must always start by reevaluating the domain model first, rather than just patching the implementation.

In this chapter, we will look at a number of possible changes to the requirements and follow them through to see how they affect our understanding of the domain model first, before changing the implementation. Furthermore, we will see that the heavy use of types in our design means we can have high confidence that the code is not accidentally broken when changes are made to the model.

We'll look at four kinds of changes:

- Adding a new step to the workflow

- Changing the input to the workflow

- Changing the definition of a key domain type (the order) and seeing how that ripples through the system

- Transforming the workflow as a whole to conform with business rules

Change 1: Adding Shipping Charges

For our first requirements change, let's look at how to calculate shipping and delivery charges. Let's say that the company wants to charge customers for shipping using a special calculation. How can we integrate this new requirement?

First we'll need a function to calculate the shipping cost. Let's say that this company is based in California, so shipping to local states is one price (say $5), shipping to remote states is another price (say $10), and shipping to another country is yet another price ($20).

Here's a first pass at implementing this calculation:

```
/// Calculate the shipping cost for an order
let calculateShippingCost validatedOrder =
  let shippingAddress = validatedOrder.ShippingAddress
  if shippingAddress.Country = "US" then
    // shipping inside USA
    match shippingAddress.State with
    | "CA" | "OR" | "AZ" | "NV" ->
      5.0 //local
    | _ ->
      10.0 //remote
  else
    // shipping outside USA
    20.0
```

Unfortunately, this kind of conditional logic, with multiple branching for special conditions, is hard to understand and maintain.

Using Active Patterns to Simplify Business Logic

One solution that makes the logic more maintainable is to separate the domain-centric "categorization" from the actual pricing logic. In F#, there's a feature called *active patterns*[1] that can be used to turn conditional logic into a set of named choices that can be pattern-matched against, just as if you had explicitly defined a discriminated union type for each choice. Active patterns are a perfect fit for this kind of categorization.

To use the active pattern approach for this requirement, we first define a set of patterns to match each of our shipping categories:

```
let (|UsLocalState|UsRemoteState|International|) address =
  if address.Country = "US" then
    match address.State with
```

---

1. https://docs.microsoft.com/en-us/dotnet/fsharp/language-reference/active-patterns

```
  | "CA" | "OR" | "AZ" | "NV" ->
    UsLocalState
  | _ ->
    UsRemoteState
else
  International
```

And then, in the shipping calculation itself, we can pattern-match against these categories:

```
let calculateShippingCost validatedOrder =
  match validatedOrder.ShippingAddress with
  | UsLocalState -> 5.0
  | UsRemoteState -> 10.0
  | International -> 20.0
```

By separating the categorization from the business logic like this, the code becomes much clearer, and the names of the active pattern cases act as documentation as well.

Defining the active patterns themselves is still complicated, of course, but that code is only doing categorization, with no business logic. If the categorization logic ever changes (such as having different states in "UsLocalState"), we only need to change the active pattern, not the pricing function. We've separated the concerns nicely.

Creating a New Stage in the Workflow

Next, we need to use this shipping cost calculation in the order-placing workflow. One option is to modify the pricing stage and add the shipping cost logic to it. But we'd be changing code that works and making it more complicated, which in turn could lead to bugs. Rather than changing stable code, let's get the most out of composition and add a new stage in the workflow to do the calculation and update the PricedOrder:

```
type AddShippingInfoToOrder = PricedOrder -> PricedOrderWithShippingInfo
```

This new stage in the workflow could then be slotted in between PriceOrder and the next stage, AcknowledgeOrder.

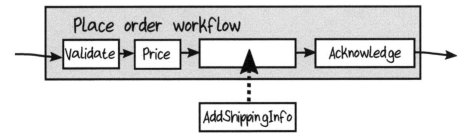

Typically, as we evolve any design, we'll discover more details that we need to keep track of. For example, the customer might want to know the shipping method (for example, FedEx or UPS) as well as the price (and even this is probably oversimplistic). So we're going to need some new types to capture this extra information:

```
type ShippingMethod =
  | PostalService
  | Fedex24
  | Fedex48
  | Ups48
type ShippingInfo = {
  ShippingMethod : ShippingMethod
  ShippingCost : Price
  }
type PricedOrderWithShippingMethod = {
  ShippingInfo : ShippingInfo
  PricedOrder : PricedOrder
  }
```

Note that we've created another order type now—PricedOrderWithShippingInfo—that contains the new shipping information. You might well think that this is overkill, and we could consider just reusing the PricedOrder type instead by adding a field for ShippingInfo. But there are some advantages to creating a whole new type:

- If the AcknowledgeOrder step is modified to expect PricedOrderWithShippingInfo as input, you cannot get the order of the stages wrong.

- If we add ShippingInfo as a field in PricedOrder, what should it be initialized to before the shipping calculation is done? Simply initializing it to a default value might be a bug waiting to happen.

One final issue: How should the shipping cost be stored in the order? Should it be a field in the header, like this?

```
type PricedOrder = {
  ...
  ShippingInfo : ShippingInfo
  OrderTotal : Price
  }
```

Or should it be a new kind of order line, like this?

```
type PricedOrderLine =
  | Product of PricedOrderProductLine
  | ShippingInfo of ShippingInfo
```

The second approach means that the order total can always be calculated from the sum of the lines, with no special logic needed to include fields from the header as well. The downside is that you could accidentally create two ShippingInfo lines by mistake, and we have to worry about printing the lines in the right order.

Let's go for storing the shipping info in the header. Now we have everything we need to complete the AddShippingInfoToOrder stage in the workflow. We just need to code up a function that follows these requirements:

- It will implement the AddShippingInfoToOrder function type defined above.

- It takes a dependency to calculate the shipping cost—the calculateShippingCost function that we designed above.

- It takes the shipping cost and adds it to the PricedOrder to make a PricedOrder-WithShippingInfo.

Because all these requirements are represented by types, it's surprisingly hard to create an incorrect implementation! Here's what it would look like:

```
let addShippingInfoToOrder calculateShippingCost : AddShippingInfoToOrder =
  fun pricedOrder ->
    // create the shipping info
    let shippingInfo = {
      ShippingMethod = ...
      ShippingCost = calculateShippingCost pricedOrder
      }
    // add it to the order
    {
    OrderId = pricedOrder.OrderId
    ...
    ShippingInfo = shippingInfo
    }
```

And it would be slotted into the top-level workflow like this:

```
// set up local versions of the pipeline stages
// using partial application to bake in the dependencies
let validateOrder unvalidatedOrder = ...
let priceOrder validatedOrder = ...
let addShippingInfo = addShippingInfoToOrder calculateShippingCost

// compose the pipeline from the new one-parameter functions
unvalidatedOrder
|> validateOrder
|> priceOrder
|> addShippingInfo
...
```

Other Reasons to Add Stages to the Pipeline

In this example, we've added a new component to the pipeline because the requirements have changed. But adding and removing components like this is a great way to add any kind of feature. As long as a stage is isolated from the other stages and conforms to the required types, you can be sure that you can add or remove it safely. Here are a few things you can do in this way:

- You can add a stage for operational transparency, making it easier to see what's going on inside the pipeline. Logging, performance metrics, auditing, and so on can all be easily added in this way.

- You can add a stage that checks for authorization, and if that fails, sends you down the failure path, skipping the rest of the pipeline.

- You can even add and remove stages dynamically in the composition root, based on configuration or context from the input.

Change 2: Adding Support for VIP Customers

Let's now look at a change that affects the overall input of the workflow. Say that the business wants to support VIP customers—customers who get special treatment, such as free shipping or a free upgrade to overnight delivery.

How should we model this?

One thing we should *not* do is model the *output* of a business rule in the domain (such as adding a "free shipping" flag to the order). Instead, we should store the input to a business rule ("the customer is a VIP") and then let the business rule work on that input. That way, if the business rules change (which they will!), we don't have to change our domain model.

We'll assume that somehow the customers' VIP status is associated with their login on the website, so we don't need to determine it ourselves in the order-taking domain. But how should we model the VIP status? Should we model it as a flag in CustomerInfo, like this?

```
type CustomerInfo = {
  ...
  IsVip : bool
  ...
  }
```

Or should we model it as one of a set of customer states, like this?

```
type CustomerStatus =
  | Normal of CustomerInfo
  | Vip of CustomerInfo
```

```
type Order = {
  ...
  CustomerStatus : CustomerStatus
  ...
  }
```

The downside of modeling this as a customer state is that there may be other customer statuses that are orthogonal to this, such as new versus returning customers, customers with loyalty cards, and so forth.

The best approach is a compromise, which is to use a choice type that represents the status along the "VIP" dimension, independent of other customer information.

```
type VipStatus =
  | Normal
  | Vip
type CustomerInfo = {
  ...
  VipStatus : VipStatus
  ...
  }
```

If we ever need other kinds of statuses, it will be easy to add them in the same way. For example:

```
type LoyaltyCardId = ...
type LoyaltyCardStatus =
  | None
  | LoyaltyCard of LoyaltyCardId
type CustomerInfo = {
  ...
  VipStatus : VipStatus
  LoyaltyCardStatus : LoyaltyCardStatus
  ...
  }
```

Adding a New Input to the Workflow

Let's assume that we're using a new VipStatus field then. As always, we'll update the domain model and then see where that leads us.

We'll first define a type for status and then add it as a field of the CustomerInfo:

```
type VipStatus = ...
type CustomerInfo = {
  ...
  VipStatus : VipStatus
  }
```

As soon as we do this, though, we get a compiler error in the code that constructs a CustomerInfo:

```
No assignment given for field 'VipStatus' of type 'CustomerInfo'
```

This demonstrates one of the nice things about F# record types: *all* fields must be provided during construction. If a new field is added, you'll get a compiler error until you provide it.

So where can we get the VipStatus from? From the UnvalidatedCustomerInfo that is the input to the workflow. And where does that come from? From the order form that the user fills in—the DTO. So we need to add a corresponding field in the UnvalidatedCustomerInfo and in the DTO as well. For both of these, though, it can be a simple string, using null to indicate a missing value.

```
module Domain =
  type UnvalidatedCustomerInfo = {
    ...
    VipStatus : string
    }
module Dto =
  type CustomerInfo = {
    ...
    VipStatus : string
    }
```

And now, finally, we can construct a ValidatedCustomerInfo using the status field from UnvalidatedCustomerInfo, along with all the other fields:

```
let validateCustomerInfo unvalidatedCustomerInfo =
  result {
    ...

    // new field
    let! vipStatus =
      VipStatus.create unvalidatedCustomerInfo.VipStatus

    let customerInfo : CustomerInfo = {
      ...
      VipStatus = vipStatus
      }
    return customerInfo
  }
```

Adding the Free Shipping Rule to the Workflow

One of the requirements was to give VIPs free shipping, so we need to add this logic to the workflow somewhere. Again, rather than modifying stable code, we'll just add another segment to the pipeline as shown in figure on page 273.

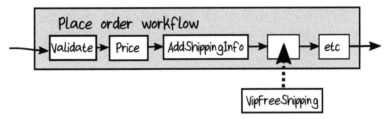

As before, we start by defining a type that represents the new segment:

```
type FreeVipShipping =
  PricedOrderWithShippingMethod -> PricedOrderWithShippingMethod
```

And then we create the workflow segment that implements that type and insert it into the workflow. There's no need to show the code—I think you know how this works by now.

Change 3: Adding Support for Promotion Codes

Let's move on to a different scenario: the sales team wants to do some promotions, and they want to offer a promotion code that can be provided when placing an order to get discounted prices.

After discussion with the sales team, we have these new requirements:

- When placing an order, the customer can provide an optional promotion code.
- If the code is present, certain products will be given different (lower) prices.
- The order should show that a promotional discount was applied.

Some of these changes are easy, but the last requirement, which looks so simple, will create surprisingly powerful ripples throughout the domain.

Adding a Promotion Code to the Domain Model

Let's start with the new promotion code field. As always, we'll update the domain model and see where that leads us.

We'll start by defining a type for the promotion code and then adding it as an optional field of the order:

```
type PromotionCode = PromotionCode of string

type ValidatedOrder = {
  ...
  PromotionCode : PromotionCode option
  }
```

There's no special validation for PromotionCode, but it's a good idea to use a type rather than just a string so that we don't mix it up with other strings in the domain.

As with the VipStatus field earlier, adding a new field will trigger a series of compiler errors. In this case, we'll need to add a corresponding field to UnvalidatedOrder and the DTO as well. Note that even though the field in ValidatedOrder is explicitly marked as optional, we can use a non-optional string in the DTO, with the assumption that null will indicate a missing value.

```
type OrderDto = {
  ...
  PromotionCode : string
  }
type UnvalidatedOrder = {
  ...
  PromotionCode : string
  }
```

Changing the Pricing Logic

If the promotion code is present, we need to do one kind of pricing calculation, and if it's absent, we need to do another. How can we model this in the domain?

Well, we've already modeled the pricing calculation using a function type:

```
type GetProductPrice = ProductCode -> Price
```

But we now need to provide a different GetProductPrice function based on the promotion code. Here's the logic:

- If the promotion code is present, provide a GetProductPrice function that returns the prices associated with that promotion code.

- If the promotion code is not present, provide the original GetProductPrice function.

What we need then is a "factory" function that, given an optional promotion code, returns the appropriate GetProductPrice function, like this:

```
type GetPricingFunction = PromotionCode option -> GetProductPrice
```

Passing in an option like this seems a bit unclear though, so perhaps we should create a new type that's more self-documenting?

```
type PricingMethod =
  | Standard
  | Promotion of PromotionCode
```

Logically, this is equivalent to an option, but it's a bit clearer when used in the domain model. The ValidatedOrder type now looks like this:

```
type ValidatedOrder = {
  ... //as before
  PricingMethod : PricingMethod
  }
```

And the GetPricingFunction looks like this:

```
type GetPricingFunction = PricingMethod -> GetProductPrice
```

One more thing has to change. In the original design, we injected a GetProduct-Price function into the pricing stage of the workflow. Now we need to inject the GetPricingFunction "factory" function into the pricing step instead.

```
type PriceOrder =
  GetPricingFunction  // new dependency
    -> ValidatedOrder // input
    -> PricedOrder    // output
```

Once you've made these changes to the domain model, you'll get a bunch of compilation errors in the implementation again. However, these compiler errors are your friends! They'll guide you in what you need to do to fix the implementation. It's a tedious but straightforward process. Once you are done, though, and the implementation compiles again, you can be very confident that everything works without error.

Implementing the **GetPricingFunction**

Let's have a quick look at how the GetPricingFunction might be implemented. We'll assume that each promotion code is associated with a dictionary of (Product-Code,Price) pairs. In that case the implementation might be something like this:

```
type GetStandardPriceTable =
  // no input -> return standard prices
  unit -> IDictionary<ProductCode,Price>

type GetPromotionPriceTable =
  // promo input -> return prices for promo
  PromotionCode -> IDictionary<ProductCode,Price>

let getPricingFunction
  (standardPrices:GetStandardPriceTable)
  (promoPrices:GetPromotionPriceTable)
  : GetPricingFunction =

  // the original pricing function
  let getStandardPrice : GetProductPrice =
    // cache the standard prices
    let standardPrices = standardPrices()
    // return the lookup function
    fun productCode -> standardPrices.[productCode]
```

```
// the promotional pricing function
let getPromotionPrice promotionCode : GetProductPrice =
  // cache the promotional prices
  let promotionPrices = promoPrices promotionCode
  // return the lookup function
  fun productCode ->
    match promotionPrices.TryGetValue productCode with
    // found in promotional prices
    | true,price -> price
    // not found in promotional prices
    // so use standard price
    | false, _ -> getStandardPrice productCode

// return a function that conforms to GetPricingFunction
fun pricingMethod ->
  match pricingMethod with
  | Standard ->
    getStandardPrice
  | Promotion promotionCode ->
    getPromotionPrice promotionCode
```

We won't go into a detailed explanation of this code—it's pretty self-explanatory. But you can see that we're using many of our favorite functional programming techniques: types to ensure that the code is correct (GetProductPrice) and to make the domain logic clear (the choices in PricingMethod), functions as parameters (promoPrices of type GetPromotionPriceTable), and functions as output (the return value of type GetPricingFunction).

Documenting the Discount in an Order Line

One of the requirements was, "The order should show that a promotional discount was applied." How should we do that?

In order to answer that, we need to know whether the downstream systems need to know about the promotion. If not, the simplest option is just to add a "comment line" to the list of order lines. We don't need to have any special detail in the comment, just some text describing the discount.

This means we need to change the definition of an "order line." So far, we've been assuming that the lines of an order always reference particular products. But now we need to say that there's a new kind of order line that does *not* reference a product. That's a change to our domain model. Let's change the PricedOrderLine definition to reflect this by making it a choice type:

```
type CommentLine = CommentLine of string

type PricedOrderLine =
  | Product of PricedOrderProductLine
  | Comment of CommentLine
```

There's no need for any special validation for the CommentLine type, except perhaps to ensure that the number of characters is not too large.

If we *did* need to track more detail than just a comment, we could have defined a DiscountApplied case instead, containing data such as the amount of the discount, and so on. The advantage of using a Comment is that the shipping context and the billing context need not know anything about promotions at all, so if the promotion logic changes, they aren't affected.

Now, because we have changed PricedOrderLine into a choice type, we also need a new PricedOrderProductLine type that contains the details of lines that are product-oriented, such as price, quantity, and so forth.

Finally, it's clear that the ValidatedOrderLine and PricedOrderLine have now diverged in their design. This demonstrates that keeping the types separate during the domain modeling is a good idea—you never know when this kind of change might be needed; and if the same type had been used for both, we wouldn't be able to keep the model clean.

To add the comment line, the priceOrder function needs to be changed:

- First, get the pricing function from the GetPricingFunction "factory."
- Next, for each line, set the price using that pricing function.
- Finally, if the promotion code was used, add a special comment line to the list of lines.

```
let toPricedOrderLine orderLine = ...

let priceOrder : PriceOrder =
  fun getPricingFunction validatedOrder ->
    // get the pricing function from the getPricingFunction "factory"
    let getProductPrice = getPricingFunction validatedOrder.PricingMethod

    // set the price for each line
    let productOrderLines =
      validatedOrder.OrderLines
      |> List.map (toPricedOrderLine getProductPrice)

    // add the special comment line if needed
    let orderLines =
        match validatedOrder.PricingMethod with
        | Standard ->
          // unchanged
          productOrderLines
        | Promotion promotion ->
          let promoCode = promotion|> PromotionCode.value
          let commentLine =
            sprintf "Applied promotion %s" promoCode
            |> CommentLine.create
            |> Comment // lift to PricedOrderLine
```

```
        List.append productOrderLines [commentLine]
    // return the new order
    {
        ...
        OrderLines = orderLines
    }
```

More Complicated Pricing Schemes

In many cases, pricing schemes can become even more complicated, with multiple sales promotions, vouchers, loyalty schemes, and so on. If this happens, it's probably a sign that pricing needs to become a separate bounded context. Remember the discussion on getting the bounded contexts right on page 18? These are the clues:

- A distinct vocabulary (with jargon such as "BOGOF"[2])

- A special team that manages prices

- Data specific to this context only (such as previous purchases and usages of vouchers)

- Ability to be autonomous

If pricing is an important part of the business, then it's just as important that it can evolve independently and stay decoupled from the order-taking, shipping, and billing domains. Here's a diagram showing pricing as a distinct bounded context closely related to order-taking but now logically separate:

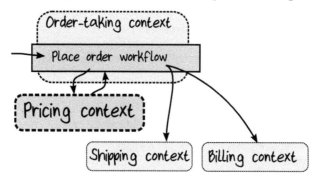

Evolving the Contract Between Bounded Contexts

We've introduced a new kind of line, CommentLine, which the shipping system will need to know about to print the order correctly. That means that the OrderPlaced event that's sent downstream will need to be changed as well.

---

2. https://en.wikipedia.org/wiki/Buy_one,_get_one_free

And now we've just broken the contract between the order-taking context and the shipping context.

Is this sustainable? That is, every time we add a new concept to the order-taking domain, do we really have to change the events and the DTOs and break the contract? Surely not. But as it stands, we've introduced coupling between bounded contexts, which is definitely not what we want.

As discussed earlier in *Contracts Between Bounded Contexts*, on page 48, a good solution to this issue is to use "consumer-driven" contracts. In this approach, the (downstream) consumer decides what's needed from the (upstream) producer, and the producer must provide that data and nothing more.

In this situation, let's think about what the shipping context *really* needs. It doesn't need the prices, it doesn't need the shipping cost, it doesn't need the discount information. All it needs is the list of products, the quantity for each one, and the shipping address. So let's design a type to represent this:

```
type ShippableOrderLine = {
  ProductCode : ProductCode
  Quantity : float
  }

type ShippableOrderPlaced = {
  OrderId : OrderId
  ShippingAddress : Address
  ShipmentLines : ShippableOrderLine list
  }
```

This is much simpler than the original OrderPlaced event type. And because it has less data, it's less likely to change when the order-taking domain changes.

With this new event type at hand, we should redesign the PlaceOrderEvent output of the order-taking workflow. We now have the following:

- An AcknowledgmentSent to log and to send to the customer service context
- A ShippableOrderPlaced to send to the shipping context
- A BillableOrderPlaced to send to the billing context

```
type PlaceOrderEvent =
  | ShippableOrderPlaced of ShippableOrderPlaced
  | BillableOrderPlaced of BillableOrderPlaced
  | AcknowledgmentSent  of OrderAcknowledgmentSent
```

Printing the Order

What about printing the order, though? When the order is packed and ready for shipping, a copy of the original order is printed out and placed in the package. How can the shipping department print out the order when we have deliberately reduced the information available to it?

The key to this is being aware that the shipping department just needs something it can print, but it doesn't actually care about the content. In other words, the order-placing context can provide the shipping department with a PDF or an HTML document and then have it print that.

This document could be provided as a binary blob in the ShippableOrderPlaced type above, or we could dump a PDF into shared storage and let the shipping context access it via the OrderId.

Change 4: Adding a Business Hours Constraint

So far, we've looked at adding new data and behavior. Now let's look at adding new constraints on how the workflow is used. Here's our new business rule:

- Orders can only be taken during business hours.

For whatever reason, the business has decided that the system should only be available during business hours (perhaps under the assumption that people accessing the site at four o'clock in the morning are probably not real customers). So how can we implement this?

We can use a trick that we've seen before, which is to create an "adapter" function. In this case we'll create a "business-hours-only" function that accepts any function as input and outputs a "wrapper" or "proxy" function that has exactly the same behavior but raises an error if called out of hours.

This transformed function will have exactly the same inputs and outputs as the original one and therefore can be used anywhere that the original one was used. Here's the code for the transformer function:

```
/// Determine the business hours
let isBusinessHour hour =
  hour >= 9 && hour <= 17

/// tranformer
let businessHoursOnly getHour onError onSuccess =
  let hour = getHour()
  if isBusinessHour hour then
    onSuccess()
  else
    onError()
```

You can see that this is completely generic code:

- The onError parameter is used to handle the case when we are outside of business hours.

- The onSuccess parameter is used to handle the case when we are inside business hours.

- The hour of day is determined by the getHour function parameter rather than being hard-coded. This allows us to inject a dummy function for easy unit testing.

In our case, the original workflow takes an UnvalidatedOrder and returns a Result where the error type is PlaceOrderError. Therefore the onError we pass in must also return a Result of the same type, so let's add an OutsideBusinessHours case to the PlaceOrderError type:

```
type PlaceOrderError =
  | Validation of ValidationError
  ...
  | OutsideBusinessHours  //new!
```

We now have everything we need to transform the original order-placing workflow:

```
let placeOrder unvalidatedOrder =
    ...

let placeOrderInBusinessHours unvalidatedOrder =
  let onError() =
    Error OutsideBusinessHours
  let onSuccess() =
    placeOrder unvalidatedOrder
  let getHour() = DateTime.Now.Hour
  businessHoursOnly getHour onError onSuccess
```

Finally, in the top level of our applications (the composition root), we replace the original placeOrder function with the new placeOrderInBusinessHours function, which is completely compatible, since it has the same inputs and outputs.

Dealing with Additional Requirements Changes

Obviously, we're just scratching the surface with the kinds of changes that could be asked for. Here are some others to think about and how they might be addressed:

- *VIPs should only get free postage for shipping inside the USA.* To support this, we just need to change the code in the freeVipShipping segment of the workflow. It should be clear by now that having lots of small segments like this really helps to keep complexity under control.

- *Customers should be able to split orders into multiple shipments.* In this case, there needs to be some logic for doing this (a new segment in the workflow). From the domain-modeling point of view, the only change is that the output of the workflow contains a *list* of shipments to send to the shipping context, rather than a single one.

- *The customer should be able to see the status of an order: whether it has shipped yet, whether it is paid in full, and so on.* This is a tricky one, because the knowledge of the state of the order is split among multiple contexts: the shipping context knows the shipping status, the billing context knows the billing status, and so on. The best approach would probably be to create a *new* context (perhaps called "Customer Service") that deals with customer questions like this. It can subscribe to events from the other contexts and update the state accordingly. Any queries about the status would then go directly to this context.

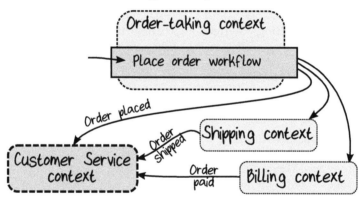

Wrapping Up

In this chapter, as we evolved the design in response to four requirements changes, we saw the benefits of type-driven domain modeling and the compositional approach to creating workflows from functions.

The type-driven design meant that when we added a new field to a domain type (such as adding VipStatus to ValidatedOrder), we immediately got compiler errors that forced us to specify where the data came from. That in turn guided us to modify other types and so on until all the compiler errors went away.

Similarly, when we changed one of the dependencies in the promotion code example (from `GetProductPrice` to the more complex `GetPricingFunction`), that also triggered a number of compiler errors. But after the code has been fixed up and the compiler errors have gone away, we can be quite confident that our implementation is working correctly again.

We also saw the advantages of using function composition to build our workflow. We could easily add new segments to the workflow, leaving the other segments untouched. And of course, no changes to existing code means less chance of introducing a bug.

Finally, in the "business hours" example, we saw that, thanks to "function types as interfaces," we could transform whole functions in powerful ways while preserving plug-in compatibility with existing code.

Wrapping Up the Book

We've covered a lot of ground in this book, from ruminations on high-level abstractions like bounded contexts all the way down to the minutia of serialization formats.

We haven't had a chance to cover many important topics: web services, security, and operational transparency, to name a few. However, in the process of working through this book, I hope you've developed some techniques and skills that you can apply to any design problem.

Let's highlight some of the most important practices that we've talked about:

- We should aim to develop a deep, shared understanding of a domain before starting the low-level design. We picked up some discovery techniques (Event Storming) and communication techniques (the use of a Ubiquitous Language) that can help immensely during this process.

- We should ensure that our solution space is partitioned into autonomous, decoupled bounded contexts that can evolve independently, and that each workflow should be represented as a standalone pipeline with explicit inputs and outputs.

- Before writing any code, we should try to capture the requirements using a type-based notation to capture both the nouns *and* the verbs of the domain. As we saw, the nouns can almost always be represented by an algebraic type system and the verbs by functions.

- We should try to capture important constraints and business rules in the type system wherever possible. Our motto is "make illegal states unrepresentable."

- We should also try to design our functions to be "pure" and "total," so that every possible input has an explicit documented output (no exceptions) and all behavior is entirely predictable (no hidden dependencies).

Having gone through this process with the order-placing workflow, we ended up with a detailed set of types that we used to guide and constrain the implementation.

Then, during the implementation process, we repeatedly used important functional programming techniques like these:

- Building a complete workflow using only composition of smaller functions

- Parameterizing functions whenever there's a dependency, or even just a decision that we want to put off

- Using partial application to bake dependencies into a function, allowing the function to be composed more easily and to hide unneeded implementation details

- Creating special functions that could transform other functions into various shapes. In particular we learned about bind—the "adapter block" that we used to convert error-returning functions into two-track functions that could easily be composed

- Solving type-mismatch problems by "lifting" disparate types into a common type

In this book I aimed to convince you that functional programming and domain modeling are a great match. I hope that I have succeeded and that you now have the confidence to go out and use what you have learned for your own applications.

Index

SYMBOLS

:: ("cons"), 72

A

ACL (Anti-Corruption Layer), 48

active patterns, 266

adapter functions
  adding workflow constraints with, 280
  changing output with, 190
  converting switches to two-track, 198–200
  creating, 170–172
  handling dead-end functions, 208
  handling exceptions, 205–208

address verification examples, 108–112, 128–130, 165–168

aggregates, 94–98, 101, 112–117

agile development, 5

algebraic types, 59, 66

AND types, 64, 66, 79, 83, see also product types

anonymous functions, 150

Anti-Corruption Layer (ACL), 48

applications, built from functions, 157

applicatives, 217–218

architecture, 43–44, 53

array type, 72

Async type, 87, 134–135

asynchronous processes, 87

AsyncResult type, 218

atomicity, 113

autonomy, 18, 34, 44, 134

B

B2B companies, 27

Behavior-Driven Development, 6

BI (Business Intelligence), 249

bias, design, 29–31

bind
  function, 198–200, 203, 209, 218
  monad, 217

Booleans
  as bad design choice, 132
  replacing flags, 122–124

boundaries, 18

bounded contexts
  autonomy of, 44
  code structure within, 52
  combining multiple commands, 121
  communication between, 45–47
  contracts between, 48–50
  creating, 18
  data storage, 248
  definition, 22
  getting data from outside, 239–244
  kinds of relationships, 48
  mapping, 19
  namespaces as, 98
  overview, 16–18, 24
  preventing scope creep, 18
  ranking, 20
  workflows within, 50

Brandolini, Alberto, 8

Brown, Simon, 43

Business Intelligence (BI), 249

business processes, 12

business rules, 108–112, 270

C

"C4" approach, 43

choice types, 64, 66
  converting events to, 176
  discriminated unions, 65
  modeling domain errors, 194
  modeling in relational databases, 252
  modeling with, 84, 101
  reading from relational databases, 258–260
  serialization of, 232
  serializing with maps, 235–238
  single-case unions, 66, 79–80, 230
  translating to DTOs, 232–235

class-driven design, avoiding, 30

classes, 43

Clean Architecture, 54

code, for this book, xi

code, within bounded contexts, 52

collection types, 72
collections, 82
    serialization of, 230
Command type, 121
command-query responsibility segregation (CQRS), 246–248
command-query separation (CQS), 244–246
commands
    combining multiple in one type, 121
    definition, 22
    documenting, 13
    as input, 120
CompilationRepresentation, 105, 225
components, 43
computation expressions
    composing, 211
    creating, 209–211
    lists, 213–216
Conformist relationship, 48
consistency
    between aggregates, 116
    between contexts, 114
    definition, 104
    multiple aggregates, 117
    overview, 112
    within aggregates, 113
constrained types, 162
constraints, 36, 81, 104–106, 280
Consumer-Driven Contract relationship, 48
"cons" operator, 72
containers, 43
Context Maps, definition, 22
context maps, 19, 49
with (copying records), 94
coupling, 48–50
CQRS (command-query responsibility segregation), 246–248
CQS (command-query separation), 244–246
cubes, 250
currying, 152
Customer/Supplier relationship, 48

D

data
    accessing outside pure functions, 239–244
    bounded context storage, 248
    consistency, 103
    CQRS, 246–248
    CQS, 244–246
    document databases, 250
    integrity, 103
    modeling null, 69
    multiple domains, 249
    relational databases, 251–262
    static, 7
    transferring between bounded contexts, 46
    transforming, 7
Data Transfer Objects (DTOs), 46, 222–223, 229–238, 250
database-driven design, avoiding, 29
DDD (domain-driven design), see domain-driven design (DDD)
dead-end functions, 208
decoupling, 45
dependencies
    composition problems, 162
    definition, 130
    "factory" functions, 274
    modeling with types, 128
    partial applications, 190
    passing, 180–183
    placement of, 130
    testing, 185–187
    too many, 183
    visibility of, 137
dependency injection, 180
dependency injections, 162
deserialization
    choice types, 234, 236
    collections, 231
    connecting to workflow, 223
    design types for, 222
    enumerations, 232
    error handling, 227
    generic types, 238
    setting up, 225
    wrapping JSON serializers, 226
development team, definition, 4

discriminated unions, serialization of, 231, see also choice types
document databases, 250
domain, documenting, 31–33
domain concepts, see ubiquitous language
domain events
    converting to choice types, 176
    creating, 175
    definition, 7, 22
    discovering, 7–11, 23
    documenting commands, 13
    extending to edges, 11
    within bounded contexts, 52
domain experts
    definition, 4, 15
    interviewing, 25–29, 33–35
    listening to, 18, 143
domain models
    aggregates, 94–98
    best practices, 283
    building, 67–69
    constraints, 36
    definition, 22
    errors, 70
    evolving, 265–283
    importance of shared, 4–6
    keeping types separate, 277
    lists, 72
    no value, 71
    objects, 46, 120, 222, 250
    optional values, 69
    order-placing example, 77, 98
    patterns, 78
    persistence, 239–263
    process overview, 284
    read-only, 11
    serialization, 221–238
    text-based languages, 31–33
    using algebraic type, 82–85
    using states, 124–128
domain types, changing, 229
domain-driven design (DDD)
    approaching, 4
    benefits, 6
    best practices, 283

not class-driven design, 30
compared to agile, 5
creating Ubiquitous Language, 21, 24
not database-driven, 29
executable documentation, 142
focusing on Domain Events, 7–14, 23
guidelines, 6
overview, 3, 22
partitioning domain into subdomains, 14–16, 23
process overview, 284
relationships between bounded contexts, 48
uses for, 3
using bounded contexts, 16–21, 24
domains
bounded contexts, 16–21
definition, 15, 22
determining inputs/outputs, 28
documenting, 36–41
non-functional requirements, 27
partitioning, 23
subdomains, 14–16
understanding, 25–29, 33–35
DTOs (Data Transfer Objects), 46, 222–223, 229–238, 250

E
edge cases, 126
effects
async, 218
composition problems, 162
documenting, 134–136
errors, 191
modeling, 87
email address verification example, 108–110
Entities
aggregates, 94–98
definition, 88–89, 98
identifiers, 89–91
implementing equality, 91–93
enumerations, serialization of, 231
equality, 89, 91–93
errors
classifying, 192

computation expressions, 209–216
dead-end functions, 208
documenting, 70
documenting effects, 134–136
domain, 192–194
exceptions, 205–208
exceptions for, 173, 191
functions for, 218
handling, 87
making explicit, 191
modeling in types, 194
overview, 191
serialization pipelines, 226
two-track handling, 196–205
ugly code, 195
unhandled edge cases, 126
event sourcing, 248
Event Storming, 7, 10–11, 23
Event Storming (Brandolini), 8
events, see domain events
exceptions, 173, 191, 195, 205–208
exn, 83
Expecto, 186

F
F#
composition of types, 64–66
function composition, 156
functions as things, 150
implementing state machines, 127–128
lists, 214
resources, xi–xii
serializers for, 229
SQL type providers, 254–258
testing tools, 186
types in, 61–63
working with types, 66–67
"factory" functions, 274
feedback loops, 5
files, organizing types, 73
flatMap function, 198–200
FsCheck, 186
FsUnit, 186
function signatures, 60

functional applications, 157
functional programming
benefits, 186
vs. object-oriented programming, 147–148
transformers, 171
types, 61–63
functions
adapters, 170–172, 190, 198–200, 205–208, 280
anonymous, 150
chaining Result-generating, 196–205
composition of, 156–160
composition problems, 162
currying, 152
dead-end functions, 208
defining function types, 69
documenting effects in signature, 87
error-handling, 218
"factory", 274
generic types, 61
I/O sandwich, 242
as input, 151
modeling workflows, 85–88
monads, 196, 217–218
as output, 151
overview, 59
partial application, 153
purity, 239–242
as things, 149–151
total, 154–155, 192
transformers, 171
type signatures for, 60
use of, 148
using types to guide implementation, 163–165
as values, 63

G
garbage in, garbage out, 3
generics, 61, 121
serialization of, 238

H
Hexagonal Architecture, 54
Hohpe, Gregor, 115, 262

I
I/O (input/output), see input/output (I/O)
identity, 88–94
immutability, 93–94

infrastructure errors, 192, 194
input/output (I/O)
    adding input to work-flows, 271
    connecting, 136, 158, 162
    at edges of workflow, 239–242
    external infrastructure, 221
    function sandwich, 242
    functions as, 151–152
    functions as output, 151
    keeping at edges, 54
    modeling complex, 85–86
    modeling rules, 270
    patterns, 79
    total functions, 154–155
    understanding, 25–29
    validation, 47
    workflows, 120–122
integrity
    business rules, 108–112
    definition, 103
    invariants, 107
    simple values, 104–106
    units of measure, 106
invariants, 107
iterative processes, 5

J
JSON, 224–229, 235–238

K
key-value maps, 235–238

L
lambda expressions, 150, 164
let keyword, 60, 150
let! keyword, 210, 212
"lifting" types, 175–177, 190
list type, 72
lists, 150, 177, 213–216
    serialization of, 230

M
map function, 199, 203, 218
Map type, 72
mapError function, 210, 212
maps, key-value, 235–238
measure types, 106
microservice premium, 44
models, *see* domain models
module definitions, 105

modules, 43
monads, 196, 217–218

N
namespaces, 98
NonEmptyList type, 107
North, Dan, 6
null, 69

O
object-oriented programming, 147–148
objects, 63
Onion Architecture, 53
online analytical processing (OLAP), 249
online transaction processing (OLTP), 249
Option type, 69
optional values, 69
options, serialization of, 230
OR types, 64, 66, 79, *see al-so* choice types
order-placing example
    acknowledge order step, 131–133, 135
    adding shipping charges, 266–270
    connecting I/O, 136
    constraints, 36, 280
    creating events, 175
    domain model, 77, 98
    error handling, 203–205, 212
    events, 133
    implementing acknowledg-ment step, 174
    implementing pricing step, 172–174
    implementing validation step, 165–172
    life cycle modeling, 38–40
    other requirements changes, 281
    piping approach overview, 161–162
    pricing step, 130, 135, 278
    printing order, 279
    process overview, 284
    promotion codes, 273–278
    shipping context, 278
    substep modeling, 40
    summary, 119
    text-based model, 31–33

    understanding in-puts/outputs, 25–29
    using states for modeling, 122–124
    validation step, 128–130, 134
    VIP support, 270–273
    workflow details, 33–35
outputs, *see* input/output (I/O)

P
panics, 192–193
paper-based systems, 13
parameters, functions, 152–154
partial application, 153, 168, 190
payment system example, 67, 240
performance, 81, 107
persistence
    atomicity, 113
    CQRS, 246–248
    CQS, 244–246
    data storage, 248–250
    definition, 221
    document databases, 250
    edges, 239–242
    overview, 239
    relational databases, 251–262
    transactions, 262
persistence ignorance, 30
pipelines, *see also* workflows
    adding new input, 271–273
    adding new stages, 267–270
    assembling, 187
    commands and, 120–122
    composing, 178–180
    creating events, 175
    dependencies, 190
    handling dependencies, 180–187
    implementation, 190
    implementing steps, 162–177
    modeling processes as, 14
    modeling workflows, 119–120
    two-track error handling, 196–205
    workflow input, 120
piping, 156, 161–162

private, 105–106

Process Managers, 142

processes
asynchronous, 87
business, 12
in domain model, 79
iterative, 5

product types, 64, 66, *see also* record types

Q

queries, 242, 251, *see also* data

R

rec keyword, 74

record types, 83, 101

records, 235–238
with for copying, 94
serialization of, 230

relational databases
choice types, 252, 258–260
functional models and, 251
using SQL type providers, 254–258
writing to, 260

reporting, importance of, 11

Repository pattern, 243

requirements, 10, 27

ResizeArray type, 72

resources
architecture approaches, 53
business analytics systems, 249
domain-driven design (DDD), 3
Event Storming, 8
F#, 147
F# libraries, 107
measure types, 107
Sagas, 142
serializers, 228
software architecture, 43
SQL type providers, 254
testing tools, 186
for this book, xi–xii

result computation expression, 212

Result type, 87, 105, 130, 192, 196, 200, 209–216, 218

return
computation expression, 209
monad, 217

S

Sagas, 140

scenarios, definition, 12

scope creep, 18

self-documenting design, 37

seq type, 72

serialization
choosing serializers, 228
connecting to workflow, 223
definition, 221
design types for, 222
error handling, 226
setting up, 224
wrapping JSON serializers, 226

Set type, 72

Shared Kernel relationship, 48

shared models, developing, 10

simple types
constrained values, 81
implementing, 162
modeling with, 101
performance issues, 81
single-case unions, 66, 79–80, 230
translating to DTOs, 230
using, 66

simple values, integrity of, 104–106

single-case unions, 66, 79–80, 230

smart constructor, 105

software architecture, *see* architecture

SQL type providers, 254–258

"Starbucks Does Not Use Two-Phase Commit" (Hohpe), 115, 262

states
modeling sets, 122–124
state machines, 124–128, 140

structs, 82

subdomains, 14–16, 23

sum types, *see* choice types

switch functions, 196, 198

system context, 43

T

teams, 10–11

text-based language models, 31–33, 36, 38–40, *see also* order-placing example

total functions, 154–155, 192

transactions, 262

trust boundaries, 47

tuples, serialization of, 232

two-track functions
adapter blocks, 198–200
error type compatibility, 201
organizing Result, 200
overview, 196
type checking, 200

type inference, 60

type signatures, 60

types, *see also* simple types
advantages, 268, 282
as documentation, 101
checking, 200
composable, 67–69
composition of, 64–66
dependency modeling, 128
documenting business rules, 108–112
documenting errors, 70
domain error modeling, 194
generics, 61, 121, 238
implementing state machines with, 127–128
keeping separate, 277
"lifting" to shared, 175–177, 190
modeling with, 142
Option, 69
organizing, 73
overview, 61–63
steps modeling, 128–136
unknown, 83
values in, 63
working with, 66–67

U

Ubiquitous Language
capturing, 37
creating, 21, 24
definition, 22

instead of developer-centric, 79, 101
modeling domain errors, 194
Undefined, 83
unit type, 71
units of measure, 106
unknown types, 83
Unquote, 186
use cases, definition, 12

V

validation, 47, 103, *see also* integrity
Value Objects, 88–89, 93, 98
value types, 82
values
    constrained, 81
    simple, 79–82
    in types, 63

variables, 63
Versioning in an Event Sourced System (Young), 229
void, 71

W

waterfall development, 143
workflows, *see also* pipelines
    active patterns, 266
    adding new input, 271–273
    adding new stages, 267–270
    composing, 136
    constraints, 36, 280
    definition, 12
    friction-free design, 18
    input, 120–122
    keeping I/O at edges, 54, 239–242

life cycle modeling, 38–40
long-running, 140
modeling, 85–88
    as pipelines, 119–120
    state machines, 124–128
    substep modeling, 40
    text-based model, 31–33
    understanding I/O, 25–29
    understanding details, 33–35
    using states for modeling, 122–124
    using types for modeling, 128–136, 142
    within bounded contexts, 50

Y

Young, Greg, 229

Thank you!

How did you enjoy this book? Please let us know. Take a moment and email us at support@pragprog.com with your feedback. Tell us your story and you could win free ebooks. Please use the subject line "Book Feedback."

Ready for your next great Pragmatic Bookshelf book? Come on over to https://pragprog.com and use the coupon code BUYANOTHER2017 to save 30% on your next ebook.

Void where prohibited, restricted, or otherwise unwelcome. Do not use ebooks near water. If rash persists, see a doctor. Doesn't apply to *The Pragmatic Programmer* ebook because it's older than the Pragmatic Bookshelf itself. Side effects may include increased knowledge and skill, increased marketability, and deep satisfaction. Increase dosage regularly.

And thank you for your continued support,

Andy Hunt, Publisher

Level Up

From data structures to architecture and design, we have what you need.

A Common-Sense Guide to Data Structures and Algorithms

If you last saw algorithms in a university course or at a job interview, you're missing out on what they can do for your code. Learn different sorting and searching techniques, and when to use each. Find out how to use recursion effectively. Discover structures for specialized applications, such as trees and graphs. Use Big O notation to decide which algorithms are best for your production environment. Beginners will learn how to use these techniques from the start, and experienced developers will rediscover approaches they may have forgotten.

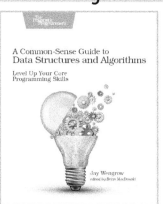

Jay Wengrow
(218 pages) ISBN: 9781680502442. $45.95
https://pragprog.com/book/jwdsal

Design It!

Don't engineer by coincidence—design it like you mean it! Grounded by fundamentals and filled with practical design methods, this is the perfect introduction to software architecture for programmers who are ready to grow their design skills. Ask the right stakeholders the right questions, explore design options, share your design decisions, and facilitate collaborative workshops that are fast, effective, and fun. Become a better programmer, leader, and designer. Use your new skills to lead your team in implementing software with the right capabilities—and develop awesome software!

Michael Keeling
(358 pages) ISBN: 9781680502091. $41.95
https://pragprog.com/book/mkdsa

Explore Testing

Explore the uncharted waters of exploratory testing and delve deeper into web testing.

Explore It!

Uncover surprises, risks, and potentially serious bugs with exploratory testing. Rather than designing all tests in advance, explorers design and execute small, rapid experiments, using what they learned from the last little experiment to inform the next. Learn essential skills of a master explorer, including how to analyze software to discover key points of vulnerability, how to design experiments on the fly, how to hone your observation skills, and how to focus your efforts.

Elisabeth Hendrickson
(186 pages) ISBN: 9781937785024. $29
https://pragprog.com/book/ehxta

The Way of the Web Tester

This book is for everyone who needs to test the web. As a tester, you'll automate your tests. As a developer, you'll build more robust solutions. And as a team, you'll gain a vocabulary and a means to coordinate how to write and organize automated tests for the web. Follow the testing pyramid and level up your skills in user interface testing, integration testing, and unit testing. Your new skills will free you up to do other, more important things while letting the computer do the one thing it's really good at: quickly running thousands of repetitive tasks.

Jonathan Rasmusson
(256 pages) ISBN: 9781680501834. $29
https://pragprog.com/book/jrtest

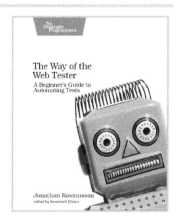

The Joy of Mazes and Math

Rediscover the joy and fascinating weirdness of mazes and pure mathematics.

Mazes for Programmers

A book on mazes? Seriously?

Yes!

Not because you spend your day creating mazes, or because you particularly like solving mazes.

But because it's fun. Remember when programming used to be fun? This book takes you back to those days when you were starting to program, and you wanted to make your code do things, draw things, and solve puzzles. It's fun because it lets you explore and grow your code, and reminds you how it feels to just think.

Sometimes it feels like you live your life in a maze of twisty little passages, all alike. Now you can code your way out.

Jamis Buck
(286 pages) ISBN: 9781680500554. $38
https://pragprog.com/book/jbmaze

Good Math

Mathematics is beautiful—and it can be fun and exciting as well as practical. *Good Math* is your guide to some of the most intriguing topics from two thousand years of mathematics: from Egyptian fractions to Turing machines; from the real meaning of numbers to proof trees, group symmetry, and mechanical computation. If you've ever wondered what lay beyond the proofs you struggled to complete in high school geometry, or what limits the capabilities of the computer on your desk, this is the book for you.

Mark C. Chu-Carroll
(282 pages) ISBN: 9781937785338. $34
https://pragprog.com/book/mcmath

Past and Present

To see where we're going, remember how we got here, and learn how to take a healthier approach to programming.

Fire in the Valley

In the 1970s, while their contemporaries were protesting the computer as a tool of dehumanization and oppression, a motley collection of college dropouts, hippies, and electronics fanatics were engaged in something much more subversive. Obsessed with the idea of getting computer power into their own hands, they launched from their garages a hobbyist movement that grew into an industry, and ultimately a social and technological revolution. What they did was invent the personal computer: not just a new device, but a watershed in the relationship between man and machine. This is their story.

Michael Swaine and Paul Freiberger
(422 pages) ISBN: 9781937785765. $34
https://pragprog.com/book/fsfire

The Healthy Programmer

To keep doing what you love, you need to maintain your own systems, not just the ones you write code for. Regular exercise and proper nutrition help you learn, remember, concentrate, and be creative—skills critical to doing your job well. Learn how to change your work habits, master exercises that make working at a computer more comfortable, and develop a plan to keep fit, healthy, and sharp for years to come.

This book is intended only as an informative guide for those wishing to know more about health issues. In no way is this book intended to replace, countermand, or conflict with the advice given to you by your own healthcare provider including Physician, Nurse Practitioner, Physician Assistant, Registered Dietician, and other licensed professionals.

Joe Kutner
(254 pages) ISBN: 9781937785314. $36
https://pragprog.com/book/jkthp

The Pragmatic Bookshelf

The Pragmatic Bookshelf features books written by developers for developers. The titles continue the well-known Pragmatic Programmer style and continue to garner awards and rave reviews. As development gets more and more difficult, the Pragmatic Programmers will be there with more titles and products to help you stay on top of your game.

Visit Us Online

This Book's Home Page
https://pragprog.com/book/swdddf
Source code from this book, errata, and other resources. Come give us feedback, too!

Register for Updates
https://pragprog.com/updates
Be notified when updates and new books become available.

Join the Community
https://pragprog.com/community
Read our weblogs, join our online discussions, participate in our mailing list, interact with our wiki, and benefit from the experience of other Pragmatic Programmers.

New and Noteworthy
https://pragprog.com/news
Check out the latest pragmatic developments, new titles and other offerings.

Save on the eBook

Save on the eBook versions of this title. Owning the paper version of this book entitles you to purchase the electronic versions at a terrific discount.

PDFs are great for carrying around on your laptop—they are hyperlinked, have color, and are fully searchable. Most titles are also available for the iPhone and iPod touch, Amazon Kindle, and other popular e-book readers.

Buy now at *https://pragprog.com/coupon*

Contact Us

Online Orders:	*https://pragprog.com/catalog*
Customer Service:	*support@pragprog.com*
International Rights:	*translations@pragprog.com*
Academic Use:	*academic@pragprog.com*
Write for Us:	*http://write-for-us.pragprog.com*
Or Call:	+1 800-699-7764